# INDIA AND CENTRAL ASIA

Edited by
Indranil Banerjie

Brunel Academic Publishers Ltd., UK

INDIA AND CENTRAL ASIA
Copyright © Indranil Banerjie 2004

ISBN  0-9547556-0-X

First Published 2004 by
Brunel Academic Publishers Ltd.
196 Church Road,
Northolt, Middlesex

Printed & bound by Brunel Academic Publishers Ltd.
for SAPRA India Foundation
201–202, II^nd Floor, 16A Uday Plaza, Uday Park New Delhi – 110 049

# INDIA AND CENTRAL ASIA

# Contents

SECTION TWO
Country Reports

# INTRODUCTION

India's foreign policy has been greatly influenced by the fact that the country is hemmed in from two sides by potentially hostile forces. On its western borders, there is Pakistan, a country that has consistently sought to damage Indian interests, and in the east, is the Peoples Republic of China (PRC), a major power that fought a short but bitter war with India four decades ago and still continues to claim thousands of square kilometres of Indian territory. Indian analysts see an attempt at encirclement by China, which has signed military agreements with Pakistan and Myanmar. Pakistan has also been helped in its nuclear weapons and ballistic missiles programmes by the PRC. In recent times, an emboldened Pakistan has sought to project its influence and military power outside its borders, most noticeably in Afghanistan which for some years was ruled by a pro-Pakistani extremist group known as the Taliban. In Kashmir, Islamist rebels backed by Islamabad have been fighting Indian security forces for over a decade. In short, Indian policy makers traditionally, have seen themselves existing in a dangerous neighbourhood. Not surprisingly therefore, when five independent republics suddenly emerged at the centre of Asia, Indian policy makers reacted instinctively by trying to reach out to them. The basic underlying aim was to ensure that the heart of Asia does not turn hostile to India. Indian policy makers knew it was in their interest to see that these countries also do not end up helping hostile forces or falling prey to the ravages of militant Islam.

Much of Indian policy towards Central Asia is easy to

comprehend if seen within this psychological framework. India's primary instinct, to put it another way, is self-preservation. Other nations view Central Asia differently: some want to integrate the region through historical ties, some just want a piece of the economic action, some want to place their flag bearers in positions of power, while some see the region as a strategic centrepiece meant to be controlled and dominated. India wants to see the Central Asian Republics (CARs) to evolve into progressive, secular democracies, neutral in disposition and independent in fact. But all this is easier wished for. And Indian policy makers know that. The inherent weakness of the some of the CARs make them extremely vulnerable to hostile forces and destabilisation. To prevent this, India needs to be proactive on various fronts. Russia's influence in the region is receding at a remarkable pace and the resultant space is being filled by various conflicting forces. If there is any consensus by the major powers on Central Asia, it is on the need to check the inroads by militant Islamist forces. But state and non-state actors from Pakistan, the Middle East and some other countries are continuing to erode the region's secular character. Economic and military competition, if not outright rivalry amongst the big powers, is also, inadvertently in some cases, adding to regional contradictions. Within the republics, a volatile mix of ethnic and religious groups is pulling in different directions. The democratic urge is battling autocratic tradition. Abruptly dispossessed economic classes are railing against the affluent. In short, Central Asia is caught in an age of turbulence. Understanding this turmoil is part of the raison d'être of this book. The other imperative is to understand the nature of India's relationship with the region.

The changes and conflicts within Central Asia have intensified since 9/11, a date that has become a sort of watershed in contemporary history. Change for most

Central Asians has been intense and often traumatic. Sheltered and smothered by the Soviet Union for decades, the region saw little upheaval after the initial years of the Bolshevik revolution and the agricultural collectivisation movement. State-controlled Islam, collective farming, socialistic welfare policies and the repression of political dissent meant that the average Soviet Central Asian experienced few signs of turmoil, although this is not to say they did not resent the political and religious restrictions or Russian racism. But few were prepared for the almost forcible divorce from the Soviet Union. This caused a social and economic shock that the region is yet to get out of. Within a very short period after independence, the region witnessed a massive upsurge in Islamist sentiments and movements. This was most pronounced in the three republics of Uzbekistan, Kyrgyzstan and Tajikistan. The reports of Islamist upheavals in Central Asia caused nothing short of consternation in New Delhi. The thought that the violence in Kashmir was becoming part of a much wider Pan-Asian pattern was extremely disturbing because it suggested that secular India was facing a much larger and widespread threat. The implications of this was becoming apparent in Afghanistan where Pakistan and its Islamist allies were getting stronger by the day. Eventually, the success of the Taliban and news of the Uighur uprising in China's Xinjiang province, confirmed India's fears about the emergence of an intensely hostile Islamist crescent stretching from Xinjiang in the east to Central Asia in the west. The epicentre of this hostile region was Pakistan. From the mid-1990s onwards, it was clear to India that this region was breeding Islamists, radicalising them, training them to carry out terrorist acts and sheltering them from probing eyes. All through the crucial period when a particularly virulent form of militant Islam was being formed in protected crucibles in Pakistan and Afghanistan,

Indian policy makers tried their best to force the world to take heed. But they failed and 9/11 happened.

In those years, India was quietly developing its policy options in Central Asia in a slow but consistent manner. Traditionally, India had no direct links with these republics and relations were almost exclusively at the government or bureaucratic level. The absence of significant people-to-people contacts between Indians and Central Asians during the Soviet period meant that the new relationship had to be policy- and not people-driven. Fortunately, as has been mentioned earlier, Indian policy makers recognised the importance of this region right from the beginning. The first imperative was to open diplomatic relations and convince the republics of the need to open missions in India. This was done fairly quickly. The second issue was how to chart out a safe physical route to the region. The land routes were out even though they were the shortest. Air links existed and were increased. But this was the expensive route. The shortest way from New Delhi to Tashkent is via Pakistan and Afghanistan. The second shortest route is through Chinese Xinjiang. But neither of these two routes were safe. India thus exploited its growing relations with Iran to develop a land-sea corridor that could be used to connect India to Central Asia and beyond into Asiatic Russia. Iran as well as a number of Central Asian states have realised the importance of this transport corridor and work on it has intensified in recent times.

Today, India's contacts with the CARs have developed at various levels. Central Asian airlines with their competitive airfares haul thousands of Indians all over the world; chartered flights come in for cargo; traders buy truckloads of garments and other goods in Delhi's bazaars; and students from all over the region come to study in premier Indian educational institutions. Indian businessmen had initially been cautious in investing in or trading with the

CARs. That diffidence has vanished, although the levels of trade and investment remain far below potential. Indian industry is also beginning to get a piece of action on the energy front. Central Asia's hydrocarbon resources have been much written about and touted. Some of the largest oil exploration, drilling, and pipeline projects of recent times have been signed in this region. China and the United States have emerged as the two biggest players in the energy sector after Russia. India has only recently signed a contract to explore and extract oil in Kazakhstan. If this contract proves lucrative, India could bid for bigger energy projects.

India does not view Central Asia as its exclusive preserve. Neither does it seek to dominate the region or ever become a regional *hegemon*. It clearly understands that its presence now and in the near future will be significant and not strategic. The fact that the region is physically cut off from India and is host today to the forces of global competition, clearly limit India's options. The entry of the United States into the region after 9/11 has further limited Indian options. This is primarily because the United States has the capacity to crowd out others. Coupled with this is the fact that India has been working in tandem with both Iran and Russia to further its policies in the region. Iran, like India, is extremely concerned about the spread of Wahabi Islam, and so is Russia. All three countries also wish to limit severely the role of Pakistan in the CARs as well as in Afghanistan. The United States, on the other hand, views Pakistan as an ally, although one that needs careful watching. The US does not welcome the entry of regional forces like Iran, India and Russia in Afghanistan even though it is clear that in the long run only these countries can prevent Islamist actors in Pakistan from controlling Afghanistan and stabilising Central Asia. Thus, even though India is keen to develop a strategic alliance with the United States at the bilateral level, it sees conflicting issues in the region, particularly in those involving Pakistan. Hence, India will remain active in Central Asia in the months and years to come. It will seek out alliances that promise to enhance its limited aims in the region. How exactly it will chart out a course through turbulent Central Asia will depend much on whether the big powers can contain, if not destroy, the forces behind the events of 9/11. This book, divided into four sections, is an attempt to understand Central Asia and India's relationship with that region. Each chapter is a personal view. Hopefully, they will collectively provide a vision of what is yet to come.

Indranil Banerjie
New Delhi, December 2003

# SECTION ONE
Country Profiles

# Chapter I
# REPUBLIC OF KAZAKHSTAN

Covering an area of 2.7 million sq km, Kazakhstan is the largest of the Central Asian states. It borders Turkmenistan, Uzbekistan and Kyrgyzstan to the south, China to the east, and the Russian Federation to the north. It is also one of the most economically prosperous countries in the region due to its massive oil and natural gas reserves, as well as an abundance of minerals and metals. A fairly strong industrial and manufacturing sector has helped the country to usher in economic reform and modernisation programmes. Nearly 56 per cent of the population lives in urban areas, making Kazakhstan the most urbanised of the Central Asian Republics. The population is also characterised by tremendous diversity, with almost half the population made up of non-Kazakhs. This diversity, however, has also been a source of internal ethnic conflict. Kazakhstan is home to the Baikonur Cosmodrome, the leading space centre of the former USSR, which has now been leased to Russia.

*Official Name*: Republic of Kazakhstan.

*Capital*: Astana.

*Area*: 2,717,300 sq km.

*Population*: 16.73 million.

*Population by Religion*: Muslim – 47 per cent; Russian Orthodox – 44 per cent; Protestant – 2 per cent; Others – 7 per cent.

*Languages*: Kazakh (Qazaq) is the state language spoken by nearly 40 per cent of the population. Russian is the official language spoken by around 65 per cent people.

*Anthem*: *We are a valiant people, sons of honour*, written by Muzafar Alimbayev, Kadyr Myrzaliyev, Tumanbai Moldagaliyev and Zhadyra Daribayeva.

## History

Between the first and the eighth century, Turkic-speaking and Mongol tribes invaded and settled in the areas that are now known as Kazakhstan and Central Asia. Arab invaders introduced Islam by the eighth century. Between 1219 and 1224, Mongol tribes led by Genghis Khan invaded Kazakhstan. By the late fifteenth century, the Khanate of Kazakhstan had been established, separating the region into three zones, and a Kazakh ethnic identity emerged by the sixteenth century. The Russian empire had established a hold over Kazakhstan by the mid-nineteenth century by waging wars against the local tribes. After the Bolshevik coup in Russia in 1917, there was civil war in Kazakhstan. In 1920, Kazakhstan turned into an autonomous republic of the USSR. By 1936, the Kazakh Autonomous Soviet Socialist Republic became a full Union Republic of the USSR, the Kazakh SSR.

Under Soviet rule, Kazakhstan saw a period of industrial growth. Huge railroads criss-crossed the region and communication improved. However, the Soviet campaign to collectivise agriculture in Kazakhstan in the early 1930s resulted in widespread devastation in the region. An estimated one million people died of starvation. The Soviet rule also saw the systematic settlement of Russians. Many of those deported from parts of the USSR during the Second World War, including Germans, Crimean, Tatars and Caucasians, settled in Kazakhstan. This led to a change in the demographic profile of the region: the proportion of Russians increased from 19.7 per cent of the population in 1926 to 42.7 per cent in 1959. The Kazakh-Russian ethnic conflict has been simmering ever since. In 1986, Kazakhs protested against the appointment of Gennadiy Kolbin, an ethnic Russian, as head of the Communist Party of Kazakhstan (CPK), replacing Dinmukhamed Kunayev, an ethnic Kazakh. In June 1989, Nursultan Nazarbayev, an ethnic Kazakh, was appointed head of the CPK. The Kazakh Supreme Soviet adopted a legislation establishing Kazakh as the official language and Russian as the language of inter-ethnic communication in September 1989.

On 25 October 1990, the Kazakh Supreme Soviet declared its sovereignty and Nazarbayev was appointed as the first Kazakh president. In 1991, Nazarbayev won the uncontested presidential elections and Kazakhstan declared independence from the Soviet Union, and joined the Commonwealth of Independent States (CIS). In 1999, Nazarbayev was re-elected president after his main rival, former Prime Minister Akezhan Kazhegeldin, was barred from standing for the elections. Later, parliamentary elections were held for the first time by a combination of party list and first-past-the-post system. The elections were criticised for various irregularities. Increased emigration from the country by ethnic Germans – nearly 300,000 of them left in the early 1990s – and Russians was accompanied by the return of ethnic Kazakhs from Kyrgyzstan, Mongolia, Tajikistan and Turkmenistan. According to a census held in February 1999, ethnic Kazakhs constituted 54.3 per cent of the total population.

## Government and Politics

*Government Type*: Presidential government and bicameral parliament comprising a forty-seven-member senate and a sixty-seven-member Majlis (lower house).

*Ruling Party*: People's Unity Party (PUP).

*Head of Government*: Prime Minister Imangali Tasmagambetov.

*Head of State*: President Nursultan A Nazarbayev.

Kazakhstan is a constitutional republic with a strong presidency. Under the 1995 Kazakh Constitution, the president of the Republic is the head of state and the commander-in-chief of the armed forces. He holds broad executive powers including that of vetoing any legislation passed by the Parliament. The president is elected directly by universal adult franchise for a seven-year term. The Constitution provides for a maximum of two consecutive terms for the president. The government is headed by the prime minister who is accountable to the president and serves at his pleasure. He chairs the Cabinet of ministers. There are four deputy prime ministers, fourteen ministers, and eleven chairmen of state agencies. The government proposes most of the legislations taken up by the Parliament.

## Conflicts

*Internal Conflicts*: The Islamic Movement of Uzbekistan (IMU), a militant group based in Afghanistan, has been carrying out terror acts in Kazakhstan in order to overthrow the government and establish an Islamic regime. Simmering ethnic tension, particularly amongst the large ethnic Russian group, is another source of internal conflict. In mid-November 1999, the arrests of fourteen separatists, including ethnic Russians, led to the discovery of an alleged plot aimed at establishing an independent republic through an armed rebellion against the authorities in several towns in the north and east of Kazakhstan.

*External Conflicts*: Kazakhstan is a party to the issue of the division of the Caspian Sea boundaries between the coastal states. The contentious issue of division of mineral resources located in the seabed has strained relations between Kazakhstan and Russia, as well as other states such as Azerbaijan, Turkmenistan and Iran.

There is a border dispute with Uzbekistan over 299,000 acres of land around two villages – Bagys and Turkestanets – with a combined population of 2000. The disputed territory is controlled by Uzbekistan while the over-whelming majority of residents are ethnic Kazakhs. Uzbek troops have also been accused of arbitrarily demarcating the border in many parts.

## Military

In May 1992, President Nazarbayev issued a decree for the establishment of Kazakhstan's armed forces. Kazakhstan inherited defence hardware from the former Soviet Union, most of which is in a depleted condition today. The Soviet-era Intercontinental Ballistic Missiles (ICBM) are positioned in Kazakh territory. A battalion of Kazakh Border Guards is deputed in Tajikistan for providing security. The Kazakh military participates in the US International Military Education and Training programme, Foreign Military Financing, as well as NATO's Partnership for Peace programme. The annual defence expenditure is around US $322 million.

## Economy

Kazakhstan has enormous fossil fuel reserves as well as significant supplies of minerals and metals. Kazakhstan's industrial sector is based on the extraction and processing of these natural resources. Its machine building sector, specialising in construction equipment, tractors, agricultural machinery and some defence products, is growing. Mining and power also contribute significantly to the economy. Kazakhstan has large areas under agriculture. It is a major producer and exporter of agricultural products including fruits, sugar beets, potatoes, vegetables, cotton, grain and cereals. Livestock breeding is another important economic activity. Kazakhstan produces the Karakul and Astrakhan wool, which are exported to different countries.

In order to reduce growing inflation, Kazakhstan launched a comprehensive programme of stabilisation and economic reform in 1993 with the assistance of the International Monetary Fund (IMF). After 1997, economic reform and privatisation programmes initiated by the government have gathered speed and private sector assets have grown substantially.

Kazakhstan has nearly fourteen billion barrels of proven oil reserves and 68.5 trillion cubic feet of natural gas deposits. Energy exports are, therefore, one of the main revenue earners of the Kazakh economy. The Offshore Kazakhstan International Operating Company (OKIOC), an international consortium, is undertaking exploration and production in the oil and gas fields of Kazakhstan. Oil and gas exports are expected to increase over the coming years as the 1,500-kilometre-long petroleum pipeline connecting the Tengiz oilfield in western Kazakhstan with Novorossisk on the Russian Black Sea coast is expected to be a major transit route for crude oil exports.

# Chapter II
# REPUBLIC OF KYRGYZ

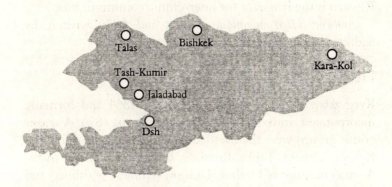

Flanked by Kazakhstan to the north, Uzbekistan to the west, Tajikistan to the south and west, and China to the east, the Kyrgyz Republic, better known as Kyrgyzstan, is a small landlocked country in eastern Central Asia. The country is almost completely mountainous with more than half of it lying at an elevation higher than 2,500 m. Lacking natural resources and an industrial base, Kyrgyzstan is one of the poorer countries within the CARs, with 40 per cent of its population living below the poverty line. It does, however, possess significant hydroelectric power potential and has also been extremely active in carrying out market reforms and stabilisation policies. Islam is the main religion of the Kyrgyz Republic with a majority of ethnic Kyrgyz being Sunni Muslims. Kyrgyzstan faces an insurgency problem with terrorists from Uzbekistan and Afghanistan using the country as a transit point to carry out terror acts in Kyrgyzstan and neighbouring countries.

*Official Name*: Kyrgyz Republic.
*Capital*: Bishkek.
*Area*: 198,500 sq km.
*Population*: 4.68 million.
*Population by Religion*: Muslim – 75 per cent; Russian Orthodox – 20 per cent; Others – 5 per cent.
*Languages*: Kirghiz (Kyrgyz) is the official language and Russian is the language for inter-ethnic communication.
*Anthem*: *High mountains, valleys and fields*, written by Sadikova and Kulueva.

## History

Kyrgyzstan was annexed by Russia in 1864 and formally incorporated into the Russian empire in 1876. Various ethnic groups were then settled in Kyrgyzstan, including the Kyrgyz, Uzbeks, Tajiks, Russians, Ukrainians and Germans. A small number of Uighur, Dungan (Chinese Muslims) and Koreans also settled in the region. In 1918, the Turkestan Autonomous Soviet Socialist Republic (ASSR) was established within the Russian Federation and it included Kyrgyzhia. In 1924, the Kara-Kyrgyz Autonomous Oblast (region) was created. In 1925, the region was renamed as the Kyrgyz Soviet Socialist Republic (SSR).

On 5 December 1986, the Kyrgyz Soviet Socialist Republic was established as a full union republic of the USSR. In 1985, the republic's Supreme Soviet recognised Kyrgyz as the official language and Russian as the language for communication. Elections for the 350-member Kyrgyz Supreme Soviet were held in February 1990. Absamat Masaliyev of the Kyrgyz Communist Party (KCP) was elected as the chairman. In December 1990, the Supreme Soviet voted to change the name of the republic from Kyrgyz Soviet Socialist Republic to Republic of Kyrgyzstan. In February 1991, the Kyrgyz capital Frunze was rechristened

Bishkek, which was the name of the city prior to 1926. On 31 August 1991, the Kyrgyz Supreme Soviet declared independence from the former Soviet Union and Askar Akaev was elected president of Kyrgyzstan on 12 October 1991. In December 1991, Kyrgyzstan became a signatory to the Almaty Declaration, signed by eleven former Soviet republics that formally established the Commonwealth of Independent States. The new constitution of independent Kyrgyzstan formally came into effect on 5 May 1993. The country's official name was changed to Kyrgyz Republic. Kyrgyzstan also introduced its own currency, the Som, in 1993 and this led to a deterioration in relations with Uzbekistan and Kazakhstan, who suspended all trade and closed the border fearing an influx of the old currency, the rouble. Relations improved after talks between leaders of the three countries and in January 1994, Kyrgyzstan joined the new economic zone established by Kazakhstan and Uzbekistan. In May 1998, Kyrgyzstan, Tajikistan, Kazakhstan and Uzbekistan formally constituted the Central Asian Economic Union, later renamed the Central Asian Economic Community in July 1998.

## Government and Politics

*Government Type*: Presidential government and a bicameral parliament.

*Ruling Party*: Party of Communists of Kyrgyzstan (KCP).

*Head of Government*: Prime Minister Nikolai Tanaev.

*Head of State*: President Askar Akaev.

Kyrgyzstan has a strong presidential form of government wherein the president is elected for a five-year term by popular vote. The prime minister and the Cabinet of ministers are appointed by the president and continue in office at his pleasure.

## Conflicts

*Internal Conflicts*: There is tension between the Kyrgyz and Uzbek communities over access to land and housing. This has led to an exodus of skilled non-Kyrgyz labour such as Russians. Incursions by guerrillas who are said to be members of the Islamic Movement of Uzbekistan (IMU) have further exacerbated the threat perception. These terrorists use Kyrgyzstan as a transit point and undertake acts of terror with the objective of removing the governments of different Central Asian states in order to replace them with an Islamic regime.

*External Conflicts*: Kyrgyzstan is involved in a territorial dispute with Tajikistan on its south-west boundary in the Isfara Valley. Another source of conflict is the infiltration of Islamic insurgents from Uzbekistan and Afghanistan. These insurgents have perpetrated acts of terrorism in Kyrgyzstan during 1999 and 2000. The dispute over Ferghana Valley with Tajikistan and Uzbekistan is a source of potential conflict.

## Economy

Kyrgyzstan is, predominantly, an agricultural economy. Forty per cent of its population lives below the poverty line and the annual GDP growth rate is around 3.4 per cent. Its external debt is around US $1.1 billion. Cotton, wool and meat are its main agricultural products and constitute a large part of exports. Other items of export are gold, mercury, uranium, and electricity. Hydroelectricity is another source of domestic energy production and export. Kyrgyzstan does not have significant oil and gas resources and therefore imports from Uzbekistan and Kazakhstan. Kyrgyzstan has small machinery, textile, food processing and cement industries. Among the Central Asian states, Kyrgyzstan has been one of the first to carry out market reforms and initiate economic programmes that have helped to bring down inflation rates from 88 per cent in 1994 to around 18 per cent in 2000 and 3.7 per cent in 2001. The government has divested most of its holdings in public enterprises. The government has also adopted a series of economic measures to reduce external debt and inflation and increase economic growth and financial independence.

# Chapter III
# REPUBLIC OF TAJIKISTAN

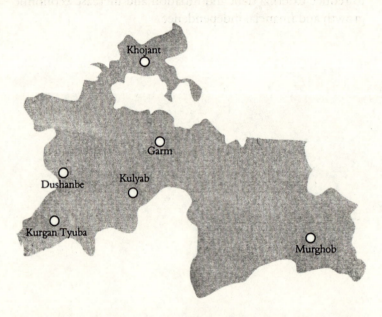

Set in the Pamir and the Tian Shan mountain ranges, Tajikistan is the most beautiful, but also the poorest, of the Central Asian states. Tajikistan shares its borders with Uzbekistan, Kyrgyzstan, China and Afghanistan. It has little or no oil and natural gas reserves, or industrial capability, and has the lowest per capita income in the region. Its most important economic resource is the cotton crop. It also has a significant, but largely unexploited, hydroelectric power potential. Socio-economic development has been hampered by continual internal strife. Terrorism and drug problems emanating from Afghanistan have led to the outflow of much needed skilled labour. Ninety per cent of the country's population is Muslim. In contrast to other countries in the region, the Tajiks are of Persian, not Turkic, descent. Tajikistan has been dependent primarily on Russia for its defence and security needs.

*Official Name*: Republic of Tajikistan.

*Capital*: Dushanbe.

*Area*: 143,100 sq km.

*Population*: 6.44 million (2002 estimates).

*Religion*: Islam is the state religion. 85 per cent of the population are Sunni Muslims; 5 per cent are Shia Muslims; and others – 10 per cent.

*Languages*: Tajik, Russian.

# History

Tajikistan, along with the other Central Asian states, became part of the Arab Caliphate in the seventh century. After the removal of the Caliphate, the region was incorporated into the Tahirid and Samanid kingdoms. The Tajiks emerged as an identifiable ethnic group in the ninth and tenth centuries. In the thirteenth century, Mongol Tatars conquered Tajikistan. From the seventeenth to the nineteenth centuries, there were small fiefdoms whose chieftains alternately submitted to or rebelled against the Khans of Bukhara. Russian and British interests in Tajikistan started in the late nineteenth century as the Russian empire advanced into Central Asia. The Tajiks joined the Basmachi rebellion against Soviet rule after the 1917 revolution in Russia, but the resistance movement crumbled in the early 1920s. Tajikistan finally became a part of the Soviet Union in 1924 as an Autonomous Soviet Socialist Republic (ASSR). In October 1929, the Tajik ASSR became a full Union Republic of the Soviet Union and its territory was enlarged by the addition of the Khujand district from the Uzbek Soviet Socialist Republic.

The movement towards independence began in February 1990, following reports that Armenian refugees were to be settled in Dushanbe, the capital of Tajikistan. As a concession to the growing Tajik nationalism, the Supreme Soviet, on 25 August 1990, adopted a declaration of sovereignty emphasising the equality of all nationalities living in Tajikistan. On 9 September 1991, Tajikistan declared independence from the Soviet Union.

The post-independence period has been marked by widespread incidents of clan and regional rivalries that led to the civil war in late 1992. The forces of the Communist government ended the civil war in early 1993. The government suspended the freedom of the press and the broadcasting media and the Supreme Court formally proscribed the opposition parties – Islamic Resistance Party (IRP), Lale Badakhshon, Rashtokehz and the Democratic Party of Tajikistan (DPT). The Communist Party of Tajikistan (CPT) remained the only legal party in the country. Even the new political parties established later in the year, the Party of Economic Freedom and the People's Democratic Party of Tajikistan (PDPT), were founded by members of the government.

## Government and Politics

*Government Type*: Presidential government and a bicameral supreme assembly.

*Ruling Party*: People's Democratic Party of Tajikistan.

*Head of Government*: Prime Minister Ogil Oqilov.

*Head of State*: President Emomali Rakhmonov.

Tajikistan has a strong presidential form of government with all powers concentrated in the office of the president. The prime minister is appointed by the president. The

Cabinet or the council of ministers is appointed by the president and approved by the Supreme Assembly (Tajik Parliament or Majlis Oli).

## Conflicts

*Internal Conflicts*: Since November 1992, there is continued civil strife in Tajikistan involving the government forces and the opposition groups known as United Tajik Opposition or UTO. The UN-mediated peace talks and ceasefire agreements have not been able to bring peace. The civil war has led to the migration of thousands of refugees to Afghanistan, Kyrgyzstan and Uzbekistan. The influx of Afghan refugees after 1996 has caused tension between different ethnic groups. Repatriation of these refugees has started following the removal of the Taliban regime in 2001.

*External Conflicts*: Tajikistan has a boundary dispute with China as the borders are not well defined. There is also the territorial dispute with a fellow member of the CIS, Kyrgyzstan, on the northern boundary in the Isfara Valley. Tajikistan also serves as a major transit point for illicit drugs from south-west Asia to Russia and Western Europe. Russia is particularly anxious to control the influx of drugs into its society and has urged Tajikistan to undertake stringent steps to cut the supply route passing through its territory.

## Military

Tajikistan's military is composed of the army, the air force, the air defence forces, the presidential national guard, and the security forces for internal and border areas. Tajikistan's border with Afghanistan is protected by Russian troops of the 201st Motorised Rifle Division. Russian forces also look after the internal security of Tajikistan. The Tajik forces have limited military hardware and missile capability.

Officer-level training is provided at the Higher Army Officers and Engineers College, Dushanbe. The June 1997 Peace Accord facilitated the integration of around 5,000 personnel of the Islamic Movement of Tajikistan into the Tajik forces. Tajikistan plans to form an air force squadron. The annual defence expenditure is around US $15 million.

## Economy

Tajikistan is a mountainous country with little oil or natural gas but with substantial hydroelectric power and significant undeveloped hydropower potential. At US $340, the per capita income of Tajikistan is the lowest in the region. The official figure for the unemployed stands at 5.7 per cent but there is a large section of underemployed and unregistered unemployed people. Tajikistan's external debt stands at nearly US $2.3 billion as in December 2001. Tajikistan has a very small oil industry with most of the country's production coming from the northern Leninobod Soghd Region. As there are no oil refineries, Tajikistan imports all petroleum products. In September 2000, an Austrian firm agreed to back Tajikistan's plans to build an oil refinery with a $3.5-million credit, but no further progress has been made to construct the refinery. The natural gas production was affected by the civil strife. Though production has resumed, the high demand and low supply makes Tajikistan dependent on natural gas imports from Uzbekistan and Turkmenistan. In the non-oil sector, cotton is its most important crop. Mineral resources are varied but limited in amount. They include silver, gold, uranium, and tungsten. Industry consists only of a large aluminium plant, hydropower facilities, and small factories mostly in light industry and food processing.

# Chapter IV

# REPUBLIC OF TURKMENISTAN

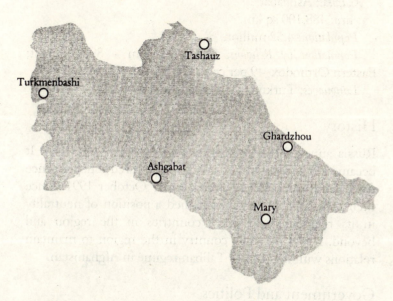

Turkmenistan, the southernmost country in Central Asia, is virtually one vast desert bordering Uzbekistan, Afghanistan, Iran and the Caspian Sea. Nearly the entire central part of the country is occupied by one of the largest deserts in the world, the Garagum (or Karakum) desert. Turkmenistan possesses the fifth largest natural gas reserves and is the tenth largest producer of cotton in the world. Its per capita income compares favourably with the other states in the region. It has adopted a very cautious approach to reforms in the economic matters, and in the foreign policy sphere, Turkmenistan has adopted a policy of 'positive neutrality'.

Turkmen President Saparmurat Niyazov has been the head of state, head of government, and supreme commander of the armed forces since 1990. His tenure was extended indefinitely in 1999. Eighty nine per cent of the population of Turkmenistan is Sunni Muslim.

*Official Name*: Republic of Turkmenistan.

*Capital*: Ashgabat.

*Area*: 488,100 sq km.

*Population*: 4.52 million.

*Population by Religion*: Sunni Muslim – 89 per cent; Eastern Orthodox – 9 per cent; Others – 2 per cent.

*Languages*: Turkmen, Russian, and Uzbek.

## History

Russia annexed Turkmenistan between 1865 and 1885. It became a Soviet republic in 1925. It declared independence from the former Soviet Union on 27 October 1991. Since then it has consistently maintained a position of neutrality in its relations with other countries in the region and beyond. It was the only country in the region to maintain relations with the former Taliban regime in Afghanistan.

## Government and Politics

*Government Type*: One-party presidential government and a bicameral parliament.

*Ruling Party*: Democratic Party of Turkmenistan (DPT).

*Head of Government and State*: President Saparmurat Niyazov.

In Turkmenistan, the president is both the chief of the state and head of the government. President Saparmurat Niyazov has held both offices since 27 October 1990. Niyazov's term was extended indefinitely on 28 December 1999 by the assembly (Majlis). The president appoints the council of ministers and the deputy chairman of the Majlis.

# Conflicts

*Internal Conflicts*: Turkmenistan faces a major threat from Islamist groups suspected of links with the Taliban. Several acts of violence have been committed by the Islamic Movement of Uzbekistan (IMU), a militant group based in Afghanistan.

*External Conflicts*: Turkmenistan is a party to the long-standing dispute over the division of the Caspian Sea into national territories. Azerbaijan, Russia, Iran and Kazakhstan are the other states claiming coastal rights over the oil-rich Caspian basin.

# Military

The 1992 Turkmen Constitution provides for universal conscription of males for service in the national armed forces. The period of regular service is eighteen months for army recruits and one year for those with higher education. Turkmenistan has an army, air force and border guards. A naval force for patrolling the Caspian Sea is also planned though Turkmenistan has some imported patrol boats currently stationed in the coastal areas. Turkmenistani officers are trained in the military institutions of the Russian Federation's ministry of defence. Limited training is provided in the military faculty established at the Turkmenistan State University. Turkmenistan has sent about 300 of its officers to training schools in Turkey, but it declined an offer from Pakistan's general staff to provide training in Pakistani military colleges. The Border Guard Command, consisting of nearly 5,000 personnel, was established in 1992 to replace the Soviet-era Central Asian Border Troops. The border guards patrol the 1,750-kilometre long mountainous Afghan and Iranian frontiers. Turkmenistan and Russia jointly command the Border

Guard Command. The total strength of Turkmen defence forces is around 16,000. The annual defence expenditure is around US $90 million.

## Economy

Turkmenistan is a desert country and the main sources of livelihood for Turkmens are nomadic cattle raising and intensive agriculture in irrigated oases. Nearly 50 per cent of its total irrigated land is devoted to cotton cultivation, making Turkmenistan the tenth largest producer of cotton in the world. Turkmenistan possesses the world's fifth largest reserves of natural gas. It has substantial oil reserves as well. At US $1,380, Turkmenistan's per capita income compares favourably with the other states in the region. But there is widespread poverty within the country. Turkmenistan's economy has benefited from the rise in oil and gas prices along with a rise in hard-currency earnings. With a strong ex-communist regime in power and a tribal-based social structure, Turkmenistan has taken a cautious approach to economic reform. It relies on gas and cotton sales to sustain its economy. Privatisation goals remain limited. Turkmenistan is keen on opening new gas export channels through Iran and Turkey to Europe, but these will take many years to realise. Another pipeline for exporting gas to India and Pakistan through Afghanistan is also under consideration.

# Chapter V
# REPUBLIC OF UZBEKISTAN

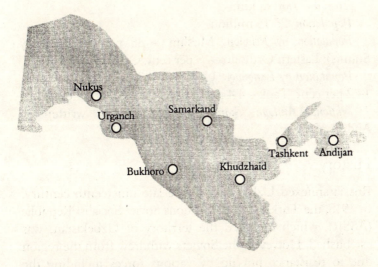

With a population of 25.15 million, Uzbekistan is the largest country in the Central Asian region in terms of population. It is also the most prosperous of the countries in the region with strong industrial and agricultural sectors and an abundance of skilled manpower. Its capital Tashkent is the most prosperous and modern city in the entire region. Uzbekistan also boasts of the largest defence forces in the region both in terms of manpower and military equipment. It faces a major terrorist threat at home in the form of the Islamic Movement of Uzbekistan (IMU), which seeks to establish an Islamic regime in the country. Uzbekistan's relations with the Russian Federation have been strained and it has emerged as a major ally of the United States, providing military bases to the US for the war in Afghanistan. The president of Uzbekistan, Islam Karimov, has proceeded cautiously on economic reforms, retaining control over most sectors of the economy.

*Official Name*: Republic of Uzbekistan.

*Capital*: Tashkent.

*Area*: 447,000 sq km.

*Population*: 25.15 million.

*Population by Religion*: Muslim – 88 per cent (mostly Sunnis); Eastern Orthodox – 9 per cent; Others – 3 per cent.

*Population by Language*: Uzbek – 74.3 per cent; Russian – 14.2 per cent, Tajik – 4.4 per cent; Others – 7.1 per cent.

*National Anthem*: *Stand Tall My Country*, written by Abdulla Oripov.

## History

Russia annexed Uzbekistan in the late nineteenth century. In 1918, the Turkestan Autonomous Soviet Socialist Republic (ASSR), which included the territory of Uzbekistan, was established. However, the Soviets withdrew from the region due to resistance put up by various forces including the nationalist Basmachi movement, the White Army, and the British.

Soviet rule was re-established in September 1919. The Khanates of Bukhara and Khiva became independent Soviet republics in 1920 and 1924 respectively and were incorporated into the Turkestan ASSR. The Uzbek Soviet Socialist Republic (SSR) was established in October 1924. In 1936, Karakalpakstan was transferred to Uzbekistan from the Russian Federation. The Communist Party of Uzbekistan (CPU) became the ruling party.

Elections to the 500-member Uzbek Supreme Soviet were held in February 1990. Birlik, the only non-communist political party, was refused permission to contest the elections. In March 1990, Islam Karimov, the First secretary of the CPU, was elected the executive president. In April 1991, Uzbekistan, along with eight other Soviet republics, agreed to sign a new Union treaty to redefine the state structure of the Union of Soviet Socialist Republics (USSR). In August 1991, Uzbekistan declared independence from the USSR and was renamed the Republic of Uzbekistan.

The CPU terminated its ties with the Communist Party of the Soviet Union (CPSU) and was rechristened the People's Democratic Party of Uzbekistan (PDPU) with Karimov as the leader. Direct presidential elections were held for the first time in December 1991. Islam Karimov won more than 85 per cent of the votes and was elected president. The only opposition party, Erk (Freedom) Party was banned from contesting. In a referendum held along with the elections, more than 98 per cent approved the independence of Uzbekistan. The new Constitution of Uzbekistan was adopted on 8 December 1992. The Constitution provided for a 250-member legislature called Oly Majlis (Supreme Assembly). In February 1995, a new political party, the Adolat (Justice) Social Democratic Party of Uzbekistan was officially registered. In March 1995, a referendum extended Karimov's term, which was to end in 1997, to 2000. In October 1995, opposition groups including the Erk, Birlik and Adolat established the Democratic Opposition Coordinating Council under the leadership of Shakurulla Mirsaidov. Karimov resigned from the position of Chairman of the PDPU in June 1996. He proposed the creation of a political opposition to the PDPU and in December 1996, the Oly Majlis passed a new law on political parties prohibiting organisation of parties on a religious or ethnic basis. In January 1988, the Majlis conferred the Amir Timur decoration on Karimov for his services to Uzbekistan. In December 1998, President

Karimov extended his support to the founding of the Fidokorlar (Self-Sacrificers) National Democratic Party (FNDP) with Erkin Norbotayev as the leader. In the elections to the Majlis held in December 1999, the PDPU won the largest representation with forty-eight seats. The FNDP won thirty-four seats and was the second largest party. Other political parties like the Adolat and the Progress of the Fatherland (PF) achieved representation in the legislature. In the presidential elections held in January 2000, Karimov secured more than 90 per cent of the votes and was elected for another five-year term.

Uzbekistan has retained full membership of the Commonwealth of Independent States (CIS). It has close relations with other Central Asian Republics (CARs) and participates in the various regional institutions jointly founded by the CARs. However, relations with the Russian Federation have been strained as Uzbekistan has refused to grant dual citizenship to the large ethnic Russian population living in the country. Relations with China, a regional power, have been improving. During Chinese President Jiang Zemin's visit in July 1996, the two countries signed a joint declaration on bilateral relations and cooperation. Relations with the United States developed rapidly after 1997, as Uzbekistan became the second largest trading partner of the US among the CARs. After 11 September 2001, Uzbek-US relations have developed significantly with Uzbekistan providing military bases for the US military campaign in Afghanistan.

## Government and Politics

*Government Type*: Presidential Government and a unicameral legislature.

*Ruling Party*: Uzbek Communist Party (UCP).

*Head of Government*: Prime Minister Otkir Sultonov.

*Head of State*: President Islam Abduganiyevich Karimov.

President Islam Karimov of Uzbekistan heads a strong presidential form of government and all powers are concentrated in the office of the president. The Cabinet of ministers is appointed by the president with the approval of the supreme assembly. The president is elected by popular vote for a five-year term. The prime minister and the deputy prime minister are appointed by the president and continue at his pleasure. Following the referendum of January 2002, the presidential term has been extended to seven years by the Supreme Assembly. Uzbekistan has also made the transition to a bicameral legislature, which was endorsed by the referendum.

## Conflicts

*Internal Conflicts*: The Islamic Movement of Uzbekistan (IMU), a radical Islamist militant outfit is seeking to overthrow the Uzbek government and establish an Islamic regime. It claimed responsibility for terrorist attacks on Uzbek soil including bomb attacks in 1999 and 2000. The IMU is headed by Jumaboy Khojiyev (known as Juma Namangani). The Uzbek government has banned the IMU. Namangani, along with Takhir Yoldoshev, the spiritual leader of IMU, were sentenced to death in absentia in November 2000. Namangani was reportedly killed during the US military campaign in Afghanistan.

*External Conflicts*: The Ferghana Valley dispute involving Tajikistan and Kyrgyzstan is a cause of tension in the region. All three countries lay claim to the Valley and little has been done to resolve the issue. The IMU is based in the Ferghana Valley and its camps are located in the mountainous tracts of Tajikistan. It has links with Osama bin Laden's Al Qaeda and is reportedly running terrorist training camps in Afghanistan. This is a source of friction as Uzbekistan accuses Tajikistan and Afghanistan of not acting against the militant outfit. Another source of tension is Uzbekistan's refusal to forge closer political ties with Russia. It has pulled out of the Commonwealth of Independent States' (CIS) Collective Security Treaty.

## Military

Uzbekistan's armed force is the largest in the region with a total strength of 55,000. The defence structure is composed of the army, air force, internal security troops, and the national guard. There is a conscription service of eighteen months. Uzbek's inventory of military equipment and hardware is the largest in the region and comprises two Corps Headquarters, 420 Main Battle Tanks, a large number of artillery, guns and other ammunition. The former Soviet Union transferred military equipment and hardware to Uzbekistan in 1991. However, the condition of this equipment has deteriorated. Uzbekistan maintains the largest internal security force in the region with an estimated strength of 17,000. The objective is to counter the operations of the Islamic Movement of Uzbekistan (IMU), a terrorist group. The Motor Rifle Division of Uzbekistan is deployed in Tajikistan. Uzbekistan's annual defence expenditure is around US $310 million.

## Economy

Uzbekistan is a dry, landlocked country. Nearly 10 per cent of its land consists of intensively cultivated, irrigated river valleys. More than 60 per cent of its population lives in densely populated rural communities. Rice, grain, vegetables and fruits are the main agricultural products. The industrial sector includes mining, manufacturing, construction and power. Uzbekistan is the world's third largest cotton exporter and a significant producer of gold and oil. Its chemical and machinery products have a significant market presence in the region. The Uzbek government, in the post-1991 period, has sought to maintain the command economy with more subsidies and greater control on production and prices. But growing inflation has forced the government to go for economic reforms with financial assistance from international financial institutions. Uzbekistan is the largest market in Central Asia. The annual GDP growth rate is around 2.1 per cent and the per capita income is around US $2,400.

# SECTION TWO
Country Reports

# Chapter VI

# KAZAKHSTAN: BEEFING UP ITS SECURITY, ECONOMY, AND ENERGY INDUSTRY

Dr Venera Galyamova

## The New Regional Security Scenario

In the aftermath of the events of 11 September 2001, a regrouping of forces has taken place in the states of the Central Asian region. The US has played the role of a major arbitrator in the heart of Eurasia and this has significant implications for the region's political process and the relationship among key players. The US-led Afghan operations have made it clear that in the new scheme of things the US is the kingpin in a unipolar world. Despite the military operations in Afghanistan, stability in the region remains elusive. This is due to the fact that the international forces have not completely destroyed the terrorist networks and their military formations. What is more, the operations have only provoked antagonism against the West. As a result of the active cooperation of Russia and Uzbekistan with NATO and the US, the balance of power in the region has been altered to some extent.

Before the establishment of US military bases in Central Asia, a regional security system was being put in place. Kazakhstan, like the other republics of Central Asia, started setting up a security system in 1991 after it gained independence. It soon became clear that the government was interested in creating a system that would not only protect the country from the old and new non-traditional threats, but would also counter the threats that terrorism and religious extremism pose to the nation. This has been manifest in the foreign policy of Kazakhstan, which has gradually become focused on the need for security. In the context of external influences, the activities of organisations created under the framework of regional cooperation, namely the Shanghai Cooperation Organisation (SCO) and the Collective Security Treaty Organisation (CSTO), face unexpected challenges. The future of these organisations is in question. Moreover, the economic cooperation among, and the processes of integration with, the Central Asian states are expected to unravel under the onslaught of global players in the region, particularly Washington.

Kazakhstan, like most other states of the region, was keen to continue with the processes of inter-regional cooperation. Uzbekistan was perhaps the only country in the region that was less than enthusiastic about the SCO. The dialogue between China, on the one side, and Russia, Kazakhstan and three other Central Asian Republics (CARs) on the other, had led to the signing of the Charter of the SCO. However, it appears that members of the SCO must re-evaluate the general geopolitical balance, assess their capabilities and strategic interests of third parties, before the organisation can become fully effective in the new regional scenario. Until it has reworked its priorities, it is unlikely that the organisation will accept new members into its fold. India, Mongolia, Iran, and recently Pakistan, have expressed their interest in joining the organisation.

The September 2001 tragedy forced the Republic of Kazakhstan to join the anti-terrorist coalition. As an opponent of terrorist forces, Kazakhstan, along with its partner-members in the SCO, was under pressure to demonstrate that it is willing to participate as a true member of the world community. Besides, it had little choice but to cooperate with Washington in its war on terrorism. Apart from providing humanitarian assistance to the people of Afghanistan, by supplying grain and other provisions, fuel-lubricating material and technology, Kazakhstan also decided to provide aerial space to the international peacekeeping forces operational in Afghanistan and its airport for airplanes engaged in humanitarian UN missions. Besides, it declared its intention to send a peacekeeping battalion 'Kazbat'.

## Implications of US Presence

Meanwhile, it was anticipated that Washington would provide thorough information about those responsible for the 11 September terrorist acts. This, however, did not happen. Thus, the United States began to implement its strategy, and the states of Central Asia and Caucasus found themselves in a situation where they could well turn into victims of the US strategy. Ten years ago, when the CARs gained independence, many doubted their ability to survive in the post-Soviet world. Similarly, today many feel that these states will inevitably be transformed into US satellites.

The American foreign policy strategy in the context of Central Asia involves:

- Creation of democratic political institutions.
- Implementation of market-oriented reforms to accelerate economic development.
- Promoting cooperation among the states of the region and their integration into the world community.
- Implementation of an effective policy in the sphere of security, including the fight against terrorism and drug trafficking.
- Prevention of illegal trafficking of weapons of mass

destruction or components of such weapons inside the
region and beyond.

- Advancement of US commercial interests, expansion
  and diversification of global energy resources.

The US is not a new player in Central Asia. When the states
acquired their independence, the US had strived to
establish itself and play a crucial role in the region. Prior to
11 September 2001, the US sphere of influence in the
region was limited. However, in the post-11 September
environment, its influence has extended to military
cooperation.

In the present situation, Washington is clearly aiming at
altering the balance of power in the region to its advantage,
as well as hoping to extend its political success to the
economic sphere as well. On the whole, following the
events of 9/11, Kazakhstan's engagement with the US has
intensified and political cooperation has strengthened.
These developments are expected to have a substantial
impact on the medium- and long-term development of
Kazakhstan. The process has begun, as is evident from the
fact that in March 2002, the US administration accorded
Kazakhstan the status of a market-oriented economy in
terms of US anti-dumping legislation.

## The Russian Response

Simultaneously, there has been a change in Russian strategy
in the region. On the one hand, Moscow has become more
West-oriented, and on the other, there are signs that it is
striving to secure its influence in the region. This is clearly
visible on many fronts. The Kremlin is actively promoting
the processes of integration in the framework of the
Commonwealth of Independent States (CIS), and encouraging
cooperation in the economic and political spheres.

In particular, there has been huge progress in negotiations

between Kazakhstan and Russia on the issue of drawing a modified middle line in the Caspian Sea. The talks are not about territorial divisions but about gaining sovereign rights on the exploitation of resources. The heads of states have signed a memorandum, according to which Kazakhstan obtains jurisdiction over the Kurmangazi fields and gains the right to participate in exploration of the Khvalinkoe and Central fields, which hold far less extractable reserves.

Moscow's efforts to strengthen its ties with the states of CIS have borne fruit, as this is in the national interests of all the players. In a landmark event, on 23 February 2003, the presidents of Russia, Kazakhstan, Ukraine and Belarus agreed to create a common economic zone. The objective is promotion of trade under a common supranational body and synchronisation of their economic processes. Significantly, Kazakhstan was favoured with the formal leadership of this new body. Clearly, this was an indication that the president's repeated statements of fostering Eurasian unity, was being acknowledged. It is evident that the geopolitical changes will give a boost to the process of economic integration in the region. And this initiative could well be an opportunity for Kazakhstan to take giant steps towards economic prosperity.

In the current political scenario in Central Asia – with the US and Russia as the key players – it appears that China will have to take a backseat in the region. Kazakhstan, however, is poised to enhance its status in the region at several levels.

## Political Instability and the Threat of Terrorism

Despite the United States' Afghan campaign, the region still faces serious threats from drug trafficking and terrorism.[1] To quote from *Critical Decade*, a newly released book by the president of Kazakhstan, N A Nazarbayev, 'The Central

Asian region constitutes a territory with a high terrorist potential. And manifestations of extremism and terrorism covered all the republics of the region in the course of their emergence as independent and sovereign states.'

Central Asia remains a highly unstable region. Tension between the regime and the political opposition is at its peak in many of the CAR states leading to political instability. As a result, the risk of terrorist threats is very high. Besides, many of these regimes are on the verge of collapse as a result of rising religious extremism. Territorial disputes between states are routinely exploited by political, religious and ethnic groups to cause further instability and tension. While the presence of US forces in the region is a stabilising factor, the situation on the ground has not altered much during the past year.

Kazakhstan is politically more stable than most of the other CAR states. As President Nazarbayev writes in *Critical Decade*, 'Till this day there were no manifestations of extremism and terrorism in our state.' However, Kazakhstan has had to face the growing problem of import of terror and extremism into the country. Therefore, it has become critical for Kazakhstan to take adequate measures to respond to rising social conflicts and resolution of issues that have a potential for proliferation of terrorism within the Republic. These conflicts need to be tackled at several levels:

- Poor socio-economic conditions and a low standard of living are the main reasons for social aggression, which is often manifest as terrorist activities. Positive advances in the economic sphere and efforts to increase employment and income levels of the population have been initiated.[2]
- Political extremism has been on the rise and steps have been taken to prevent conflicts.
- Kazakhstan's active participation in the initiatives of international and regional security organisations is also

bearing fruit. Kazakhstan is playing a key role in the development of the SCO. Measures have been taken to further the agenda of the CSTO and make it a forum for multilateral cooperation in the sphere of security. It is actively supporting this agenda by joining hands with the anti-terrorist coalition.

- The adoption of special legal measures to fight terrorism is aimed at further strengthening the nation's stability. In February 2002, additional clauses were added to the Criminal Code of the country to deal with acts of terrorism. More such legislation is being proposed to ensure that the country is equipped to deal with any emergency that may threaten its security.

- Measures have also been taken to crack down on organised crime, illegal migration and drug trafficking, which can pose tremendous security hazards to a nation. Drug trafficking is almost always a fund-raising activity for terrorist networks. These networks have been using Kazakhstan as a transit route for drugs. The government is actively working on blocking the corridors through which drugs travel to other states in the region.

- Porous borders are used by terrorist networks to smuggle in their arms and drugs. Kazakhstan has signed a number of agreements with its neighbours and is negotiating with Uzbekistan and the Russian Federation to 'delimit' its borders. Kazakhstan's border problems with Kyrgyzstan have been resolved.

- Efforts are being made to strengthen the country's southern borders. The formation of the southern military district and three other military districts in western, eastern, and central Kazakhstan are steps that have been taken to secure the country against aggressors.

President Nazarbayev has emphasised in *Critical Decade* that 'Kazakhstan is in a winning position, as we have time to thoroughly analyse the ... proliferation of terrorism in the world, as well as the experience of resisting this phenomenon. At the same time, a substantial level of terrorist activity in regions, close to Kazakhstan, keeps the security system in the condition of high alert.' As a result, following the events of September 2001, Kazakhstan perceives that it needs to empower itself by realigning its foreign policy in a manner that is aimed at preserving stability in Central Asia and ensuring its own security interests.

## Carving a National Identity

In the past, Kazakhstan's brush with modernisation was indirect as it was a part of the Russian empire and later the USSR. After gaining independence, Kazakhstan entered a new phase with the national government initiating reforms in a limited manner. The transition to a market-oriented economy and democratic institutions has had a lasting impact on the nation. It has meant a dramatic change from the old political and economic systems and has therefore been a difficult process. The impact has been felt in all spheres of life, particularly politics.

Western analysts and critics have pointed out that in Kazakhstan, power is vested in the president and therefore there is a tendency towards authoritarianism and weak opposition. Despite many flaws, Kazakhstan has had many achievements during its decade of independence. First of all, the structure of the government – with authority resting in one individual – has enabled it to embark on swift political and economic reforms, which has helped Kazakhstan establish itself as a regional leader. It has ensured domestic stability in critical times, prevented inter-ethnic rivalries from assuming critical proportions and helped stem the rise of divisive forces. Besides, it is unlikely that a straightforward replication of the Western model would have been successful in the Kazakhstan context.[3] Instead, Kazakhstan has adopted a gradual reform process to transform itself politically and economically. It is evident that this strategy is working, as it can be witnessed from the strengthening of the Opposition political parties. As political parties mature, democratic institutions will get strengthened and in the process Kazakhstan will evolve into a democracy in the true sense of the word.

Kazakhstan could easily have disintegrated into a battle-ground of rivals hailing from different ethnic backgrounds, spurred by the rapid rise in religious and extremist movements. But fortunately for Kazakhstan society, the people have been able to transcend the interethnic rivalries. While it is alleged that the Kazakh government has suppressed the religious and ethnic minorities, that is far from true. In fact, religious and ethnic self-awareness has grown over the years, even as people have gained a new national identity as 'Kazakhstanis'.

The rise in religious extremist movements in Kazakhstan continues to be a cause of concern, more so, in a scenario where world events have completely changed the region's geopolitical dynamics. The defeat of the Taliban in Afghanistan and the presence of NATO troops on the territories of some Central Asian Republics have provoked anti-West attitudes and this could spark off religious fanaticism. Supporters of the Taliban and other such groups could easily exploit such sentiments to resuscitate their movements. To minimise such a risk, it is necessary to mobilise special forces that can take on the role of strengthening national security. Simultaneously, conditions have to be created for development of the state and society.

The well-being of a society and the viability of a state are often reflected by the degree of religious harmony and ideological unity of the people. In the post-Soviet era, the CARs have struggled to establish a 'national identity'. In

Kazakhstan, for instance, ethnic identity is very diverse and there are as many as fifty-six ethnic groupings. Not surprisingly, carving a common identity has been a difficult process. In the absence of a common ideological base for the people, the impact of globalisation can often lead to disastrous consequences. The religious and moral marginalisation of youth, combined with the lack of a progressive education system and employment opportunities, often results in the rapid expansion of fundamentalist groups that seek to exploit the situation. The marginalisation of Kazakh-speaking youth and those from the rural areas is a major cause for concern. Forced to migrate to cities, this section of the population often end up as lumpen elements.

In the wake of an independent Kazakhstan, the state authorities sought to use the 'independence' platform to create unity among its people. But the strategy did not work, as the fruits of independence have not resulted in economic prosperity for a majority of the people. Moreover, a section of the population was also unhappy about the disintegration of the USSR. In order to create a new ideological orientation, the government resorted to creating a theoretical concept of socio-economic well-being, by harping on its achievements in creating new employment opportunities. It is also focusing on the emergence of a new Kazakh middle-class which it hopes will drive economic growth in the country. A lot remains to be done by the government to boost this progress. The new focus on socio-economic well-being could not have been more timely. As a result, in a short period of time, the ideology has begun to be accepted. Identifying oneself as a citizen of the Republic of Kazakhstan has become fashionable and this further strengthens the notion of national identity. The new urban, middle-class Kazakhstanis are increasingly acquiring a higher profile. On the other hand, there is also an increase in the lumpenisation of the rural population, which poses a potential threat to national security and, if left untackled, could be disastrous.

## Steps towards Political Reform

Today Kazakhstan is at an important stage in its development, on the threshold of what was described recently by President Nursultan Nazarbayev as 'our readiness to leave behind our past and enter a new historical stage of development of an Independent Kazakhstan.' Among the most significant events have been the government's gradual steps towards political reforms. Consider these:

- By introducing the job of Secretary of State, the government is making an effort to improve the administrative set-up, strengthening authority from the top down. The fact that this job was awarded to the minister of foreign affairs, Kasimjomart Tokaev, is an indication of the priority given to foreign policy in Kazakhstan today.
- Two new actors have arrived on the political stage of Kazakhstan, namely, the Democratic Choice of Kazakhstan and Ak Jol.
- The increasingly anti-establishment stance taken by leaders of Opposition political parties is likely to be a feature of the political movement. In the past, Opposition leaders remained largely loyal to the central authority. The new anti-establishment posture has resulted in arrests of some leaders. While these events have shaken up the Kazakhstani society, it indicates a churn in the political system in modern Kazakhstan.
- The government has introduced the position of an ombudsman, demonstrating its willingness to meet international norms on protection of civil rights and liberties.

- The enactment of new legislation on political parties in July 2002, which determines the legal framework for formation, registration and activities of political parties, is another significant development. The law states that the major function of a political party is to represent the interests of citizens and participate in elections. The formation of political parties on ethnic and religious grounds is prohibited in the Republic.
- Elections for the municipal heads of rural districts were held in an effort to create conditions for effective administration and decentralising authority.
- There are ongoing efforts to build consensus for political reform of the state. Conferences are convened at which representatives of the government and civil society come together to devise strategies on liberalisation of the political system.

The process of political development depends on further democratisation of the political system, gradual politicisation of the business elite as well as the development of a strong political Opposition, building up political awareness among the Kazakh people and ensuring a mix of centralisation as well as decentralisation of power.

The political system in Kazakhstan has for long been practically bipolar – on one side there is a powerful government and on the other, a weak Opposition. Such a structure of political system is characteristic of new states that are making the transition to nationhood. Among the main issues that need to be resolved is the division of power among various interest groups representing different political ideologies and sections of the population. The bipolar structure, being simple and containing proficient mechanisms, satisfies the ruling elite of the country.

In the second half of 2001, various groups comprising both the Opposition political parties and members of the elite began to put forward their political demands. Technocrats, business organisations and groups that included former high-ranking state officials were part of the new elite groups. The creation of a new Opposition movement, the Democratic Choice of Kazakhstan (DCK), and then the political party Ak Jol, both of which became publicly active, was the turning point in the political development in Kazakhstan. The DCK is headed by former state officials of the country and representatives of the political and economic elite while the Ak Jol has a strong financial base and is better equipped than its political rivals to make a mark. Ak Jol's charter points to its readiness to act in the framework of the existing state Constitution and work constructively with the government. The leaders of the party have repeatedly been emphasising and demonstrating that their measures of democratisation do not clash with the strategic course of the development of the society and the state.

It is no secret that since Kazakhstan gained independence influential political agencies in the West and international organisations have been putting pressure on the country to usher in democracy. The most active in this regard have been the United Nations, Organisation for Security and Cooperation in Europe (OSCE), the US State Department and international non-government human rights organisations. They have been calling for the democratisation of state and society, strengthening of rights and liberties, and the development of civil society. As a result of their influence, the nature and content of the development of domestic political processes have been altered to a certain extent.

The events of 9/11 were expected to increase the influence of these organisations, particularly in the context of Kazakhstan's military cooperation with the US and other state members of NATO. This impact has been reflected in the strengthening of the Opposition political parties and their new-found activism. The Opposition is keen to privatise public sector enterprises and pave the way for foreign investment and they have now found Western support for this cause. The revival of the political parties will inevitably lead to a disruption of the present regime, which is widely perceived as being corrupt.

Despite the 'external' influence on political processes in Kazakhstan, these Western organisations have not been able to translate their influence into real political change, and this in turn has led to a weakening of these influences in the past year. As far as the local Opposition is concerned, its main aim is to influence the regime to allow the creation of political parties and their representation in Parliament. They have been using their external influence to gain recognition and thereby exert pressure on the development of the internal political system. As a result, a new hierarchy of relations between the central authority on the one hand and the political and business elite on the other is taking place. This in turn provokes an active involvement of the groups of elite, who aim to obtain maximum dividends from the present situation. The involvement of the mass media in this process is also a crucial factor. The Kazakhstani mass media has been effective in highlighting the activities of the Opposition parties and the business elite. This has in turn forced the central authority to crack down and restrain the rights of some of the most radical media groups, in the 'interests of societal security'. In 2002, the effect of domestic pressure on politics was more pronounced than external ones. The participation of various social groups as well as major actors in the political arena has further strengthened this movement.

Corruption is a major barrier to economic and social prosperity in Kazakhstan. There have been efforts to rein in corruption, particularly in the sphere of administrative offence. Special commissions have been established to deal with this problem and the agency of state services has set up a department to curb corruption. But this is unlikely to yield quick results unless the bureaucratic processes are changed. The existing system of recruiting government personnel has led to the proliferation of corrupt practices. And the complex bureaucratic system defies any initiative by the government to track those indulging in corruption. This, in turn, is highlighted by the media as a failure on the part of the regime. Currently, specific efforts towards decentralisation and limiting the powers of regional state bodies are aimed at curbing corruption. Providing financial autonomy to regions is being seen as one of the measures to fight corruption.

## Reviving the Economy

The process of economic reforms has been quite successful and has established Kazakhstan as a leader in the region. Today, the country is on the threshold of a new liberalised, market economy. A number of major events promise more prosperous times for the nation: These include:

- The president has announced a three-year action plan (2003–2005) for developing the rural economy, transport infrastructure and standard of living of the population, and further integration of the economy of the country with regional common markets. Under the programme, a framework for financial assistance to villages and development of accommodation for inhabitants of rural regions has been drawn up. It also aims at stimulating domestic migration from unfavourable regions to regional centres and small cities. Prime Minister I Tasmagambetov pointed out in his 6 February 2003 speech, 'The government is faced with four priority objectives on revival of villages: stabilisation of food market of the country; avoiding a sharp downfall in provision of domestic products for the people under the pressure from imported goods; creation of preconditions for sustainable economic growth by the means of correlation of agrarian and industrial sectors; and halting the degradation of rural infrastructure.'

- The European Union and the US have granted Kazakhstan the status of a country with market economy.

- A new law on investors has been enacted, which, according to critics, gives the government more opportunities to regulate foreign companies.

- Kazakhstan has been propagating economic integration with the states of the CIS, including Russia, Ukraine and Belarus. It is not by accident that this initiative was undertaken by the president of Kazakhstan. The economies of the other CARs have yet to reach the level of development necessary for an integration that can lead to realistic gains.

- The first phase of exploration of the Kazakhstani part of the Caspian Sea is one of the priorities for the government this year.

- A new legislation is sought to be brought into force to ensure rights of ownership to private property. This will further give a boost to privatisation and place Kazakhstan way ahead of its Central Asian neighbours.

The country's oil production plants have given a boost to overall economic growth. The country's oil production totalled 42 million tonnes in 2002, which is a rise of 17 per cent over the previous year. The oilfields of KazMunaiGas, Mangistaumunaigas and Hurricane Kumkol Munai have obtained the largest oil production surpluses. The Tengiz deposit has registered a growth of 13 million tonnes. The domestic oil-processing plants processed 7.8 million tonnes of oil, which is 25 per cent more than in 2001. The production of oil products increased by 6 per cent. In 2003, the ministry of energy and mineral resources estimates that the production will increase by 10 million tonnes, largely due to the activities of KazMunaiGas, Karachaganak, Kasgermunai and SNPS-Aktobemunaigas. It is forecast that the oil-processing output will reach 8.5 million tonnes.

Almost all regions of Kazakhstan witnessed growth in energy production in 2002. The biggest growth was in the Western region due to the installation of the Karachaganak gas turbine station and also in Aktube region after the installation of steam turbine in Akturbo. Energy production grew by 5.6 per cent last year compared to 2001 and energy consumption too rose by 2.6 per cent.

The annual GDP growth in 2001 was 13.2 per cent (2002: 9.2 per cent). The country registered a growth in oil production of 17 per cent; production volumes in the chemical industry grew 1.6 times; the food industry grew by 26 per cent and the agrarian industry by 17 per cent. However, the contribution of exports to the Kazakhstani GDP was as high as 80 per cent in 2001. Of this, 52 per cent was accounted for by oil sales, and the rest were mainly non-ferrous metals. Thus, the mainstay of economic activity is raw material export. Consequently, in the aftermath of 9/11, the economy witnessed a slowdown due to its dependence on the external market.

Kazakhstan has substantial gold reserves which gives it a certain amount of stability. The growth in the oil and gas industry has had a positive impact on the other sectors as well. This has, in turn, spurred growth in enterprise and consumer demand. One positive factor is that 50 per cent of the investment that was made in the economy in 2001 was generated through the domestic industry's own resources. In 2002, Kazakhstani banks' credit ratings grew as a result of the growth in bank deposits by the people and increased money flow up to 18.5 per cent of GDP. The government's initiatives in strengthening the banking sector and the drawing up of a taxation policy have helped the Kazakhstan financial sector emerge as one of the strongest in the CIS. However, there are many issues that need to be resolved. For instance, what measures will the government take to ensure that the economy is protected from any volatility in the external market scenario, considering that the Kazakhstan economy is dependent on export of raw material? The other significant issue is the policy towards foreign investment. This is still under development and its absence continues to be an inhibiting factor in attracting investment.

## Outlook for the Future

The events of 9/11 have had a huge impact on the geopolitical situation in the region. But even so, Kazakhstan has remained more of a witness to the changes taking place than an active participant. As is apparent, Kazakhstan has not altered either its foreign policy or domestic policy dramatically. It has managed to keep its 'distance' from the West. However, it has made a few adjustments and these have primarily to do with closer ties with Russia and China within the framework of the Shanghai Cooperation Organisation.

During this period, Kazakhstan has not veered from its objectives of economic growth, protection against the impact of a global economic downturn, development of mutual cooperation with world powers and regional neighbours, creation of a stable country, and warding off existing and potential threats to its security. In the future, Kazakhstan can be expected to balance its relationship with the West on the one hand and Russia and China on the other. This is dictated by the fact that the US is striving to pressure Astana to move towards democracy and protection of human rights and, at the same time, to ensure continued access to Kazakhstan's energy resources in the future. It is, therefore, not surprising that Kazakhstan should try to build closer relations with Russia and China to balance its relationship with Washington. Such a strategy will also ensure the long-term interests of the country, as these will be the main economic partners of Kazakhstan in the future.

There is tremendous uncertainty about the future as a result of the establishment of the foreign military bases in the region; the consequent shift in the geopolitical situation and the tenuous alliances between the regional states; and the potential threat of terrorism. Besides these factors, it is also uncertain as to how George Bush's foreign policy and the emergence of a new world order is likely to affect the region. The future outlook of the Central Asian Region, therefore, is difficult to predict. A lot will depend on the shifts in strategies of the key players in the region – the US, Russia, the EU, and China.

A thorough assessment of the geopolitical scenario in the Central Asian Region and its impact on Kazakhstan cannot be complete without considering the Caspian Sea factor. The new situation points to a stronger position for the US in the region and it is expected that the US will leverage its new position to access the Caspian oil. This would not only help in eliminating the domination of the OPEC countries in determining oil prices but also effectively lead to US control over hydrocarbon resources.

For Kazakhstan, this would translate into further development of its energy industry and an inflow of foreign investments. It is clear that for all Central Asian states the new situation is likely to result in economic gain. As the strategic significance of Central Asia increases, it is apparent that the development of transport and communication infrastructure will be beefed up to access the region's energy resources. It is also clear that projects dealing with oil and gas sector development, including the TRACECA programme (Transport Corridor – Europe, Caucasus and

Asia), will be given top priority. The region is expected to be quickly integrated with global markets.

In conclusion, the geopolitical crisis following the events of 9/11 have apparently been resolved without a breakdown in dialogue and has even created favourable conditions for the development of the Central Asian states and deeper cooperation between Kazakhstan and its regional neighbours as well as with the big powers.

## Notes

1. In Kazakhstan, Kyrgyzstan, Tajikistan and Uzbekistan alone, the consumption of drug has tripled in the period between 1992 and 2000. This in turn has led to an increase in the number of those who are HIV-positive. In the course of the past seven years the number of infected people in these countries has increased by 600 times.

2. For example, a deep crisis in the neighbouring Kyrgyz Republic, which became the subject of discussion for many researchers, was to a large extent provoked by recommendations put forward by Western analysts.

3. 'About the main course of domestic and foreign policy in 2003', from the address of the president to the people of Kazakhstan, Astana, April 2002.

4. Under the framework of the US Freedom Act, a sum of 576 million dollars was allocated for the year 2004. This money was for programmes on integration of Eurasia into the Euro-Atlantic community and strengthening of stability of regional states in the fight against terrorism.

   The current allocation of 179 million dollars is an amount much smaller than the one for 2003 fiscal year. This decrease, partly reflects transfer of financial resources to the educational and professional exchange programmes, allocation to the programmes of educational and cultural exchange in the framework of the ministry of trade, the state department, and the ministry of justice. In 2002 fiscal year, the allocation for such exchanges stood at 110 million dollars. Moreover, 11.4 million dollars were allocated for exchanges by the means of additional financing in 2002 fiscal year.

   All over Eurasia, the programmes under the US Freedom Act for the year 2004 fiscal year have two priority goals dominating: Decentralisation of authority and strengthening of civil society (by the means of strengthening NGOs, independent mass media, local authorities, and judicial branch of government) and strengthening of the power of law (by fighting against corruption and effective conduct of the system of provision of order).

5. 'About the main course of domestic and foreign policy in 2003', from the address of the president to the people of Kazakhstan, Astana, April 2002.

6. It is known that in the Republic of Kazakhstan, about one million people live by the minimal standard of self-sustainability, as far as the quality of land, natural and social conditions are concerned.

7. For example, in October 2002, a sum of 350 million dollars was paid in Eurobonds and direct state debt had thus decreased to $3.7 billion.

8. Even if the military bases are temporary and will be removed soon (which is highly unlikely), the fact remains that the US was able to build up its presence in the region and secured the fulfilment of its future interests.

# Chapter VII

# KYRGYZSTAN – THE SIEGE WITHIN

Gulsara Osorova

## Introduction

The terrorist attacks on the United States on 11 September 2001 have irreversibly changed perceptions of security across the world. Nations are reassessing their priorities in the face of a threat that is multi-faceted and poses enormous challenges on a global scale. The substantial impact of the very clear and present danger that terrorism poses to the world has compelled every country, culture, region, race, religion and creed to make efforts to pool their strengths in a bid to refurbish their security infrastructure and policies. The terrorist threat in Central Asia, in this context, has enormous significance for the region and the world.

Much has been written about the Central Asian states and their attempts to establish themselves as independent, sovereign states in a post-Soviet world. The CARs have been a source of concern for Western security analysts who recognise the fact that after the break up of the USSR, these states are a potential source of instability and vulnerability. This threat of instability is further exacerbated due to the turmoil in neighbouring Afghanistan, which has for years been pumping drugs, terror and arms into a region that is a potentially rich source of oil and natural gas.

The five states – Kazakhstan, Kyrgyzstan, Tajikistan,

Turkmenistan and Uzbekistan – have made fundamental changes in their political, social, economic, military and security set-up during the last decade to foster stability and counter the threats that they face. The emergence of opposition Islamist groups in the region has posed tremendous challenges to the security of the CARs. Since the late 1990s, these groups have been particularly active in the south of Kyrgzstan. During 1999 and 2000, Kyrgyzstan, for instance, has had to cope with several Islamic Movement of Uzbekistan (IMU) incursions. Coupled with the Afghan civil war and the emergence of the Taliban as an exporter of terror, the threat to regional security increased perceptibly, culminating in the events of 11 September 2001. Some of the Central Asian states, which had no military infrastructure, took steps to preserve and safeguard their territorial integrity. As a result, in 2001, Kyrgyzstan approached Russia for help in fighting the Islamic guerrillas who had taken twenty hostages near the Tajikistan border. Later the Kyrgyz Republic created the Southern Group of Forces comprising approximately 6,000 troops from various components of the armed forces that are deployed in the southern Batken Oblast to defend against renewed IMU incursions. Further, the five countries have taken steps to boost regional security: the Collective Security Treaty signed in Tashkent in 2001 led to the creation of the Bishkek-based Collective Rapid Deployment Forces.

All the countries in the region face tremendous challenges in curtailing the spread of the terror network, and putting up effective defence mechanisms to safeguard their national interests. The task is made even more difficult in the light of the social and economic security measures that these countries need to implement to beef up their national security. This paper focuses on the impact of 9/11 on, and the challenges faced by, Kyrgyzstan.

## Striving for Economic Growth

Kyrgyzstan is one of the smallest states in Central Asia with a population of approximately 4.7 million spread over a territory of 198.5 thousand square kilometre. Most of the country is mountainous with the Tian Shan mountain range forming a spectacular backdrop. The state is flanked by the Republic of Kazakhstan in the north, the Republic of Uzbekistan in the west, the Republic of Tajikistan in the south-west and the People's Republic of China in the south-east.

Reforms have been an important feature of the development of the Kyrgyz Republic during the last decade. These reforms are aimed at creating sustainable economic growth and giving a fillip to the principles of democracy, good governance, transparency, human rights protection and market economics. In order to join the mainstream of global development and integrate itself with international society, Kyrgyzstan has consciously sought to revise outdated approaches and methods of resolving social, political and economic issues, while remaining strongly committed to the principles of democracy, good governance and human rights protection. As a result, the country has gained support from international development agencies and donor organisations.

## US Support

Ever since Kyrgyzstan gained independence in the early 1990s, it has been pursuing a policy of transition to a market economy. It has also concentrated on infrastructure development and the creation of an efficient monetary system. The decision to put in place mechanisms that would ensure sustainable economic growth has been taken in order to integrate the state into the world economy. However, it has been a difficult task and attempts to create a better market system and involve reputed institutions and professionals for better macroeconomic management have not been successful. The main reasons for this are the lack of stability in economic growth, failure to complete the process of economic reforms in all sectors and a lengthy and arduous public sector reform process. As a result, financial markets are not functioning in an efficient manner, and the conditions necessary for growth of private business enterprise and investment are not in place. There are other barriers that make sustainable economic growth a difficult proposition. Prominent among them are the high degree of dependence on international financial aid, lack of access to international commodity and financial markets, difficulties in trading with neighbouring countries as well as threats from international terrorism.

Events following the terrorist attacks of 11 September 2001, have also had an impact on the economy of Kyrgyzstan. The emergence of a global consensus on the 'war on terrorism' led to Kyrgyzstan granting the US access to its Manas airbase near Bishkek to facilitate anti-Taliban operations in Afghanistan. According to the terms of agreement between the US and Kyrgyzstan, the former will pay between $5,000 and $7,000 per day towards the use of the air base's facilities, including landing rights, rent and use of the airbase.[1] The agreement has also led to an increase in American assistance to the Kyrgyzstan economy.[2] The assistance is being provided under the aegis of a bilateral memorandum on mutual understanding, cooperation and support of economic reforms in the Kyrgyz Republic. Towards that end, in April 2002, Bill Taylor, coordinator of US assistance to the newly independent states at the State Department, visited Kyrgyzstan. During his visit, Taylor revealed that efforts were being made to lobby the US Congress to double its financial support to Kyrgyzstan, from the present US $30 million. The US has also promised to assist in the development of the private sector including small business development, provide assistance in securing borders as well as help in reforming and developing crucial sectors such as water and health.[3]

US financial assistance to Kyrgyzstan in the year 2002 added up to $50.2 million and comprised the following:

- Programmes to support democracy – $11.4 million
- Market reform programmes – $12 million
- Security programmes – $12 million
- Humanitarian aid – $6.2 million
- Inter-sectoral initiatives – $8.3 million

Besides, the US Minister of Finance, Paul O'Neil has also announced that the US will continue to support Kyrgyzstan in its efforts to stabilise the economy and strengthen its security and defence infrastructure. While it is apprehended that US financial assistance will diminish in the wake of the Iraq conflict, the US Ambassador to Kyrgyzstan has stated that the US will maintain the standards and norms of financial and other support to Kyrgyzstan's economy, notwithstanding any changes in US external policy.[4]

## The Socio-Economic Crisis

The only silver lining in Kyrgyzstan's grim economic scenario is the energy sector. There is a huge potential for attracting investment in this sector, particularly in hydroelectric power generation. Kyrgyzstan has enormous sources of hydroelectric power and this sector is already generating revenues for the state. The state's hydroelectric power potential is estimated at about 52 billion kW per year and is expected to rise to 99 billion kW per year by the year 2020. Kyrgyzstan can therefore hope to become a major exporter of energy by supplying power to the markets of China, the new independent states and Iran. However, at present, only 3 per cent of this potential is being met. To achieve its potential, this sector would have to attract investments, for which an efficient administrative and legal framework would need to be put in place. Currently, due to the lack of such a framework, investment in this sector too is beginning to decline.

Despite significant contributions to the economy of Kyrgyzstan by the energy sector, the current situation is far from optimistic. The state budget deficit remains high, external debt to donor countries has risen to $1.5 billion, which is quite significant for a state with a population of about five million, and higher than the annual GDP of Kyrgyzstan[5]. The standard of living for the majority of people remains low – about 55 per cent of the population has been officially declared as 'poor' of which 23 per cent are in the category of 'very poor'. Income inequality is growing and living conditions have deteriorated, especially in the rural areas, while the ranks of the unemployed are growing.[6]

This has led to social insecurity among the people, thereby making the society vulnerable to conflict and instability. Despite the well-developed social security system of providing support to the poorest, inefficient functioning has led to delays in payments. Besides, the lack of direction and unclear commitment towards providing financial support to the poorest of the poor and the economic reforms process have further worsened the socio-economic condition. As a result, social insecurity among people is high, which, in turn, tends to make society vulnerable to ethnic conflicts, social destabilisation and crises.

Coupled with the rise in international terrorism and religious extremism, social and economic insecurity have led to a volatile situation, which needs to be set right urgently by the political establishment. Socio-economic insecurity has major implications for the stability and security of the state. Lack of economic growth, and the consequent inability of the government to offer people employment opportunities, on the one hand, and the growing incidence of poverty on the other, have led to a rise in drug trafficking, religious extremism, prostitution and slavery. Often people are forced to become drug couriers and provide other illegal services (which are euphemistically known as 'welfare services') to eke out a living and improve their economic status. Growing poverty and the desperation to use radical means to survive create a potential for conflict that is as debilitating as any armed conflict. At the round-table meeting of the Bishkek Global Summit, it was noted by one of the speakers that 'governments should equally react to the existence of armed conflicts and social and economic problems that gave rise to conflict in the first place'.[7]

Clearly, unsolved economic and social issues have a tendency to pose a major threat to the stability and security of a nation. Greater dependence on foreign investments, insufficient economic reforms, lack of strategically significant natural resources are some of the factors that have contributed to the social insecurity in Kyrgyzstan. Unless these issues are addressed urgently, they have the potential of threatening the nation's immediate and long-term security.

## Security and Geostrategic Concerns

In the aftermath of 9/11, Kyrgyzstan's main priority has been to beef up its defence infrastructure. The need for this was first felt, as has been mentioned earlier, during the IMU[8] incursions between 1998 and 2000. The rise in Islamic fundamentalism and the increase in drug trafficking in the region further posed threats to the nation's security. To meet these challenges, Kyrgyzstan has taken a number of measures.

Islamic militancy poses problems for not just Kyrgyzstan but other countries in the Ferghana Valley[9] and threatens Russia as well. To counter this threat, the framework of the Collective Security Treaty – signed by heads of governments of Russia, Belarus, Armenia, Kazakhstan, Kyrgyzstan and Tajikistan in Tashkent in May 1992[10] – mooted the creation of the Collective Rapid Deployment Forces (CRDF) in April 2001. The CRDF is mandated to function as a joint coordinating force with headquarters at Bishkek. An 'anti-terrorist centre', headquartered in Moscow, was established in mid-2000 by the member states of the Commonwealth of Independent States, to combat the growing menace of terrorism collectively. A subsidiary branch of this centre is located at Bishkek. At a meeting of the heads of member countries of the Shanghai Cooperation Organisation in 1999, a decision was taken to set up a regional anti-terrorist centre under the aegis of the SCO. This centre is expected to begin operations soon.

From 6 January 2002, the United States was allowed the use of the Manas airbase near Bishkek. While the objective was clearly to combat terrorism emanating from Afghanistan and rebuilding it after the war, Kyrgyzstan also had much to gain from this US involvement. The IMU had been using the Afghan civil war to create tensions within Kyrgyzstan's borders. This also soured the state's relations with Uzbekistan. The other major issue was the spurt in drug trafficking. The agreement between the Kyrgyz Republic and the US was seen to have a positive impact, not just in tackling terrorism but also in engaging with Uzbekistan on border issues. Initially, the agreement with the US was signed for a period of one year and was limited to the period of the Afghanistan operations. In 2003, the agreement was further extended. It now appears that American military presence is likely to be a long-term affair. Some troops belonging to the West European countries and to the American air forces have also been deployed at Gansi. Many feel that the presence of US troops in Kyrgyzstan will have a positive effect, particularly in terms of establishing a more secure environment on its southern borders and improving relations with Tajikistan and Uzbekistan. Another positive fallout of the American military presence is that Kyrgyzstan can now reorganise its armed forces.[11] Under US supervision, the Kyrgyz armed forces can be transformed into a professional and efficient force.

US presence in Kyrgyzstan has major geostrategic implications. The Collective Security Treaty and the Collective Rapid Deployment Forces,[12] created in 2001, were the outcome of a coordinated initiative launched by Russia to ensure a commitment of the countries in the region in the event of a crisis or conflict.[13] After the deployment of US forces in Kyrgyzstan and other Central Asian states, it soon became clear that Russia would strengthen its capacities on its 'southern borders'. Russia called on the CRDF to enhance regional security[14] and Russian forces were deployed at the Kant airbase.

The deployment of American air forces in Kyrgyzstan and Central Asia was perceived by the Russians as security threat to its 'southern borders'. Similarly, another neighbour, China, was concerned by the American presence in the region. China stated publicly, and unapologetically, that it viewed the US presence as a hindrance to its strategic objectives of dominating the region.[15]

Both Russia and China are key players in the region though they have played different roles. China's diplomatic relations with Kyrgyzstan were established when the state gained independence. Over the years, China has gained in importance in Kyrgyzstan's foreign policy. This is evident the increased interactions between the two countries, culminating in the official visit of the president of the

Kyrgyz Republic, A Akayev, to China. During the visit, the two countries agreed to broaden bilateral relations, cooperate in the political, cultural and economic spheres and cooperate in education, infrastructure development and investment. The highlight of the visit was an agreement signed by the two countries propagating friendship, cooperation and neighbourly relations. Kyrgyzstan is only the third country – after Russia and Mongolia – with which China has signed such an agreement. China has promised to invest, in up to 500 projects, an amount estimated US $30 million. Chinese involvement in trade too has been significant. In 2002, trade between China and Kyrgyzstan amounted to $120,900 million.

Russia has for long been a provider of markets and assistance, including security assistance, to Kyrgyzstan. The official language of Kyrgyzstan is Russian and culturally, the people have common ties with Russia. Kyrgyzstan also features prominently in Russia's foreign policy. Therefore, Russia remains Kyrgyzstan's closest strategic partner. But clearly the deployment of US air forces in Kyrgyzstan will have an impact on this relationship. For the present, Kyrgyzstan feels more secure as both the IMU and the Taliban movements have been defeated and in the aftermath of the Afghan war, its relations with Uzbekistan and Tajikistan have improved. However, the presence of three major international players, Russia, the USA and China, could inevitably lead to a clash of interests which could have huge implications for Krygyzstan's national and security interests.

## Conclusion

The biggest impact of 9/11 on Kyrgyzstan has been the elimination of threats posed by groups such as the IMU and the Taliban. Further, it has led to an increasing awareness of the need to counter terrorist threats by forging regional cooperation. American military presence also has led to a perception of greater security. However, Kyrgyzstan is on the verge of economic and social collapse and this makes it more vulnerable to external as well as internal threats. Greater dependence on foreign investments, insufficient economic reforms, and lack of strategically significant natural resources do not offer much optimism on the economic front. The volatile political and social environment pose more of a security threat to the nation than any external factor and unless these issues are addressed by the political leadership of Kyrgyzstan, the nation cannot hope to provide safety and security to its people.

## Notes

1. Local newspaper, *Vechernii Bishkek*, January 2002.
2. Anna Kirey, Coordinator of US assistance to NIS countries, *Central Asia-Caucasus Analyst*, 24 April 2002.
3. M Ashimbaev, M Laumulin, Ye, Tukumov, L Gusseva, D Kalieva, A Kozhikov, *New Challenges and new geopolitics in Central Asia after September 11*, pp.45–49, 2003.
4. Local newspaper, *Vechernii Bishkek*, March 2003.
5. GDP consisted of 14.4 per cent in 2002 and has a trend towards decreasing.
6. National Statistic Committee of the Kyrgyz Republic – 2003.
7. S Frederick Starr, *'Conflict and Peace in Mountain Societies'*, Section: 'Mountain Cultures and Civil Society', Bishkek Global Mountain Summit, Kyrgyz Republic, Autumn 2002.
8. Islamic Movement of Uzbekistan.
9. The largest valley in Central Asia and comprises most parts, Uzbekistan, Tajikistan and Kyrgyzstan.
10. Summit of the heads of States, May 1992, Tashkent, Uzbekistan.
11. M Ashimbaev, M Laumulin, Ye, Tukumov, L Gusseva, D Kalieva, A Kozhikov, *New Challenges and new geopolitics in Central Asia after September 11*, pp.45–49, 2003.
12. Summit of the heads of States, May 1992, Tashkent, Uzbekistan.
13. William D O'Malley and Roger N McDermott, 'The Russian Air Force in Kyrgyzstan: The Security Dynamics', *Central Asia-Caucasus Analyst*, 9 April 2003.
14. Ibid.
15. Robert Cutler, 'Redrawing the architecture of Central Asian security', *Central Asia-Caucasus Analyst*, 27 February 2002.

# Chapter VIII

# ISLAMIC REVIVALISM IN TAJIKISTAN

Dr Suchandana Chatterjee

## Introduction

The world of Islam continues to be a focal point of study for scholars who are keen to observe social and political trends in Central Asia. In the post-Soviet period, there has been an emphasis on the cultural attributes of Islam and discussions revolve round Islam as a 'way of life', the social origins of the Islamic community, and diversity within Islam. Such discussions not only create awareness about 'tradition' in Central Asia, but also help reverse stereotyped explanations about the relationship between religion and politics. This interest in 'tradition' tends to get lost in the jargon about 'Islamic fundamentalism'. The terms 'political Islam' and 'Islamic fundamentalism' are often used interchangeably. Referring to Islamic revivalism in Central Asia, experts on security-related issues often take the extreme position of identifying Islamic radical groups as terrorist organisations. Hence, it is Islamic 'revival' or 'regeneration' that is the most sought-after topic of debate among scholars.

In various studies of Islamic revivalism in Central Asia, the dominant trend has been to view 'revival of religiosity' as a negative influence on society in general. Scholars tend to project 1991 as the landmark year as it represents a 'break' from the Soviet past. In post-Soviet literature, there has been a tendency to compare and contrast the Soviet and post-Soviet periods. The emphasis is on the atheist mentality of Soviet authorities and their unwillingness to accommodate Islam in Central Asia. The argument is that such an attitude alienated people of Central Asia who held more conservative beliefs. With the collapse of the Soviet Union, the religiously alienated eventually became the flag bearers of Islamic revivalism.[1]

This argument, however, does not hold as it does not seriously take into consideration the works of Soviet ethnographers who have analysed Central Asian *byt* (way of life). Second, it is erroneous to take a lopsided view of revivalism by only studying contemporary revivalist trends in Central Asia. The fact is that there have been revivalist movements in the seventeenth, eighteenth and nineteenth centuries in Central, South and West Asia. As among *jadids* (reformers), there was good deal of contact among *qadimis* (traditionalists) in the entire region and their ideas spread mainly through the dissemination of literature. Therefore, it is wrong to assume that resurgence or revival is a new phenomenon and is exclusive to the post-Soviet period.

This paper examines the metamorphosis of Islamic revivalism in Tajikistan which is the southernmost independent republic of Central Asia. Tajikistan is home to people and political parties with conflicting interests. Most prominent among them is the Islamic Renaissance Party (IRP), which is associated with a 'resurgence mentality' and has networked with revivalist groups in the Middle East, and West and Central Asia since the 1970s. The IRP subsequently split into various factions after the Civil War of 1992. Most of its members have been inducted into the political mainstream. Due to its fragmentation, the radical groups within the Islamic movement have been marginalised to a great extent. Today, the ideological battle between communists and Islamists no longer exists. The antagonistic relationship between the state and the revivalists has come to an end. In this context, it is worth exploring the symbiotic relationship between the state and society in general and the forces of tradition in particular. Lastly, the paper focuses on the post-9/11 scenario and the growing awareness among its neighbours of the social implications of Islamic jihad in Tajikistan.

## Social Character of Islamic Revivalism in Tajikistan

For quite sometime now there has been a growing interest in the Central Asian 'tradition'. Sergei Panarin, a noted ethnographer, points out that what we see today, it is the expression of a set of cultural traits and patterns of behaviour which have developed since the pre-Soviet days. There is a strong fabric of *perezhtiki* (existential structures) that is integral to Central Asian living and that permeates every aspect of the lives of those comprising a particular ethnic community in Central Asia.[2]

The influence of Islam was strongest in Mawarannahr, i.e. the river valleys between the Amu Darya and the Syr Darya where Islam acquired local characteristics. For instance, people revered their guardian deities as cult saints. Fortune-tellers, witch doctors and shamans had considerable social prestige. These were the characteristics of 'folk Islam' and included diverse rites, faiths and rituals. Pre-Islamic traditions have been a part of the religious lives of the people – in festivals on a national scale, in the ritual practices of village communities and within the family. They have been retained in various spheres of religious life, in the activities of Sufi orders and various groups in the priesthood, in household religious practices, and in customs related to the life cycle of the family and wider kinship groups (birth, circumcision, marriage, reaching the age of the Prophet, death, etc.).[3] The practice of Islamic rituals and local cults was prevalent in the USSR and continues today.

Often these rituals represent the uniqueness of ethnic groups in Central Asia and therefore have become identified as a 'way of life' rather than with the Victorian image of the 'religion of Mahomet'.[4]

The Central Asian way of life has evoked a lot of interest among scholars in recent times. The social characteristics of Islamic tradition in Central Asia and its neighbourhood, since the late eighteenth century, are of particular interest. Reflections on the world of Islam – the faith, social structures (communities), the literati (*udaba*), the clergy (ulema) in Central Eurasia and on the birth of community identity – are all part of the discourse. It is argued that in pre-Soviet times, Muslim-institutionalised property (*zakat, waqf*) was the principal means of exercising spiritual control over members of the society. Some charismatic religious leaders like Domla Hindustani found favour with Soviet authorities. 'Traditionalists' like Hindustani, who found their own status as intellectuals after acquiring their education in centres of Islamic learning in Tajikistan, Kyrgyzstan, Kazakhstan, Afghanistan and the Indian part of the Kashmir Valley, later extended their sphere of influence to the entire region.

The strongest influence of tradition in Tajikistan has been in Garm. This has facilitated the growth of Islamic radicalism as a political form of opposition. Also significant are the social composition and origins of the Islamic groups and the nature of leadership in Garm. Since the late 1970s and the early 1980s, leaders of the Islamic movement in Tajikistan have been mostly interested in the study, reform and expansion of Islam. Most of these leaders were mullahs who were a part of the informal (underground) non-registered clergy which appeared in Tajikistan in the 1970s. Most of their ideas had taken shape during their education in the underground school of the reformist theologian Domla Hindustani in Dushanbe.[5] These mullahs were sharply critical of the state-sponsored *qaziyat* led by charismatic *murids* or *ishans*.[6] Their network and profession[7] gave them a very distinct role in society. Their programmes included propagation of women's rights and involvement of the educated youth.[8] One of their main representatives was Said Abdullo Nuri, head of the Islamic movement in Tajikistan and later the UTO (United Tajik Opposition) chairman who propagated both tradition and reform. Nuri's career began as a representative of the rural mullahs of *Nahzot* and the Garmi community that migrated from Kurgan Tyube to Dushanbe where many of them gained prominence as academicians. Nuri styled himself as an Islamic modernist and came into prominence as a demonstrator working on behalf of the Afghan mujahideen in the late 1980s. His demonstrations were held mostly along the Pyandzh River on the Afghan side of the Tajik-Afghan border. His Soviet education enabled him to protest against the institutionalisation of power. He acquired his Islamic education from Domla Hindustani and soon started conducting clandestine operations for Domla Hindustani's school in Dushanbe. He helped smuggle out revivalist literature across the subcontinent and set up a network of links. These links later became sources of funding and sustenance. Nuri's brand of blending tradition and reform resulted in the integration of other social groups within the Republic (till 1993) and enabled the movement to survive for some time. Therefore, Islamic revivalism in Garm was the expression of a culture that survived the Soviet era.

## Politicisation of the Islamic Revivalist Movement and Fissures Within

Discussions about Islam as a tradition in Tajikistan were not very common in the early 1990s. It was conventional to speak about the role of political Islam in the aftermath of the Tajik Civil War. Some writings indicated that an Islamo-democratic-nationalist alternative was created during the late perestroika years. Other writings, however, emphasised that rifts within the Tajik society proved to be the greatest barrier to political revival in Tajikistan.[9] An analysis of the revivalist trends in Tajikistan therefore needs a consideration of both these viewpoints.

Political renewal in Tajikistan began not with the Islamists but with the nationalists who, since the mid-1970s began working on the reconstruction of a national identity. Therefore, the intellectuals first became vocal about national revivalism. Under the protection of Tajik official institutions and creative unions, they obtained social and political recognition. The IRP, initially created in Astrakhan in 1990, had established its Tajik branch in 1991. The Tajik branch of the IRP was known as the *Hizb-I-Nahzat-I-Islami*. As elsewhere in the Soviet Union, the Tajik IRP's discourse was classically neo-fundamentalist and voiced protests against the official clergy of the Soviet era and advocated social justice. It was a determined opponent of the apparatus intelligentsia as well as the republic's *qaziyat* under the leadership of the dynamic Qazi Turadzhonzoda. However, the leaders were cautious enough not to be labelled fundamentalists. Gradually, the Tajik IRP leadership seceded from the Party's Moscow headquarters and moved closer to the Tajik intelligentsia and received widespread public attention. Backed by their allies within the nationalist-democratic bloc, they started appealing for the 'rehabilitation' of Islamic tradition. Their slogans became anti-Russian and anti-colonial in nature and content.

The return to ancestral customs was considered essential to free Tajiks from the memories of a Russian and colonial past. They sought refuge in the Persian Islamist heritage and were drawn nearer to the Islamic Republic of Iran. It was a strange situation as the Iranians did not trust the IRP leaders in Tajikistan. In fact, Iran even acted as a mediator in the intra-Tajik dialogue pressuring the leaders of the IRP to sink their differences with the Tajik authorities. The IRP leaders tried to 'internationalise' their image by getting closer to Iran and moving away from Soviet disorder. The IRP had to tone down its fundamentalist slogans because the nationalist groups were not influenced by its religious convictions. Public opinion was limited only to the capital city of Dushanbe. Here the IRP leaders managed to have some clout, but that too with the help of their allies in the nationalist-democratic bloc. In the countryside, it was difficult for them to promote their mixed agenda by outsmarting local heavyweights and regional chiefs who wielded enormous power. In the words of Dudoignon, 'Tajikistan is the most barren terrain imaginable for a fundamentalist organisation because with the notable exception of Dushanbe, it is practically bereft of the large modern towns and industrial suburbs where classic Islamist movements have traditionally flourished.'[10]

The IRP's political ambitions were stymied. Lack of unity among the leaders was the principal reason for its declining popularity. Though Islamic political movements became the only channel for voicing sentiments of the population dissatisfied with official policies, it became difficult for the IRP's top-ranking leaders to oppose the Tajik authorities directly. Its co-option within government structures after the 1997 Peace Accord helped in bringing about a semblance of peace and restoring differences at the official level.[11] But it did not prevent the warlords from resorting to radical measures such as taking-hostage, bombing road links in Tajikistan and Krgyzstan and indulging in other subversive activities.

Not surprisingly, the perception among Tajiks is that the Accord has not been very successful and that it further detracted the leaders from a revivalist agenda. Despite being the main player in the domestic political scenario, the IRP almost immediately began losing its image as an opposition force. Their decline coincided with the fact that the Islamists were clearly divided on the strategy that they should adopt. The IRP network which had once established itself throughout the USSR was subsequently divided into national branches. These branches are often at loggerheads with each other. For instance, the Russian branch of the IRP vociferously condemned the adventurism of its Tajik counterpart.[12]

The IRP was replaced by radical foreign Islamic groups that began using Tajikistan as an entry point.[13] Parviz Mullajanov points to the rising criticism about the co-optation of religious figures in Tajikistan. For instance, Qazi Akbar Turadzhonzoda, who shared the charisma of Domla Hindustani, was not able to unify his followers. Simultaneously, there was a schism within the ranks of the umma. The young mullahs wavered and reoriented their ideology according to the fluid political situation in the republic.[14] The renowned political scientist Olivier Roy also pointed out that the Tajik IRP was largely discredited after the Civil War for proving incapable of ensuring the safety of the population and by identifying itself with the Garmis. After 1992–93, its leaders operated mostly from Afghanistan, a country that held no fascination for the Tajik people. The importance of training camps in Afghanistan has been exaggerated, and these camps serve at best as meeting places and in fomenting trouble on the border. Hence, the Islamist movement in Tajikistan has been rendered politically impotent. Such arguments point to the cracks within the Islamic movement and the myth created about the potency of an Islamic threat in Tajikistan.

## Regional Implications

There is mixed reaction among Tajikistan's neighbours about the resurgence of Islam. There is suspicion about the involvement of foreign forces in the spread of fundamentalism. Uzbekistan and Russia are particularly sensitive to political developments within Tajikistan and are wary of the implications of revivalism. Russia is uncomfortable with opposition movements and fears that the mujahideen who follow Islamist ideas and live by warfare cannot be deterred by political agreements.[15] The fear of religion being used in regional politics and diplomacy started gaining ground in the wake of the disintegration of the Soviet Union.

Pakistani authorities were jubilant about the turn of events as it presented a unique opportunity for Pakistan to carve a corridor into Central Asia through Afghanistan. Observations made by Pakistani analysts point to the rationale behind this argument. Hafeez Malik remarked that the element of Islam provides a thread of religious unity not only within the former Soviet states but also with South-west Asia. His conviction was that resurgent Islam can be used both for the purposes of national self-determination and regional cooperation. The return of the mujahideens to power in Afghanistan after the Soviet withdrawal in 1989 offered Pakistan the first opportunity to take the initiative of building what the Pakistan Central Asia Friendship Society called, a 'commonwealth of Central and South-west Asian Islamic states'.[16] Subsequently, the Pakistani rhetoric of economics and culture created awareness about Central Asia opening up to new initiatives. One such initiative was the attempt to reach Asian frontiers up to Xinjiang in the north by means of the Karakoram Highway via sub-routes running through Gorno-Badakhshan in Tajikistan and Ferghana Valley in Kyrgyzstan. Geopolitical considerations have been at the root of Pakistan's strategy for economic cooperation and trade contacts with the Central Asian states, particularly Tajikistan. Following the mujahideen's comeback in Afghanistan, Pakistan found it within its interests to claim a 'new security environment', which was backed up by public opinion in Pakistan. Proximity to Tajikistan and Afghanistan via the Wakhan Corridor led to harmony with the mujahideen's Islamic ethos.[17]

According to Olivier Roy, following the liberalisation campaign of the perestroika period, it was the official ulema in Central Asia that became the primary beneficiary of international Islamic support. Generally speaking, the IRP did not find in the Muslim Brotherhood the political support it might have expected.[18] While some local members of the IRP, by virtue of their education in Arab educational institutions, developed personal contacts with the Arab world, the leaders of the movement kept aloof from political involvement. Vice versa, there were others in Asia who exercised caution in taking sides with the IRP in Tajikistan. Iran for instance was not particularly interested in exporting Islamic revolution to Central Asia. This was primarily due to the fact that there was hardly any Shi'ite support in Central Asia. Besides, while the Tajiks are Sunnis and anti-Uzbek, the Iranians are Shi'ite and regionally motivated. Tehran was also eager to maintain cordial relations with Moscow in order to thwart the steady progress that American and Turkish interests were making into the region. Despite the rhetoric about a Tajik-Iranian heritage and the endeavour to restore an 'Islamic Persian identity'[19] through cultural contacts[20] throughout the 1990s, Iran refused to get involved in Tajik politics. At that time, Iran's only interest was to propagate the idea of an 'eternal Iran' that would be an effective counterweight to the hegemony of the Turkic race in Central Asia.[21]

In recent times, there has been growing recognition in

Iran of the opportunities that landlocked Central Asia and Caucasus can offer. The Central Asian states lie on Iran's northern borders and are trying to reach out to the world via Iran while reducing their dependence on Russia. Iran, therefore, is keen on establishing close links with its northern neighbours by opening up transport and infrastructure 'corridors'.[22] Iran's newly acquired regional status has enabled it to improve its profile and enhance its prestige vis-à-vis the West, particularly America, by expanding ties with Asian economies that are trying to emerge from the shadow of western dominance and memories of colonial rule. The new regional constellation features countries like Syria, Jordan, the Trans-Caucasian republics of Armenia and Azerbaijan, Russia, Pakistan, Afghanistan, India and China.[23] In the post-9/11 scenario, there is growing interdependence between many of these countries – Iran and China, Iran and Pakistan – and this has further implications for the region.[24]

A significant player in Tajikistan is Russia which became militarily involved in Tajikistan during the last days of the Soviet regime. The Russian 201st Motorized Division has been stationed along the Tajik-Afghan border in order to 'guard' Tajikistan's southern and south-eastern tier by observing neutrality and taking no part in the intra-Tajik strife. Gradually, however, the Division has found itself in an increasingly difficult situation. As public opinion against the Division mounts in Moscow, verbal attacks on the Russian military during public rallies are often followed by open threats.[25] The military involvement in Tajikistan has been the most sensitive issue for Russian peacekeepers who have a double responsibility: preventing armed clashes in the interior of the country with active UN monitoring; and preventing narcoterrorism across the porous borders. The Russian guards have been trained for the former but not for the second. Narcoterrorism across Afghan-Tajik borders flourishes through trans-border networks that have become almost impossible for Russian border guards to check. The Russian frontier guards estimate that there are about 5,000 narco-barons operating in this area since the end of the Civil War. Their activities have rendered defunct the Russian border posts which can hardly cope with the incessant flow of contraband items from Afghanistan through Tajikistan and Kyrgyzstan into Russia and Western Europe. Pushed into an uncomfortable situation, the Russian military has on several occasions expressed its unwillingness to fight in an unwieldy terrain. Nevertheless, Russia has been struggling to maintain the image of protector of its client state Tajikistan.

The other sensitive issue for the Russian authorities in the wake of the Tajik Civil War has been the exodus of Russian skilled labour from Tajikistan. According to surveys by the Tajik agency Sharq, the percentage of Russian population in Dushanbe declined from 32.4 per cent in 1989 to 17 per cent in December 1996.[26] It is also estimated that in 1996, Russians represented only 2 per cent of the population in Tajikistan with a majority of them concentrated in the large cities.[27] The exodus of Russian industrial workers, health care professionals, teachers in higher educational institutions and administrators in the wake of the Civil War was seen as a loss to the Tajik economy. There were several attempts to stop their exodus and the leadership toyed with the idea of dual citizenship and giving representation to Russian minorities in the Tajik Parliament. But these attempts were not seriously followed up due to the lack of employment opportunities. Not surprisingly, the situation fanned patriotic sentiments in Russia. It also gave the Russian army commanders an opportunity to express their apathy about sending their soldiers to defend a terrain that offered no security to their compatriots.

The Tajik authorities were well aware of these and other

sentiments. Since the beginning of the reconciliation efforts in 1994, Tajik authorities have suspected that 'a third force' has inhibited the progress of Tajikistan. This 'third force' could have meant Russia, Uzbekistan, the West or the Muslim radicals.[28] The most common allegation is that the Uzbeks (representing 30 per cent of the population in Tajikistan) have been trying to sabotage the reconciliation efforts of the government.

Such charges perhaps indicate that the notion of an Uzbek-Tajik symbiotic relationship is, at best, superficial. It is almost impossible to ignore the apathy of the Uzbeks in Khatlon regarding the Garmi community's rise to prominence as a persevering group of labourers settled in south and central Tajikistan. Tajiks are also very sensitive about their marginalised status vis-à-vis the Uzbeks. This sensitivity is reflected in the writings of Rahim Masov, a Tajik historian[29] who argues that the Tajiks received peripheral importance in the state-building process of the 1920s while the Uzbeks monopolised the highest posts and climbed to the pinnacle of Soviet power. There are other scholars who are sympathetic about the Tajiks and point to the Tajik intelligentsia's significant contribution towards the construction of 'a Tajik national identity' in the 1920s. A rich intellectual tradition existed among the Tajiks and Tajik intellectuals engaged themselves in literary debates while their publications received widespread attention during the 1920s.[30] Such details have not been adequately emphasised in regional histories of Central Asia. Recent developments also demonstrate the Tajiks' mistrust of the Uzbeks. A lot has been said about the Uzbeks trying to prop up a third front under the leadership of Abdumalik Abdullajanov. There have been allegations of the presence of Uzbek saboteurs – working to abort the reconciliation process – within the Tajik establishment. The Uzbeks, who dominated the Khojenti lobby, were keen to override the control of the Kulyabis who came to power in 1993. The purge of the Uzbek ministers from Khojent led to acts of defiance by members of this lobby who combined their forces in 1996 against the Kulyabi government. This aspect of an internal challenge became clear during the spurt of revolts in January 1996 initiated by General Mahmud Khudoberdiyev, commander of the 1st Brigade at Kurgan Tyube and Ibod Boimatov, formerly the mayor of Tursunzade, the capital of Hissar. Both, ethnic Uzbeks from Tajikistan, demanded the government's resignation.

However, these dissident acts were not masterminded by the revivalists. There were pressures within Tajik society – represented by regional cleavages and ethnic rifts – and not within the revivalist movement in particular. The 'challenges' symbolised the divergence in Tajik society. Therefore, it is fallacious to argue that Islamic revivalist trends disrupted the peace process within Tajikistan and led to the destabilisation of the whole region. The influx of refugees, internal displacement and health hazards were social issues that created far greater concerns about stability in the aftermath of the Tajik Civil War and more particularly after 9/11.

## Conclusion

This paper deals with the character of Islamic revivalism in Tajikistan. It tries to indicate the stereotypes of fundamentalism and the general features of a social phenomenon. In Tajikistan as elsewhere, the revivalist movement got involved in mainstream politics and disintegrated with time. Therefore, there are aberrations that have been highlighted by a group of Islamic scholars. While there is an attempt to reconsider the notion of fundamentalism, critics point to the ways in which Islamic revivalism has degenerated. In the words of a scholar who is a theorist of tradition:

The Islamic revivalism we have known has been driven more by euphoria than rational thought, more by politically explosive action than patient effort to develop workable ideas and solutions to problems. It may be still early to say that Islamic resurgence is bringing its case from street procession and popular agitation to the reflective environment of rationalist planning and debate. This however seems inevitable if a constructive engagement of the various strata of Muslim society in such a process were to be desired. Whether the religious leaders, the ulema, the intelligentsia and the government leaders can engage themselves in proactive roles of planning a more participatory future of receptiveness toward each other, to a healthy modernity, and to Islam cannot yet be clearly visualised. Politicisation of Islam has also meant politicisation of issues, a pattern of development that has undermined the prospects of reflective *ijtihad* (independent reasoning). The religious leaders, the governments and the Muslim intellectuals are on the whole, scarcely engaged in consultation and exchange of views over issues of common concern, and the challenge of making *ijtihad* an engaging process of concern to mainstream society has yet to be adequately responded.[31]

There is yet another version of religious revivalism in Central Asia. Theorists of pluralism argue that the revivalist movement in Central Asia today has assumed a 'transnational' character.[32] This is a new feature and enables the movement to survive on its own. Given these sets of arguments, one might conclude that the religious revivalist movement continues to be in flux in Central Asia. There are strains within as well as the means to support and sustain it.

Notes

1. Stephane A Dudoignon and Komatsu Hisao (eds.), *Islam in Politics in Russia and Central Asia (Early Eighteenth to Late Twentieth Centuries)*, London: Kegan Paul International Ltd, 2001. Henceforth cited as *Islam in Politics*.
2. Sergei Panarin, 'Muslims of the Former USSR: Dynamics of Survival', *Central Asian Survey*, 12 (2), 1993, p.138.
3. V N Basilov, 'Popular Islam in Central Asia and Kazakhstan,' *Journal Institute of Muslim Minority Affairs*, Vol. 8/1, January 1987, pp.7–8.
4. This is how Central Asian religious life is described in nineteenth-century and early twentieth-century British travel literature. Stephen Graham, *Through Russian Central Asia*, London: Cassel, 1916, pp.53–54; Ella R Christie, *Through Khiva to Golden Samarkand*, London: Seely, Service and Co., 1925, pp.161–165; Henry Lansdell, *Russian Central Asia including Kuldja, Khiva and Merv*, 12 (20), Vol. II, London: Sampson Low, 1885, pp.296–297.
5. Parviz Mullajanov, 'The Islamic Clergy in Tajikistan since the end of the Soviet period', in Stephane A Dudoignon and Hisao Komatsu (eds.) *Islam in Politics...*, p.226; Bakhtiyar Babadjanov and Muzaffar Kamilov, 'Muhammadjan Hindustani (1892–1989) and the beginning of the "Great Schism" among the Muslims of Uzbekistan', in S A Dudoignon and Hisao Komatsu (eds.) *Islam in Politics...*, pp.200–206.
6. Despite the initial strains between the official and unofficial clergy in Tajikistan, there was a political alliance between the two after 1992.
7. The young reformist mullahs often worked as lift-operators, guards and night watchmen.
8. They became critical about social practices, like playing music at Muslim wedding parties and ostentatious

marriages and were endorsed by the official clergy. Such protests indicated their reformist thinking and gave them social recognition.

9. Stephane A Dudoignon, 'Political Parties and Forces in Tajikistan, 1989–1993', in Mohammed Reza Djalili, Frederic Grare and Shirin Akiner (eds.) *Tajikistan: The Trials of Independence*, Surrey: Curzon, 1998, p.53.

10. Dudoignon, 'Political Parties…', p.67.

11. Kamoluddin Abdullaev, 'Including Islamists in Legal Politics: The Case of Tajikistan', Paper presented in ESCAS VIII Conference, Bordeaux, 25–27 September 2002.

12. Olivier Roy, 'Is Conflict in Tajikistan a model for conflicts in Central Asia?', in Mohammed Reza Djalili, Frederic Grare and Shirin Akiner (eds.) *Tajikistan: The Trials of Independence*, Surrey: Curzon, 1998, p.141.

13. M A Olimov and S K Olimova, 'Religious roots of terrorism in Central Asia', Paper presented at the International Terrorism and Religious Extremism: Challenges to Central and West Asia, New Delhi, 31 January–1 February 2003, p.11.

14. Parviz Mullajanov.

15. Irina Zviagekskaya, *The Tajik Conflict*, Moscow: The Russian Centre for Strategic Research and International Studies, 1997, p.27.

16. Hafeez Malik, 'New Relationships between Central and Southern Asia: Regional Politics of Pakistan', *National Development and Security*, Vol. 1, No. 2, 1992, p.87.

17. Hafeez Malik, op. cit., p.62.

18. Olivier Roy, *The Foreign Policy of the Central Asian Islamic Renaissance Party*, New York: Council on Foreign Relations, 2000, p.7.

19. Olivier Roy, op. cit., p.11.

20. Social gatherings and meetings in honour of Tajik and Persian poets were common. Also the Persian language

and script were adopted as the official means of communication for which Iran promised support. Teheran also offered a large number of scholarships to Tajik students and agreed to train Tajik diplomats. Iran Radio started broadcasting special programmes for Tajikistan and TV news from Iran were broadcast live once a day for Tajik television. Data compiled from Hafeez Malik, op. cit., and Jawaid Iqbal, 'Iran and Turkey in Central Asia: Allies or Adversaries?', *Journal of West Asian Studies*, No. 9, 1993, p.55.

21. Roy, op. cit., p.14.
22. Mehdi Sanai, *Otnosheniya Irana s Tsentral'nmoaziatskimi Stranami SNG*, Moscow, 2002, pp.4–7.
23. Breffni O' Rourke, 'Central Asia: Iran Profiles itself as a Regional Power', RFERL, 12 February 1998; Rodger Baker, 'Oil Corridor Strengthens Trade Links', The Washington Times, 1 February 2003.
24. Nazi Hussain, 'Pak-Iran Relations in Post 9/11 Period: Regional and Global Impact', *Regional Studies*, Vol. XX, No. 4, Autumn 2002, p.48. Another study deals with development projects in Pakistan's Baluchistan province. Maqsudul Hasan Nuri, 'The Afghan Corridor: Prospects for Pak-CAR relations, Post-Taliban', *Regional Studies*, Vol. XX, No. 4, Autumn 2002, pp.35–42.
25. Irina Zviagekskaya, op. cit., pp.12–13.
26. Saodat Olimova, 'Etnicheskaya I Grazhdanskaya identichnost' I ikh vliyanie na migratsionnoe povedenie naseleniya Tadzhikistana', in *Sovremennye Etnopoliticheskie Protsessy I Migratsionnaya Situatsiya v Srednei Azii*, Moscow, 2001.
27. Shahrbanou Tadjbaksh, 'National Reconciliation: the Imperfect Whim', *Central Asian Survey*, 15, 3–4, 1996, p.339.
28. Tadjbaksh, op. cit., p.330.
29. Rahim Masov, *Tadzhiki: Istoriya s Grifom 'Sovershenno*

*Sekretno'*, Dushanbe: Tsentr Izdaniya Naslediya, 1991; R Masov, *Istoriya Topornovo Razdeleniya*, Dushanbe: Irfon, 1995.

30. Guissou Jahangiri, 'The Premises for the Construction of a Tajik National Identity, 1920–1930', in Mohammed Reza Djalili, Frederic Grare and Shirin Akiner (eds.), *Tajikistan: The Trials of Independence*, Surrey: Curzon, 1998, pp.14–16.

31. Mohammed Hashim Kamali, 'Issues in the Understanding of Jihad and *Ijtihad*', *Islamic Studies*, (Islamabad), Vol. 41, No. 4, Winter 1423/2002, pp.633–634.

32. Shirin Akiner, 'Ekstremism: Global'ny Fenomen', in *Religioznyi Ekstremizm v Tsentral'noi Azii: Problemy I Perspektivy*, (*Materialy Konferentsii, Dushanbe, 25 Apreliya 2002 goda*), Dushanbe, 2002, pp.17–21.

# Chapter IX

# TURKMENISTAN: ECONOMIC DEVELOPMENT AND REGIONAL COOPERATION

Dr Archana Srivastava

In the Central Asian Republic of Turkmenistan, regulatory and legal foundations of a market economy are still in the process of being developed. This has led to chronic problems with repayment of foreign loans and the implementation of signed contracts. Moreover, Turkmenistan, like other Central Asian countries, has had to deal with the economic shock of the break-up of the Soviet Union and the transition from a state-controlled to a market-driven economy. Trade and transit have been hampered by new borders, illegal checkpoints, loss of subsidies, loss of access to secure water and energy resources, loss of administrative structure and skilled labour. As a result, Turkmenistan has sustained heavy economic losses since its independence.

Turkmenistan ranks among the world's top ten countries in terms of proven reserves of gas and oil. Its proven gas reserves are estimated at 2.86 trillion cubic metres, and there are possible additional reserves of 4.5 trillion cubic metres. Oil, gas and cotton exports are estimated to account for over 80 per cent of the country's revenues. This makes Turkmenistan one of the leading actors in the world energy market. Turkmenistan's ambitious economic programme for 2002 included high production targets for the oil and gas sector. But it is not clear if this will actually help the economy. For, at the same time, President Niyazov has also made populistic promises, announcing that gas, electricity, flour and salt would be free in the long term.

Turkmenistan has shown some stability in the economic sector. GDP has shown strong double-digit gains during the 1999–2002 period, culminating in a 21.2 per cent growth rate reported in 2002. But much of the increase is misleading, since it represents growth in gas production meant for Ukraine, which pays for only half of the exports in cash. Turkmenistan's problem is that its economy is almost wholly dependent on export of gas, oil and cotton. As for gas, Turkmenistan does not have too many options regarding its evacuation to potential export markets. Old Soviet era pipelines connect its pipelines to Russia and Ukraine, who are the only two major importers of Turkmen gas.

Given the fact that Moscow controls all export routes from the north, dependence on Russia is the biggest economic challenge for Turkmenistan. Russian energy giants such as Gazprom and Itera rule over exports of Turkmen gas. In 1994, Russia's refusal to export Turkmen gas to hard currency markets and mounting debts of its major customers in the former USSR for gas deliveries, contributed to a sharp fall in industrial production and led to an increase in the budget deficit. In 1995 Turkmenistan signed bilateral agreements with Russia to expand economic and political cooperation. But a new dispute over gas prices in 1997 again halted exports, leading to a massive decline in GDP that year. In February 2001, the Turkmen government signed a new agreement with Itera under which it was to sell 10 billion cubic metres of gas to Russia in 2001. Russia announced it would buy up to 20 billion cubic metres by 2008, but both sides have yet to come to an agreement on the final price. Turkmen gas is crucial to Russia since this feeds the southern Urals and Sverdlovsk regions. Without it, these regions would have no energy at all, since Siberian producers want to sell their gas to the West for hard currency, and the government is not able to provide balanced redistribution within Russia. Yet, no long-term gas export agreement is expected in the near future, and the uncertainty on the crucial northern export route continues to prevail.

Ukraine pays for half its gas via construction works in Turkmenistan. It is supposed to pay the rest in cash but has accumulated a debt estimated at US $380 million. Turkmenistan has little option but to continue to do business with Ukraine, despite non-payment of dues. Worse, it now has to contend with two new competitors, Kazakhstan and Uzbekistan. Both countries have announced plans to increase gas exports to Russia through the same pipeline, thereby reducing Turkmenistan's quotas.

Turkmenistan has built a small pipeline that delivers about three billion cubic metres of gas to Iran. It has also mooted an alternative route, a 1,500-km pipeline from Turkmenistan through Afghanistan to Pakistan, and potentially on to India. It will pump gas from the southern Daulatabad fields, across 764 km of Afghan territory, link up with Pakistan's gas grid and reach the Indian Ocean. Niyazov met Pakistani President Pervez Musharraf and Afghan interim leader Hamid Karzai in May 2002 to discuss renewing the Trans-Afghan plan. US officials have also been involved in reviving the project, and the Asian Development Bank has offered financing for a feasibility study. But with the cost of the project estimated between US $2 billion and $3 billion, so far only Japan has shown some interest in investing in it. The US has political motives to support the pipeline, as it would provide energy for its allies, Afghanistan and Pakistan, and challenge Russia's monopoly over the northern routes for energy exports.

Nevertheless, even if the regional political situation improves and the project finds investors, it will be at least a decade before Turkmenistan can benefit from the Trans-Afghan pipeline and become less dependent on the northern route via Kazakhstan and Russia.

Most of Turkmenistan's oil is extracted from fields at Koturtepe, Nebitdag, and Chekelen near the Caspian Sea, which have estimated reserves of up to eighty billion barrels. Production fell dramatically in 1995 but recovered in 1999, levelling off at about 150,000 barrels per day over the past three years. Efforts have been made to develop the refinery capacity in the port of Turkmenbashi on the Caspian Sea. Turkmenistan's aim is to produce 1 million barrels per day by 2010, a goal that requires an estimated foreign investment of US $25 billion.

Turkmen officials have drawn up plans for an investment of US $45 billion in the country's oil and gas sector. While some foreign companies have shown an interest in investing in this sector, lack of rules, regulations and policies have kept them away. Corruption is a serious obstacle throughout the system, even for foreign companies. Key industries are still owned by the state and the government's over-regulation of the economy is a barrier to foreign investment. Privatisation is still not being pursued wholeheartedly by the government. By mid-2000, only 200 small scale companies, from an original list of 4,300, had been sold and just six medium-sized enterprises, out of 280, had been privatised. Niyazov's new rule for energy exports has further created problems for investors. The rule, which took effect on 1 January 2002, calls for weekly auctions of gas, oil and electricity, which are to be supervised by an 'Observer Council'. The council includes officials from the government as well as tax and law enforcement agencies. Under the system one must file an application and make a monetary deposit to demonstrate the 'seriousness of their intentions', i.e. buyers will have to put up a non-refundable deposit if they want to do business with Turkmenistan.

Another barrier to economic growth is the prohibitive rules that prevent companies using sub-surface resources to export hydrocarbons. Since foreign investors do not have access to export pipelines – the state-run oil and natural gas marketing company, Turkmenneft, Turkmengaz and Turkmenneftgaz, currently owns all of the country's pipelines – they are forced to sell the oil and gas they produce in Turkmenistan through the state commodities exchange or send it to refineries. Oil and gas are sold in Turkmenistan at fixed prices that are well below world market levels. Not surprisingly, several energy projects are stalled.

Turkey and the United States are the largest investors, in terms of number of ventures in Turkmenistan, followed by South Korea, Indonesia, the United Kingdom and Japan. Business entities in these countries feel deterred by Turkmenistan's significant number of non-tariff barriers to trade. In addition, the government sets prices that lead to the import of products and services of low quality. The state restricts investments in a number of 'strategic' sectors, such as utilities and oil and gas. Foreign exchange restrictions and opaque regulations governing foreign investment also pose barriers. For instance, foreigners may not own land but can lease it. After the events of 11 September 2001, Russia launched an economic integration initiative amongst the CIS countries (Belarus, Ukraine, Kazakhstan) at a summit held on 23 February 2003. Turkmenistan, however, did not join this initiative.

Turkmenistan is among the ten largest producers of cotton in the world. There is little arable land in Turkmenistan, only about 3 per cent of the total territory, but nearly 50 per cent of this is planted with cotton. Turkmen cotton is highly valued in the international market because of its superior-quality fibre. But poor management and lack of commercial incentives for farmers have led to consistently declining harvests. After a 50 per cent fall in production in 1997, the industry is trying to revive. In 2002, however, cotton harvest plummeted to a new low, reaching only 25 per cent of the production target of 2 million tonnes. While Niyazov blamed the weather, publicly dismissed officials for failing to work and imposed fines of three months salary on ministers, the real reason for low production is the lack of incentives.

Non-convertibility of the Turkmen currency, Manat, ensures that investment in the non-energy sectors is also minimal. The most active foreign companies are those who win lucrative government tenders for construction and other services. Foremost among these is the French group Bouygues. The construction sector is now emerging as the fourth force in the economy.

The state control on the energy sector, lack of privatisation and investment and imposition of barriers through a network of state institutions are the primary reasons for the lack of economic growth. The Foreign Exchange Reserve Fund (FERF), an off-budget account, is under the personal control of President Niyazov. Money from this fund has reportedly been used for the construction of statues, monuments and other grandiose projects. Drug trafficking also offers an important alternative source of income. There have been allegations of some government officials' involvement in drug trafficking.

## The Role of Regional Dynamics

Turkmenistan is a landlocked country and its economy is solely dependent on hydrocarbon and cotton exports to international markets. For economic development and stability, Turkmenistan needs to have cordial relations with other countries, i.e. both the 'near abroad' and the 'far abroad'. At the same time, Turkmenistan finds itself wedged between conflicting geopolitical interests and has sought to remain as neutral as possible. These factors have dictated its foreign policies beginning with its membership of the United Nations in 1992. Turkmenistan has declared that 'positive neutrality' (or permanent neutrality) and 'open doors' are the two major components of its foreign policy. 'Positive neutrality' (recognised by the United Nations in 1995) is defined as gaining international recognition of the republic's independence, agreeing upon mutual non-interference in internal affairs, and maintaining neutrality in external conflicts. The 'open doors' policy has been adopted to encourage foreign investment and exports, especially through the development of a transport infrastructure.

Table I: *Turkmenistan's Economic Performance*

| Years | 1995 | 1996 | 1997 | 1998 | 1999 | 2000 | 2001 | 2002 |
|---|---|---|---|---|---|---|---|---|
| GDP Growth Rate in % | –8.2 | –7.7 | –25.9 | –1.0 | 16 | 16 | 20.5 | 21.2 |
| Inflation % | 1005 | 992 | 84 | 19.8 | 19.7 | 14 | 20.5 | NA |
| Trade: Total Exports (Million US $) | 2084 | 1692 | 774 | 614 | 1078 | NA | 2.4 bl | NA |
| Total Imports (Million US $) | 1644 | 1338 | 1005 | 1137 | 1259 | NA | 1.65 bl | NA |
| Total Direct Investment (Million US $) | 233 | 129 | 108 | 62 | 89 | 113 | 100 | NA |

Turkmenistan has avoided multilateral arrangements with other Central Asian Republics. It is a member of the Commonwealth of Independent States (CIS), but does not participate in its military structures and agreements.

Turkmenistan, however, has not kept itself completely isolated from its powerful neighbours and global players. Security agreements have focused on military cooperation with Russia and on border security with Iran and Afghanistan.

In the economic area, President Niyazov has concentrated on developing gas and oil exports, and on pipeline transport infrastructure, especially in cooperation with Iran, Turkey, and Pakistan.

## Relations with Immediate Neighbours

The resolution of border issues in a peaceful and transparent manner would have had a positive impact on regional security, economic cooperation, ethnic relations, anti-drug trafficking efforts and on the fight against religious extremism. However, regional relations have often been uneasy for a variety of reasons, and border disputes exacerbated matters.

UZBEKISTAN

Uzbekistan is one of the dominant powers of the region, especially in the aftermath of 11 September, as it has successfully forged close ties with the United States. Disputes over the region's resources is the main reason for tensions between the two neighbours. Turkmenistan's 162-km common border with Uzbekistan divides water and gas resources and creates problems of migration on both sides. The Amu Darya River forms most of the border. The two countries have failed to come to a bilateral or regional agreement on water distribution. Oil and gas fields located on the border have also caused relations between the countries to deteriorate. Each country accuses the other of stealing energy resources.

Talks on border issues between Turkmenistan and Uzbekistan have almost ceased. Turkmenistan claims the Uzbek regions of Khiva and Khorezm as part of its territory. Nationalists argue that the majority of the inhabitants there are of Turkmen descent and Khiva was home to one of the most influential regional Khanates during the nineteenth century. At the same time, Uzbek nationalists assert that the majority of the people living in the Tashauz and Turkmenabad areas in Turkmenistan are Uzbeks and therefore Uzbekistan has a rightful claim to this territory.

The dispute over the territorial leasing of oil and gas facilities surfaced after independence. Turkmenistan voiced its unhappiness over Uzbekistan's long-term leases on facilities with Turkmenistan, claiming that it deprived the country of substantial revenues. In turn, Uzbekistan demanded that it be granted ownership of these facilities. Relations became so strained over the issue that trade between the two countries almost stopped in the mid-1990s and rail, air and bus links were suspended.

In a joint presidential meeting in 1996, Uzbekistan recognised Turkmenistan's right to neutrality. In exchange, Turkmenistan allowed Uzbeks to own property within Turkmenistan. Uzbekistan increased payments for existing lease arrangements. It also agreed to pay Turkmenistan a portion of the revenues generated from the oil extracted on Turkmenistan's soil. In 1998, Turkmenistan imposed visa requirements on Uzbekistan, quickly leading to retaliation. Free border travel has now been allowed for ten days and up to 150 kilometres into each other's territory. This has effectively eased the effects of the visa regime on traders and border residents.

According to the joint Turkmen-Uzbek commission agreement, a 1,700-km fence was to be installed by the decree passed in March 2001 by President Niyazov. The increased border patrolling has actually provoked tension. In June 2001, clashes between Uzbek citizens and Turkmen border guards led to the death of four persons. By the end of 2001, at least seven new posts had been constructed by Turkmenistan along the Uzbekistan border and on 1 January 2002 the Uzbek authorities introduced a US $6 charge on any Turkmen citizen crossing the border. The

Turkmen authorities had introduced a similar fee a year earlier.

Tensions rose further in January 2002 with several reports of shooting incidents and protests by residents of border zones. Discontent has fuelled a popular protest in the Turkmen regional capital of Tashauz. It drew 700 people who called for immediate removal of all travel restrictions and withdrawal of visa fees. The border restrictions have prompted illegal border crossings. In 2001, Turkmen border guards killed two Uzbeks who were trying to cross the border illegally. In January 2002, Turkmen guards also accidentally shot a fourteen-year-old boy, who was keeping watch over a herd of cows near the border.

Such localised clashes demonstrate how difficult socio-economic conditions and tough border regimes can combine to provoke unrest. In the absence of close relations at higher political levels it is all too easy for local conflicts to slip out of control. Border tensions between Turkmenistan and Uzbekistan remains a cause for concern as neither side is ready to broker a compromise that offers freedom of movement in the border region.

Turkmen regulations that discriminate against ethnic Russians and Uzbeks in education and employment is another potential source for conflict. For appointments in government positions, candidates' family backgrounds are screened going back three generations. This prevents minorities from applying for government jobs. Ethnic Uzbeks in the northern Turkmen city of Tashauz are registering their children as ethnic Turkmen to avoid discrimination.

Turkmenistan has better relationship with Kazakhstan, although the two countries are competitors in the gas market. The two countries differ on their policy towards the division of the Caspian Sea basin.

AFGHANISTAN

Turkmenistan has good relations with Afghanistan, with which it shares a 744-kilometre border. It is now renewing its connections with the new political elite of Afghanistan in an effort to kick-start economic cooperation and embark on its most ambitious project, the Trans-Afghan pipeline, designed to transport Turkmen gas to the Pakistani market. Niyazov's visit to Islamabad during 29–30 May 2002 resulted in the signing of a 'tripartite agreement on construction of the gas and oil pipeline with the leadership of Pakistan and Afghanistan'. The 1,500-km pipeline is expected to transport thirty billion cubic metres of gas. The project is bogged down by continued political instability in Turkmenistan, Afghanistan and Pakistan. India, which is an important market, is reluctant to support the project.

Close relations with the Taliban led to the emergence of Turkmenistan as a key drug transit route. The border is largely uncontrolled and Turkmen and Afghans living on both sides of the border have been crossing it with impunity. Unconfirmed reports suggested that Turkmenistan served as a transit route for several groups of Taliban and Al Qaeda fighters fleeing Afghanistan in late 2001. It was even suggested that Turkmen diplomatic officials provided the Taliban and Al Qaeda supporters with transit visas to pass through Turkmenistan, as they headed for Europe or Russia. While it is impossible to confirm such reports, they are plausible given the level of corruption in the security forces. The United Nations Drug Control Programme report published in 2000 said that 50 per cent of drugs consumed in Western Europe is trafficked through Central Asian States, via Turkmenistan and Afghanistan.

Afghanistan is reported to have about two million ethnic Turkmen. Living largely in the north-eastern areas controlled by the ethnic Uzbek leader, General Abdul

Rashid Dostum, they eke out a living by practising traditional crafts such as carpet weaving or by farming. In an effort to play a greater role in Afghanistan's nation-building exercise, Turkmen community leaders have formed a 'shura' or 'Council', to interact with top officials of the Karzai administration. The council is composed of intellectuals from the Turkmen refugee community in Pakistan and elders and other leaders of the Turkmen population in Afghanistan.

## IRAN

In the south-west, Turkmenistan shares a 992-km border with Iran. Predominantly Shi'ite, Iran has friendly relations with secular Turkmenistan (where Sunni Islam dominates). Iran provides alternative existing routes for Turkmenistan's small volume of gas exports. Russia's erratic attitude forced Turkmenistan to look for alternative trading partners for oil and gas exports and Iran proved to be a promising partner.

Iran purchases cotton and chemical products in exchange for food products, road and construction services. Iran is also a key corridor for the import and export of goods to and from Uzbekistan and Kazakhstan via Turkmenistan's road and railway network. Regionally, Tehran and Ashgabat have a shared position on Russia's growing control over the Caspian Sea and the region's pipeline routes. Turkmenistan is the only littoral country that supports Iran's position in the ongoing multilateral Caspian Sea negotiations. The two states have also signed bilateral agreements under which Iranian specialists will help renovate the Turkmenbashi Oil Refinery and the Mary Cotton Processing Plant. The Iranians will also help build the Turkmenistan-Iran-Europe gas pipeline, and Ashgabat-Tehran, Mary-Mashhad-Turkmenbashy, and the Gudurol-Gorgan highways. In January 1996, Niyazov signed agreements with Iran linking the two countries' electric power networks and constructing a joint dam on the Hari River. Another agreement was signed to forge cooperation in oil, gas, and agriculture sectors. A joint statement expressed concern about Azerbaijan's exploitation of Caspian Sea resources, although Turkmenistan has generally supported Azerbaijan and Kazakhstan, against Iran and Russia, on resource rights in the Caspian.

Increasingly isolated from other regional powers, Turkmenistan may forge even closer relations with Tehran as a foreign policy option. Tehran's intelligence services are reportedly active in Ashgabat, primarily to counter US influence, but also with the long-term aim of boosting the country's standing in the region and increasing its options for bypassing Washington's economic embargo.

## Near Abroad: Russia

Russia remains important for Turkmenistan because of economic and security reasons. Their relationship has seen several ups and downs in the last few years but they have kept their differences at a manageable level. The Treaty on Joint Measures signed by Russia and Turkmenistan in July 1992 provided for the Russian Federation to act as a guarantor of the latter's security and made former Soviet army units in the republic the basis of the new national armed forces. Under the agreement, Russia would provide the logistical support and pay Turkmenistan for the right to maintain special installations, while Turkmenistan would bear the cost of housing, utilities and administration. Despite this, Turkmenistan has not joined the CIS Collective Security Agreement.

As Turkmenistan does not have the infrastructure to export its gas and oil resources, it has to depend on Russia to a large extent. Moscow has ensured that Turkmen gas reaches only as far as Ukraine, where it cannot compete with Russian gas exports to Europe. Not surprisingly, Turkmenistan is exploring other opportunities to find alternative gas export routes. On 10 April 2003, President Putin and President Niyazov signed a strategic energy accord in Moscow under which Turkmenistan will supply natural gas to Russia till 2008. Russia's gas multinationals, primarily Itera and Gazprom, have considerable influence over Moscow's policy towards Turkmenistan. As monopoly buyers of Turkmen gas, they have been able to keep prices well below world benchmarks, even at the occasional risk to bilateral relations.

Russian leaders are also concerned about President Niyazov's policies towards ethnic Russians. Moscow sought to resolve the issue by persuading Turkmenistan to accept dual citizenship for ethnic Russians but it has not been very active in supporting the ethnic Russian community or pressing Ashgabat on the issue. However, on 10 April 2003, both presidents signed a protocol cancelling the 1993 agreement on dual citizenship. Niyazov even issued a decree advising citizens with dual Russian-Turkmen citizenship to choose one or the other within two months. Over 100,000 people living in Turkmenistan hold dual citizenship.

Turkmenistan's opposition to Russian proposals on the division of the Caspian Sea has also harmed relations. Most recently the Turkmen government has criticised Moscow for sheltering Turkmen opposition activists, many of whom live in Moscow.

## The United States

The 11 September terrorist attack has redefined US foreign policy, including its policy towards Central Asia. With the US playing the role of the chief economic donor and security manager in the region, a realignment of power has taken place. The Central Asian Republics have responded by welcoming stronger strategic ties with the US, hoping that such cooperation would lead to greater economic assistance.

Turkmenistan's political relations with the US however, have not changed dramatically. President Niyazov continues to harp on neutrality though he has expressed general support for attempts to form an international coalition to combat global terrorism. Even so, he has declared that such a coalition should be coordinated by the United Nations rather than the US. Niyazov has consented to the use of Turkmenistan's ground and air transport 'corridors' for the delivery of humanitarian aid to Afghanistan during air strikes against Al Qaeda and the Taliban. But he has refused access to Turkmenistan's military bases, given the country's policy of non-interference. Turkmenistan, along with other Central Asian States, except Uzbekistan, is wary of the Bush administration's war against Iraq and worried about the consequences. However, in accordance with its policy of neutrality, Ashgabat has largely refrained from commenting on the Iraq crisis.

The US would like to see Turkmenistan move out of the Iranian and Russian spheres of influence. The US would like Turkmenistan to develop a pipeline network that can export Caspian oil and gas to world markets by circumventing Russia and Iran. The US-conceived idea of linking Turkmenistan's oil with the Baku-Ceyhan pipeline looks politically and financially impractical. The project was stalled in 2000 after the Turkmen government essentially removed itself from the negotiations by making unrealistic demands for pre-financing. Instead, the US seems to be focusing its efforts to make the proposed Trans-Afghan pipeline viable.

At the same time, Washington is also concerned about President Niyazov's regime, which it terms 'authoritarian'.

The US raised the human rights issue at the OSCE meet in late 2002, with the EU and others. The report in the OSCE meeting suggested that Turkmenistan should take some steps to 'help steer Turkmenistan out of its self-imposed isolation and back on to the path of full integration in the international community'. To protect human rights, prohibit torture and uphold the rule of law, Turkmenistan, in the opinion of the US, should allow access to family members, lawyers, the International Committee of Red Cross and NGOs to all prisoners; cooperate with the OSCE on legal and judicial review, including review of trials related to the events of November 2002; repeal the re-imposition of exit visas and the 'draconian' betrayers of the motherland law; and reverse its actions on property confiscation and forced resettlement.

The media attack launched on the US ambassador, Laura Kennedy, following the arrest of former foreign minister Boris Shikhmuradov indicates Washington's relative lack of influence in Ashgabat. On 8 January 2003, the state-controlled media implied that Kennedy tried to help the former foreign minister flee the country after the failed assassination attempt. Earlier, the Turkmen media sharply criticised the US State Department spokesman Philip Reeker for making allegedly false accusations about massive arrests following the assassination attempt. The US clearly lacks effective tools with which to usher in political change in Turkmenistan.

US aid to Turkmenistan amounted to US $18.1 million in fiscal year 2002, of which US $8 million went to the security sector, mostly towards border security to control the spread of weapons of mass destruction and drug trafficking. Given the evidence of government officials' involvement in smuggling, it is unlikely that such aid will help in eradicating the problem.

Table II: *Trade with India (in million US $) (January–November 1999)*

| Imports from India | 1.17 |
|--------------------|------|
| Exports from India | 1.17 |
| Balance of Trade | + 7.33 |

## India

India's relation with Turkmenistan is friendly and supportive on vital issues. India recognised Turkmenistan's independence and an embassy in Ashgabat was established on 30 June 1994. Turkmenistan's embassy started functioning in India in January 1995. President Niyazov visited New Delhi twice to discuss economic cooperation (18–20 April 1992 and 25–26 February 1997). India's trade relation with Turkmenistan is favourable. India exports medical equipment, machines, construction materials, electrical items, leather goods and tea while Turkmenistan exports silk, wool and yarn to India. On 5 September 2000, a new initiative in bilateral cooperation was taken, with the creation of a joint working group to focus on power engineering projects. Niyazov met the Indian minister of culture and tourism, Ananth Kumar, and signed the document.

India is a promising energy market and supplying hydrocarbon resources to India could benefit Turkmenistan. India's energy demand is growing at a rate of 7 per cent per annum. A consortium comprising Japanese and US firms has been working on a project that would link Turkmenistan's gas fields with India through neighbouring Afghanistan and Pakistan. While Russia and Iran are keen that Turkmenistan's pipeline should pass through their territory, the US wants the pipeline to reach India via Afghanistan and Pakistan, keeping Iran and Russia, out of the picture. On the other hand, because of the strained relations with Pakistan, India is not keen on this project.

Indian officials admit that it would be cheaper to build the pipeline over land through Pakistan but they say that the security risk would be too high. The alternative – laying a pipeline under the Arabian Sea – is much more expensive. 'The Pakistan route would be too juicy a target for Islamist terrorists,' said one Indian official.

## Conclusion

Turkmenistan is clearly seeking ways and means to expand its international relations with a view to enlarging its economic options, particularly those related to energy exports. At the same time, it is having to grapple with contentious internal issues, including ethnic problems. President Niyazov, despite the criticism surrounding many of his decisions, is also attempting to balance various geopolitical realities by adopting a policy of positive neutrality. He needs to circumvent the Russian stranglehold on his country's energy resources and yet he must not cause a serious breach in relations that would lead to an overnight collapse of his economy. At another level, he must not antagonise the powerful United States and at the same time he must forge closer ties with Iran, a country that promises to be the lifeline of his economy. He must stand up against global terrorism and yet must maintain cordial relations with the Afghans, even those of extreme views, in order to avoid destabilisation of his eastern borders. The big issue is whether the current Turkmen leadership will be able to grapple successfully with these and other complicated issues given its history of operating in a rigid Soviet system that has long proved to be ineffective in grappling with today's crises.

# SECTION THREE
## Time of Turbulence

# Chapter X

# RUSSIA, THE US AND CENTRAL ASIAN RIVALRY

Lena Jonson

## Introduction

Developments after 11 September 2001 created a new political landscape in Central Asia. Russian President Putin's consent to Western use of Central Asian airfields and airspace during operations in Afghanistan changed the international climate, improved Russian-US cooperation, and paved the way for increased cooperation between the US and Central Asian governments. The direct US presence in Central Asia resulted in an acceleration of certain trends that had been observed in Central Asia since the mid-1990s. These trends consisted of a Russian decline, a growing foreign engagement by both state and non-state actors, and increased foreign policy activity on the part of the Central Asian governments.

The purpose of this paper is to analyse the new geopolitical situation in Central Asia in an effort to identify trends for the future with regard to the policies of Russia and the USA in the region. The focus is on the distribution of power and influence in the region as reflected in the evolving patterns of cooperation in the fields of energy and security.

A focus only on Russian and US engagement in Central Asia in the analysis involves several limitations. First, it gives the impression that the geopolitical map of Central Asia is determined only by these two actors, when, in reality, present Central Asia is characterised by the engagement of a larger number of foreign actors, state as well as non-state; and, second, it gives too much emphasis to a rivalry between Russia and the USA, when the relationship also includes a component of cooperation. To view developments in Central Asia in terms of a zero-sum game between Russia and the USA may seem tempting. With such an approach the main contours of foreign engagement seem to be easy to grasp: what is won by one side is lost by the other. This approach introduces distortions, and there is a serious risk that the opportunities for international cooperation will be neglected. Thus, it is argued in this paper that, although Russia and the USA are major powers engaging in the region, other actors contribute to form the setting. Moreover, although Russian and US state interests differ, this contest does not exclude a component of cooperation between the states. In order to grasp this dual relationship, the term 'competition' will be used in this text instead of 'rivalry'.

The paper describes the political landscape in Central Asia after 11 September 2001. It also gives an analysis of US interests and policies in the region with regard to security and energy. Issues regarding the Russian policy response have been dealt with and finally some conclusions with regard to the trends and prospects for geopolitical change in the region are presented.

## The Central Asian Setting after 11 September 2001

*Putin's Crucial Decision*
In September 2001, President Vladimir Putin made two crucial decisions which resulted in a radical change of Russian policy in Central Asia and meant that Russia's

Central Asia policy became directly linked to its policy towards the West.

In his telephone call to President George W Bush as the first foreign head of state to call him immediately after the terrorist attacks on the USA, Putin expressed solidarity with Bush and his right to respond in self-defence against the terrorists and those supporting the terrorists, which meant Osama bin Laden, Al Qaeda and the Taliban regime in Afghanistan. On 13 September 2001, Russia and NATO issued a joint statement condemning the terrorist attacks. On 24 September 2001, Putin announced his decision to consent to the use by US troops of Central Asian airspace and airfields during military operations against Afghanistan.

While the first decision was easy, the second was much more complicated. The Russian consent to US troops was given since Moscow understood it would not be able to stop the Central Asian governments from participating in the US-led anti-terrorist coalition.

Among the Russian military there was strong opposition to allowing US military access to the territories of Central Asian states in the near neighbourhood of Afghanistan. On 14 September 2001 Russian Defence Minister Sergei Ivanov stated: 'Central Asia is within the zone of competence of the Collective Security Treaty of the Commonwealth of Independent States. I see no reasons whatsoever, even hypothetical, for any suppositions about NATO operations being conducted from the territories of Central Asian countries which are members of the CIS.'[1] The Central Asian states, however, did not share his conviction. On 16 September 2001, Uzbekistan's Foreign Minister Abdulaziz Kamilov declared that Uzbekistan was open to 'any form of anti-terrorist cooperation with the United States', including the possible use of Uzbek territory for strikes on terrorist camps in Afghanistan.[2] The Tajik foreign minister also indicated interest in cooperation with the USA, but, as he was uncertain what Moscow's policy would be, he said consultations with Moscow would take place first.[3]

Yet Putin managed to coordinate a basic common view on what Central Asian support for US operations in Afghanistan would be. He had telephone conversations with all the Central Asian presidents on Monday, 17 September and again on Sunday, 23 September.[4] In the meantime the secretary of the Russian Security Council, Vladimir Rushailo, and the chief of the Russian General Staff, Anatolii Kvashnin, went to Central Asia for consultations. On 19 September they had consultations with President Rakhmonov of Tajikistan, and thereafter attended a meeting in Astana of the security officials of the participating states of the Collective Security Treaty (CST). On 23 September Putin received military and intelligence officials to discuss the Central Asian situation and coordination with the governments of the region.[5] On 24 September 2001, Putin declared that Russia and the Central Asian allies would allow the USA and its allies access to their air corridors and airfields – for humanitarian, rescue and intelligence missions but not for military operations. Defence Minister Sergey Ivanov confirmed on 26 September that Russia and the Central Asian states were prepared to make air corridors available and place their airfields at the coalition's disposal. Their support, Ivanov said, was the result of a weekend of intensive consultations between the Central Asian states and Russia.[6] When on 28 September the CIS prime ministers met, they backed the formula of Putin.

The first US troops arrived in Uzbekistan in late September 2001. On 5 October 2001, President Islam Karimov repeated that these troops were allowed only for humanitarian and search and rescue operations.[7] On 7 October, the US bombing of Afghan territory was initiated. More US and Western troops followed to Central

Asia. By February 2002 there were about 1,500 in Uzbekistan, altogether about 2,000 in Kyrgyzstan, and less than 300 in Tajikistan.

Putin had used the opportunity which the terrorist acts of 11 September 2001 had opened up to make a breakthrough in relations with the West. His speeches at the German Parliament and at the NATO headquarters in late September clearly reflected his intention to improve relations with the US government and with Europe.[8] From the Russian side there were great expectations regarding what would follow from closer cooperation with the USA. Reports from the meeting between Putin and NATO Secretary General George Robertson on 3 October 2001 seemed to bear out to these expectations: 'The global threat from international terrorism, and interests in building a long-term and balanced system of European and global security demand deep changes in the format and content of cooperation between Russia and NATO.'[9] The Russian media speculated that Russian support for the US government at this difficult juncture would improve Russian-US cooperation, increase Russia's international role, bring Russia closer to membership of the World Trade Organization (WTO), and contribute to a more understanding approach from the West towards Russia's war in Chechnya.

Putin's September 2001 policy has extended his anti-terrorist agenda, which had been formulated in 1999 as a policy to rally the states of the CIS – first of all the Central Asian states – and made it a platform for improving Russia's relations with the West in a struggle against a common enemy. While previously Moscow had regarded Central Asia as an arena separated from its policy towards the West, now it became part of Putin's Western agenda.

The overthrow of the Taliban regime by the forces of the US-led international coalition reduced the external threat to the Central Asian states and improved the general security situation in the region. However, it also created a dilemma and a challenge to Russian policy. Russia was left behind as the USA took the lead in the political reconstruction of Afghanistan and developed security cooperation with Central Asia in the US-led international anti-terrorist coalition. Thus, while the USA improved the general security situation in the region, to Russian policy makers the situation remained complex. Moreover, with a reduced external threat, the domestic problems of Central Asian countries came to the forefront, and they were no less complex. In the post-September situation with other states engaging in Central Asia, it became more evident than before that if Russia was to regain influence in the region in the future, it had to prove itself useful to the Central Asian states.

## Central Asian Desire for Cooperation with the USA

In Central Asia the post-11 September developments meant a breakthrough for a US and Western presence. As Putin had seized the opportunity, so did the Central Asian governments.

Uzbekistan was the country, most ready to cooperate with the USA. On 12 October the US government, in a joint statement with President Karimov, gave extended security guarantees to Uzbekistan.[10] The USA, Britain and Turkey promised assistance in the development of a military training centre within the framework of the NATO Partnership for Peace (PFP) programme.[11] The increased US presence in Uzbekistan meant that the role of security guarantor for Uzbekistan was de facto transferred to the USA from Russia. Russia was already past having any means by which to influence Uzbek policy. Uzbekistan had stayed aloof from Russian-led security cooperation since it left the CST in April 1999. It participated in anti-terrorist cooperation with the CST states after 1999, but it did not return to membership of the CST. In official statements President Karimov repeatedly stressed the importance of Russia for Central Asian stability, yet it became obvious that official Tashkent regarded Russian-led security cooperation as being without substance and largely insignificant for the future of Uzbekistan.

In Kyrgyzstan, on 28 December 2001, the parliament agreed to let the US military set up a base at Manas International Airport outside Bishkek for one year.[12] In January 2002, President Askar Akaev announced that he was prepared to prolong the agreement for a US military presence on Kyrgyz territory.[13] In the event, about 2000 soldiers from NATO countries came to be located at the Manas base, although the agreement allowed for as many as 5,000. In mid-March 2002, the Kyrgyz Parliament followed up its previous decision and approved a one-year deployment of troops at Manas from NATO countries, Canada, Denmark, France and Italy, and Australia.[14] Kazakhstan, although willing to give its support to the anti-terrorist coalition, was too far away from Afghanistan to be useful to US aircraft.

President Niyazov of Turkmenistan, on 14 September 2001, responded positively to a US proposal for support for retaliatory strikes, as he said 'organisers of the terrorist assault prove to be in Afghanistan'.[15] Niyazov had nevertheless immediately pointed out that the coalition's goals, mandate, procedures, and missions had to be clearly defined and it should function under UN aegis.[16] He also had to reconcile his actions with the status of Turkmenistan as a permanently neutral country, and accordingly did not allow foreign troops on Turkmen territory. Turkmenistan did come to play an important role for the transit of international humanitarian aid for Afghanistan, but the new situation did not do much to increase the presence of international organisations, nor did it break the isolation of Turkmenistan.

With regard to Tajikistan's position, the change was remarkable. As Russia's most loyal ally in Central Asia, Tajikistan had been exclusively Russia's domain before 11 September. In late September, the Tajik government let the US government know that it was willing to open its territory for over-flights, landing and basing if needed. It offered all available sites and left it up to the Americans to state their preferences.[17] After a telephone conversation between Putin and Rakhmonov on 5 October 2001, the Tajik government made its offer public on 8 October. In mid-October, Foreign Minister Talbak Nazarov declared that Tajikistan 'does not rule out the stationing of US forces in the country'.[18] On 3 November 2001, during a visit by US Defence Secretary Donald Rumsfeld to Dushanbe, Tajikistan publicly gave its consent to the use of three military airfields by the US-led coalition.[19] A US assessment team found, however, that of the three airfields under discussion (Dushanbe, Kulyab and Kurgan-Tyube) only Dushanbe could be used and, as it was not suitable for heavy aircraft to land and take off, it was to be used only for refuelling of cargo planes. During Rumsfeld's visit, President Rakhmonov agreed to initiate regular exchanges of information on anti-terrorist operations and to establish permanent military-to-military contacts between the USA and Tajikistan. Rumsfeld confirmed that Tajikistan would provide assistance with regard to 'over-flights, intelligence gathering and various types of military-to-military cooperation'.[20] In December 2001 troops started to arrive: among the first were French marines arriving on 6 December to be transferred to Afghanistan.

The US government offered Tajikistan support and assistance to strengthen its border security system, although

Russian troops carried the major responsibility for guarding the Tajik-Afghan border. A bilateral agreement signed on 5 February 2002 stated that the USA was to provide support to the Tajik Border Force in training and in purchase of technical and communications equipment. As part of Tajikistan's participation in the US-led anti-terrorist coalition, Tajikistan and the USA also developed full cooperation in intelligence gathering, especially with regard to movements, events and people on both sides of the Tajik-Afghan border.

Although Tajikistan remained Russia's most loyal ally, and the numbers of coalition troops there were small, the US presence brought a new element into the Tajik political debate. The new international attention being paid to Tajikistan brought hopes and expectations, as well as the beginning of a more critical stance towards Russia within Tajikistan. Problems in bilateral relations developed, when Russia started the process of regulating the presence of foreign labour migrants in Russia, and deported Tajiks. Tajikistan reacted strongly. Rumours appeared from time to time that the Tajik authorities had started to claim compensation for the presence of Russian troops, although the authorities denied it.

In January 2002, the USA lifted its ban on the export of weapons to Tajikistan. On 22 February 2002, Tajikistan formally joined the PFP as the last state of Central Asia to do so, and this gave further input to its cooperation with the USA and NATO countries. It was expected that Tajikistan would work together with the PFP in civil emergency planning, scientific affairs, environmental programmes and military reform.[21] Although the Western military presence in Tajikistan was small (150 US troops at the most, and 50 in September 2002; and 500 French at the most, 150 in September 2002), there was a marked shift in Tajikistan's strategic situation.[22]

The Central Asian governments showed no interest in

setting a deadline for the US military presence in their countries to end. President Karimov expressed to a great extent the attitude of the Kyrgyz and Tajik governments as well when in August 2002 he declared that the US troops could stay as long as they needed. 'They came here to carry out their mission and function which they had made known to the entire world, that is, to create a coalition the main aim of which is to destroy the machine of terrorism. In this situation the Americans came and only they, thanks to their military power, I am saying this with full responsibility, only they played the leading role here. Only their operations made it possible to liquidate camps and bases and the machine of the Taliban, to deal a blow and break the backbone of terrorist organisations and gangs,' the president said. 'My opinion is that they will be here for as long as it takes to ensure a guarantee.'[23]

During 2002, President Karimov, President Rakhmonov and President Akaev visited the USA.[24] For Rakhmonov the visit, in early December 2002, was his first ever to the USA. It was successful and Tajikistan's role in the international anti-terrorist coalition was highly praised in Washington. The prospects for 'long-term strategic partnership' were the focus of the talks, as reported by the Tajik Foreign Ministry.[25] Rakhmonov brought home a credit for agricultural development and the promise of food aid. Times had changed when Russia's closest ally also wanted to host US and NATO troops.

By early March 2003, shortly before the US/British military operations against Iraq were initiated, the Central Asian states had taken their positions on the forthcoming war. President Karimov expressed strong support for US military action in Iraq, even downplaying the need for a second UN Security Council resolution on the crisis. He said that Uzbekistan unequivocally supported the US position on resolving the Iraq problem.[26] 'If you ask me about the motives for Uzbekistan's position, I would like to draw a comparison. Just imagine a genie, sitting in a vessel, with a narrow neck. Once the genie is let out of the bottle, it will not be possible to put it back in. If there are programmes to develop chemical, biological and bacteriological weapons in Iraq, and they are not stopped in time, tomorrow these weapons will fall into the hands of terrorists and religious extremists, and then, believe me, the whole world will tackle this problem, but it will be too late, and the situation will be uncontrollable.' Karimov went on to say that the USA had grounds for a military campaign even if it meant going ahead with it without a UN resolution. 'We support the position of the United States to resolve the Iraq problem. It is all we want to say. There is no need to clarify this point.'

Turkmenistan made very different statements on Iraq. President Niyazov had said to the Organisation for Security and Cooperation in Europe (OSCE) Chairman-in-Office and Dutch Foreign Minister de Hoop Scheffer, that Turkmenistan supported the US position.[27] To Iranian representatives, however, Niyazov said that he supported Iran's critical stance towards the USA. Tajikistan and Kyrgyzstan took on a low profile, emphasising the role of the UN Security Council for decisions on the use of force but avoiding direct criticism of the USA.[28]

## The USA's Interest and Policy in Central Asia

To a great extent the energy resources in the Caspian Sea region explain the US interest in Central Asia. Although only the littoral states, Kazakhstan and Turkmenistan, have sizeable deposits, Uzbekistan, Kyrgyzstan and Tajikistan are part of the strategic environment in which the Caspian's resources will be exploited. The security of this wider area is crucial when developing the energy resources. Securing the diversified supply of energy to the world market is a crucial component in US foreign and security policy. In the contemporary US worldview, Central Asia constitutes a part of the extended Middle East. When responsibility for relations between the US military and the militaries of the Central Asian states was transferred in 1999 from the US European Command to the US Central Command (CENTCOM), covering the Middle East, this reflected a shift in perspective. Lieutenant General William E Odom explained in 1997 why it would benefit Central Asia and the Caucasus to include these regions in CENTCOM: 'Because we and they share huge mutual interests, interests arising from three sets of realities. First, the oil and natural gas reserves in the Caspian Sea basin approach the size of those in the Persian Gulf. Given the added demands for energy caused by the rapidly growing economies of China, India, and other late developing states, the importance of these additional reserves is obvious. Second, political and military conditions in the Trans-Caucasus and Central Asia present obstacles to bringing this energy to the global market. Third, both regions are the objects of outside states competing for influence there. Not only Russia, but also China, Turkey, Iran, Pakistan, and Saudi Arabia, are competitively engaged, often in non-constructive ways. Also, some of the problems in the Persian Gulf region and Afghanistan are refracted into Central Asia and the Trans-Caucasus.'[29]

In testimony in December 2002 to the Senate Foreign Relations Subcommittee on Central Asia and the Caucasus, Assistant Secretary of State Elisabeth Jones outlined three sets of long-term interests of the USA in Central Asia: preventing the spread of terrorism; assisting the Central Asian states with economic and political reform and the rule of law; and ensuring the security and transparent development of Caspian energy resources.[30]

US companies discovered the Caspian region early and took the lead in the international consortia which emerged in Azerbaijan and Kazakhstan during the first half of the 1990s. The USA's commitment to the principle of multiple pipelines resulted in its backing the Baku-Ceyhan option in February 1995, which was intended to prevent first Russia but also Iran from dominating future decisions on pipelines. Yet it was not until 1997 and the second administration of President Bill Clinton that the USA's strategic objectives in the Caspian region were formulated.[31] In March 1997, then National Security Adviser Sandy Berger singled out the region as a priority for US policy and stated Washington's intention to step up its involvement in the Caucasus and Central Asia. In July 1997, US Deputy Secretary of State Strobe Talbott stated in a speech that what happened in the Caspian region 'matters profoundly' to the USA.[32] The Clinton administration's National Security Strategy elaborated on the security interests underpinning US policy towards Central Asia.[33]

From the beginning of the Baku-Ceyhan project the US government invested much time and effort to get it accepted by the states concerned. When the decision to build the Baku-Tbilisi-Ceyhan oil pipeline was taken in August 2002, it was a success for the US government. Construction work started in early 2003 and was expected to be completed in 2005. The US administration strongly encouraged Kazakhstan to join the Baku-Ceyhan pipeline by initially shipping oil across the Caspian Sea in order to develop an underwater pipeline later, but Kazakhstan remained hesitant.

The project of a gas pipeline from Turkmenistan across Afghanistan to Pakistan, which to a large extent had been a 'baby' of the US company Unocal in the 1990s but had to be abandoned after the Taliban established control in Afghanistan, was reinvigorated in 2002. In early 2002, a memorandum was signed between Turkmenistan, Afghanistan and Pakistan on a feasibility study in preparation for building a 1,500 km-long gas export pipeline from Dovletabat in Turkmenistan via Kandahar in Afghanistan to Multan in Pakistan.[34] On 17 October 2002, Afghan, Pakistani and Turkmen officials drew up an intergovernmental agreement to study the capacity of the pipeline to supply thirty billion cubic metres (bcm) annually of Turkmen gas to Pakistan and the costs of this. However, implementation of the project seems to be a matter for the distant future since Afghanistan remains unstable and Russia, in April 2003, secured a firm agreement on the export of Turkmenistan's gas through Russia for the next twenty-five years.[35]

In testimony before a subcommittee of the Senate Committee on Foreign Relations, in late April 2003, Leonard L Coburn from the US Energy Department reported that the Bush administration had been 'extremely proactive' in its efforts to enhance energy cooperation with Russia and the Caucasian and Central Asian states. With respect to the situation in the Central Asia-Caspian region, he concluded that there had been substantial investment successes by Western and US companies in the region, but he also cited a lack of export outlets and the unresolved legal status of the Caspian Sea as two major factors inhibiting the development of the oil and gas resources there.[36]

The Central Asian states had joined NATO's PFP programme in 1994 (except for Tajikistan, which joined in February 2002). During the following years several multi-lateral exercises within the PFP framework took place in the USA with participating Central Asian militaries. The USA encouraged Kazakhstan, Kyrgyzstan and Uzbekistan to create the Central Asian peacekeeping battalion in 1996 and to carry out annual exercises in which US troops and troops from NATO countries participated after 1997. The USA regarded bilateral and multilateral cooperation under the PFP as a key mechanism for promoting Central Asian integration into Western political-military institutions, encouraging civilian control over their militaries and institutionalising cooperative relations with the US military, while at the same time dissuading other regional powers – especially Russia, China and Iran – from seeking to dominate the region.

The incursions into Kyrgyzstan by Uzbek Islamist rebels in August 1999 led the USA to give more emphasis to security and anti-terrorist issues in its cooperation with the Central Asian states. During her round tour of the Central Asian states in April 2000, Secretary of State Madeleine Albright announced a new Central Asian Border Security Initiative, which provided US $3 million in security assistance, initially to Kyrgyzstan, Kazakhstan and Uzbekistan, and later to Turkmenistan and Tajikistan. When George W Bush came to power he maintained the core elements of Clinton's policy but accentuated the energy issues.[37]

The 11 September attacks greatly increased the US engagement in the region, and security cooperation in particular expanded dramatically. Anti-terrorism became the defining principle of US foreign policy. In October 2001, the US Department of Defense's Quadrennial Defense Review summarised the general principles underlying US security interests in Central Asia as: preventing the hostile domination of key areas and maintaining a stable balance of power; maintaining access to key markets and strategic resources; addressing threats from territories of weak states; sustaining coalitions; and preparing to intervene in unexpected crises.[38]

Although there seems to exist a consensus in the US administration on the need for a general US engagement in Central Asia, different views remain with regard to the form and degree of this engagement in the short-term and long-term perspective.

## The Russian Policy Response in Central Asia

Several factors explain why Putin gave his consent to a US military presence in Central Asia in September. First, as already mentioned, his policy turn can be explained by his desire to improve relations with the West, and above all the USA. Improved relations with the West is considered by the Russian government a necessary external condition for a successful carrying out of domestic reforms of Russia. Second, the local setting in Central Asia set the limits to the kind of policy response Russia could come up with. Russia's role and influence in Central Asia had declined rapidly during the second half of the 1990s, and Russia was no longer able to control the local scene. The decline was reflected in the economic, political, military and cultural spheres.[39] As a consequence Russia was unable to prevent either the negative impact on Central Asia of the turmoil and Islamic radicalism in Afghanistan or the growing engagement of other foreign countries and governments.

When Vladimir Putin came to power as Russian prime minister in 1999 he made a determined effort, responding to Russian security and strategic concerns, to rally the Central Asian states against a common threat in the shape of 'international terrorism' and to counter the growing foreign engagement on security matters in the region, in particular that of the USA.[40] He tried to make the CST the key instrument for the anti-terrorist struggle, and in late 1999 and early 2000 Uzbekistan participated in joint exercises with CST states. Yet Uzbekistan did not return to the Treaty, and Turkmenistan never joined. When the US government became more active in Central Asia after 11 September 2001, the CST anti-terrorist structures seemed to be marginalised as the US government did not turn to the CST with requests for assistance and cooperation but instead turned to the Central Asian governments directly.

During the first half of 2002 it seemed as if Russia did not object to the US engagement in Central Asia, since it and the USA had become allies in a struggle against the common enemy of terrorism. The common anti-terrorist struggle was the main purpose of the NATO-Russia Council, created in May 2002.[41]

From the summer of 2002 it became apparent that Russia was determined to find a policy to secure its future presence in Central Asia. It continued its efforts to develop security cooperation within the CST, and at the ceremonies to mark the tenth anniversary of the Treaty in May 2002, the six member states (Russia, Kazakhstan, Kyrgyzstan, Tajikistan, Belarus and Armenia), in a joint statement, agreed to raise the status of the organisation by formalising and reorganising it, and to seek international recognition as a regional organisation according to Chapter VIII of the UN Charter.[42] Efforts to strengthen multilateral economic cooperation were made within the Eurasian Economic Community (of which the members are the same countries as are signatories to the CST). Difficulties in developing multilateral cooperation made it necessary for Russia to put more effort into bilateral relations. Towards the end of 2002 Russia had improved relations with Kazakhstan, Kyrgyzstan and Turkmenistan, in doing so taking the opportunity to exploit the domestic difficulties of the governments in the latter two countries. The shooting of five people during demonstrations in Kyrgyzstan in March 2002, the repeated cleansing of state structures in Turkmenistan in 2002 and the arrest of former Turkmen foreign minister, Boris Shikhmuradov, in November 2002 indicated the fear and weakness of these regimes. In this situation both turned to

Russia for assistance.

A series of agreements were concluded with Kyrgyzstan when President Putin visited Bishkek in early December 2002. During his visit a Russian airbase was opened at Kant – just outside Bishkek and not far from the US base at Manas International Airport. The Kant base was planned to host about twenty planes under the responsibility of the Rapid Reaction Force of the CST. Although so far it was only a symbolic gesture without military significance, the opening of the base was a signal of Russia's intention to maintain military presence in the region. The CST Rapid Reaction Force is to include in the future 1,500 men from Russia, Kazakhstan, Kyrgyzstan and Tajikistan, the Central Asians deployed at their home bases. An Anti-Terrorist Centre is located in Bishkek. The Russian 201$^{st}$ Motorized Rifle Division in Tajikistan (about 8,000 men) is being reorganised into a Russian military base. The Russian border troops (about 11,000 men) remain on guard at the Tajik–Afghan border.

As soon as Putin came to power in 1999 he had indicated a stronger emphasis on the role of energy in Russian foreign policy. In April 2000, at the Russian Security Council, he declared that Russia should become more active in the Caspian region, called for greater Russian engagement in the exploitation of the Caspian energy resources, and the coordination of policies by Russian companies and ministries. A position of representative of the president in the Caspian region was created, and a former minister for energy, Viktor Kalyuzhny, was appointed with responsibility for coordinating policy and dealing with all foreign policy issues concerning the region, including the legal division of the Caspian Sea.[43] Putin's focus on energy resulted in the launching in November 1999 of work on the extension by the Caspian Pipeline Consortium (of which Russia was a major member, together with the US company Chevron) of the northern route from the Tengiz field in Kazakhstan to Novorossisk at the Black Sea. The extension was completed in 2001. As Russian policy in Central Asia was activated in 2002, energy issues were given stronger emphasis.

A major agreement on the export of Turkmen gas to Russia had been in preparation for a long time. Russia is the main provider of outlets for gas from Turkmenistan. Disagreement over the price level, as well as Turkmenistan's expectations of a future pipeline across Afghanistan, had held up new deals. When Putin came to power in 1999 he renewed the discussions on an increase of Russian imports of Turkmen gas, and when he visited Turkmenistan in May 2000, a document of intent was signed whereby Russia was to increase its purchases of Turkmen gas by 10 billion cubic metre each year from 2001 to a level of 60 billion cubic metre by 2004. The agreement was for long term and covered a period of thirty years. However, agreements over prices and payment mechanism were left to further negotiations,[44] and the two countries continued to disagree over price. In September 2002, a Russian delegation visited Ashgabat for a meeting with the Russian-Turkmen Inter-Governmental Economic Commission.[45] The head of the Russian delegation, Energy Minister Yusufov, announced that President Niyazov supported Russia's proposals on gas purchases for the period up to 2020. Until 2005, Russia would base its proposals on Turkmenistan's residual potential and the capacity of the Central Asia-Centre gas pipeline, which runs from Ashgabat to Aleksandrov Gay on the border between Kazakhstan and Russia. Russia agreed to repair and restore the sections of the pipeline that run across Uzbek and Kazakh territory, and according to Yusufov, Russia intended to make huge investments to expand the gas transportation system. The Russian companies Gazprom and Zarubezhneft were planning to participate in the development of the hydrocarbon resources on the Turkmen shelf of the Caspian Sea.

When President Niyazov visited Moscow in April 2003 the agreement on the buying and selling of gas was signed within a framework of twenty-five years. Gazprom was given the right to buy all Turkmen gas excluding what was already committed under existing agreements with other partners.[46] Turkmenistan's current export obligations – notably with Ukraine and Iran – expire in 2006. The short-term price deal was favourable to Turkmenistan, at US $44 per cubic metre – the rate Niyazov had been holding out for over several years of negotiations.[47] For Russia the deal was crucial in several respects. It made it possible for Russia to meet its gas obligations to Europe in spite of its own difficulties with production and investment in its own fields. The agreement covered not only Russian purchases of Turkmen gas but also modernisation of the gas pipeline networks and Russian participation in the development of Turkmenistan's gas fields.

Putin moved the energy issue up on the Russian agenda for cooperation with Central Asia. In 2000 he had launched the general idea of a gas alliance of Russia together with Turkmenistan, Uzbekistan and Kazakhstan. In January 2002, he presented a proposal to set up a Eurasian Alliance of Natural Gas Producers, to include these four states, and on 1 March 2002, the leaders of all four states agreed on a joint statement on 'cooperation in energy policy and measures to defend the interests of natural gas producers'. Putin stressed the importance of uniting the efforts of Russia and Turkmenistan – the major gas producers – and Kazakhstan and Uzbekistan, which provide essential transit routes. The four countries intended to coordinate import-export and investment policies and to promote a common 'energy security' strategy. Natural gas cooperation would ensure 'stable supplies to the world and CIS markets', the joint statement said.[48] A statement signed on 23 October 2002 confirmed the intention.

A gas alliance would open up the Russian natural gas pipeline network to Central Asian producers, which are eager to access European markets. There was also the prospect of a new pipeline through Ukraine running along an existing route from Aleksandrov Gay to Novopskov in the north of Lugansk Oblast in Ukraine. As the pipeline infrastructure in Central Asia already exists, it is more a question of coming to an agreement on exit to the European market. The Central Asia-Centre pipeline system is, however, deteriorating with decrepit pipelines and limited capacity, and needs major investment.[49]

Russia's interest in forming a gas alliance should also be seen against the background of the revived plans for a gas pipeline from Turkmenistan across Afghanistan to Pakistan. It was a priority of Russian policy to prevent this project from becoming the first choice of Turkmenistan for the future. Nevertheless, on 17 October 2002, Russian Deputy Foreign Minister Andrey Denisov declared Russia's interest in the project, and so did the Russian gas and oil company Itera.[50] Denisov stated that the Russian foreign ministry believed that 'any initiative of this type will promote Afghanistan's speedy reconstruction and the development of regional cooperation on the whole'.[51] The Asian Development Bank was to finance the feasibility study. But, because of the continuing instability in Afghanistan, the project did not seem even close to being started.

In 2002 Russia also demonstrated interest in developing the hydroenergy resources of Tajikistan and Kyrgyzstan by completing and reconstructing some large power stations. At the Eurasian Economic Community summit in April 2003 it was announced that Russia and Kazakhstan were to take on the financing.[52]

It is a priority of President Putin to maintain good relations with the USA. This does not exclude, however, that Russia will try to expand its cooperation with Central Asian states in order to secure its influence over the area with regard to energy and security cooperation. Thus, during 2002–03 Russia activated its policy in Central Asia in response to the post September 2001 situation in the region.

## Prospects for the Future

The post-September 2001 developments accelerated the trends which had already begun in Central Asia. The US military presence paved the way for other governments and international organisations to engage in the region. All Central Asian governments were willing to develop cooperation with the USA within the US-led anti-terrorist coalition, illustrated also by Tajikistan, Russia's closest ally in Central Asia.

The US showed interest in all Central Asian countries, although US military was deployed only in Uzbekistan, Kyrgyzstan and Tajikistan. All three remain members of the Russian-led Treaty of Collective Security. Still security cooperation with the USA on the bilateral and multilateral (Partnership for Peace) levels are ongoing. In that sense parallel security arrangements are developing in Central Asia, one Russian-led and one US-led. Both Russia and the US have declared their common interest in fighting the threat of 'international terrorism'. Some observers regard the evolution of two parallel arrangements as a temporary phenomenon, which can only contribute to increasing insecurity and the potential for instability in the region. Others, among them several Central Asian observers, instead see this situation as a strengthening of regional security. The Kyrgyz scholars Kaana Aoidarkul and Mels Omarov write: 'In the final analysis this created what can be called "intersecting" systems in the global security landscape, an involvement in which gives the regional countries additional security guarantees.'[53]

Although it seems most likely that the US military presence in Central Asia will be reduced in the future, US engagement in the region can be expected to remain high. Charles William Maynes, director of the Eurasia Foundation and former editor (1980–97) of the US journal *Foreign Policy*, wrote in spring 2003: 'Although the Bush administration promises a timely end to the military presence there, many believe the United States will remain engaged through an enhanced political and military presence for years to come; after all, staying until the "job is done", as the administration has promised, means rooting out the conditions that breed terrorism in the first place. And that formidable goal suggests a quasi-permanent US interest in Central Asia'.[54] However, this does not automatically mean that the US will engage in major financial aid and investments in the region.[55] The present US administration is taking on far-going obligations and expenses in other countries. This is illustrated by the US/British military invasion of Iraq in April 2003 and the consequent obligation to rebuild Iraqi society. There is, therefore, a risk that the interest of the US administration, and thereby also that of several of the international organisations, may turn to other directions than Central Asia.

Although it looked in spring 2002 as if Russia was content with playing the role of a minor partner to the USA, and had lost interest in Central Asia, by summer 2003 this proved to be wrong. In Putin's policy, close relations with the USA remain first priority, which he demonstrated during the war in Iraq when he set limits to Russian criticism of US Iraq policy. Nevertheless, Russia's policy in Central Asia was activated during 2002. Russia has a historical interest in Central Asia, and Russia will not abandon Central Asia.

Russia's interest in Central Asia is long-term. At present Russia is still struggling with a decline of its influence and does not have enough to offer the Central Asian governments in order to successfully develop multilateral economic and military cooperation with them. The Russian government is therefore trying to make the most of bilateral relations with Central Asian states. The Central Asian states are in desperate need of assistance for developing their economies, and they do not expect Russia to be able to help them in this regard; they are therefore looking for assistance from other directions. The ongoing reconfiguration of influence in the region means that it will be difficult for Russia ever to come back to the role of a 'hegemon', although it may develop into a strong and active partner of Central Asian countries.

Russia Central Asian policy after 11 September 2001 has to be understood in the larger context of Russian-US relations. Vladimir Putin has invested in cooperation with the USA in order to implement his domestic reform agenda, first of all, but also as a way to win back a role on the international scene. Thus, Russia's Central Asian policy has become incorporated into Russia's Western, primarily, its US policy. Thus, although, competition will remain between Russia and the USA in the region, Central Asia has become part of Russian-US general foreign policy relations. As long as both countries are interested in maintaining good mutual relations on the global scale, competition in Central Asia will be complemented by a large potential for cooperation.

The engagement of states other than the USA and Russia in Central Asia contributes to reduction in the negative implications of Russian-US competition by strengthening its cooperation with powers in the neighbourhood. Economic relations now develop between Asian and Central Asian states. Projects, which as yet are only at an early stage or still on the drawing board, will gradually be implemented. New pipeline routes and connections by road and rail will open up Central Asia to a wider Asian region in the future. Among these powers China has the largest potential for cooperation with Central Asian states in the future, first of all with regard to Kazakhstan, Kyrgyzstan, and Tajikistan. So far China has acted mainly as an economic player, but it is now engaging in security cooperation within the framework of the Shanghai Cooperation Organisation. Iran, which played a crucial role in the inter-Tajik negotiations to end the Tajik civil war, demonstrates interest in large economic and infrastructure development projects.

The Central Asian states have a potential for conflict and instability. Their regimes are all authoritarian to some degree and afraid of popular demands and political freedom. The societies are going through a difficult transition period, when both market reforms and democratisation are necessary in order to allow the countries to develop and raise standards of living. If the governments do not allow channels for discontent and political demands to be articulated, there is a risk that large sections of their societies will reject modernisation and go instead for radical political options like those presented by radical Islamism. The Central Asian countries therefore need the attention and engagement of the international community. Engagement by international organisations is important in order to help create the conditions for economic development and democracy. When development towards the rule of law is secured, international investment will eventually follow.

The present Russian and US administrations share a common view on the terrorist threat as the major threat to the security of their countries. Although the focus on the anti-terrorist struggle may seem narrow, it is likely to become a take-off for a broader understanding of the need for cooperation with regard to both security and energy issues in Central Asia. The present close relations between Russia and the USA on the global level have to be transformed into closer cooperation in Central Asia, and structures for multilateral cooperation to be developed. No such structures exist in Central Asia in which both Russia and the USA are members. The Shanghai Cooperation Organisation has only Russia and China as members of the powers engaging in the region. The cooperative component of Russian-US relations needs to be developed in Central Asia.

## Notes

1. ORT Vremya Programme, 14 September 2001/ ITAR-TASS, 14 September 2001, *Jamestown Monitor*, Issue 170, 18 September 2001.
2. *Jamestown Monitor*, Issue 170, 18 September 2001.
3. *Jamestown Monitor*, Issue 170, 18 September 2001.
4. BBC, *Inside Central Asia*, 393, 17–23 September 2001.
5. BBC, *Inside Central Asia*, 393, 17–23 September 2001.
6. See statement by Foreign Minister Igor Ivanov: 'President Putin reached agreement on this issue with the leaders of the five Central Asian countries over the weekend' and 'only flights with humanitarian cargo are meant here'. Interfax, 26 September 2001.
7. BBC, *Inside Central Asia*, 395, 1–7 October 2001.
8. Daily News Bulletin, IPD, Ministry of Foreign Affairs, Moscow, 25 September 2001, www.mid.ru.
9. *Diplomaticheskii vestnik*, 2001, No. 11, p.26.
10. BBC, *Inside Central Asia*, 396, 8–14 October 2001.
11. Nezavisimaya Gazeta, 9 April 2002.
12. RFE/RL, 11 January 2002.
13. *Asia Plus*, 17 January 2002.
14. Interfax/*Asia Plus*, 15 March 2002.
15. *Jamestown Monitor*, 170, 18 September 2001.
16. ITAR-TASS, 14 September 2001.
17. At the end of September, Rakhmonov had told Secretary of State, Colin Powell that Tajikistan would cooperate with the USA to fight terrorism. BBC, *Inside Central Asia*, 395, 1–7 October 2001.
18. DPA, 18 October 2001; and *Jamestown Monitor*, 204, 6 November 2001.
19. *Jamestown Monitor*, 204, 6 November 2001.
20. Raffi Khatchadourian, 'US Eyes Bases in Tajikistan', *Eurasia Insight*, 6 November 2001.

21. BBC, *Inside Central Asia*, 414, 18–24 February 2002.
22. *Asia Plus*, 24 September 2002.
23. Uzbek Radio first programme, Tashkent, in Russian, 1120 GMT, 29 August 2002; BBC Monitoring Central Asia, 29 August 2002.
24. President Karimov visited the USA during 11–14 March, President Akaev on 23–29 September, and President Rakhmonov in early December 2002.
25. BBC, *Inside Central Asia*, 456, December 2002.
26. Uzbek TV on Thursday, 6 March 2003; BBC, *Inside Central Asia*, 9 March 2003.
27. BBC, *Inside Central Asia*, 9 March 2003.
28. Tajikistan and Kyrgyzstan were supporters of Moscow on the Iraq issue according to Viktoriya Panfilova, 'Slozhnaya rol statista', *N G Dipkurer*, 24 March 2003, No. 5 (49).
29. Lt. Gen. William E Odom, 'US policy toward Central Asia and the South Caucasus', *Caspian Cross Roads*, Vol. 3, No. 1, Summer 1997. However, John Roberts wrote in 2001: 'It is possible to make some reasonable estimates that the oil and gas resources of the Caspian region are significantly higher than, and may even be double, those of the North Sea, while falling far short of those in the Persian Gulf – some 40–60 billion barrels of oil, or 4–6 per cent of world proven recoverable oil reserves.' John Roberts, 'Energy reserves, pipeline routes and the legal regime in the Caspian Sea', in *The Security of the Caspian Sea Region*, edited by Gennady Chufrin, SIPRI/Oxford University Press, 2001, p.34.
30. A Elisabeth Jones, 'US–Central Asian Cooperation', Testimony to the Subcommittee on Central Asia and the Caucasus', Foreign Relations Committee, US Senate, 13 December 2001, p.9.
31. Stephen Blank, 'The USA and Central Asia', in Allison Roy and Lena Jonson (eds.), *Central Asian Security: The New International Context* (Washington, DC: Brookings

Institution Press and Royal Institute of International Affairs, 2001).

32. 'A Farewell to Flashman: American policy in the Caucasus and the Central Asia', Address by Deputy Secretary of State, Strobe Talbott at the Paul H Nietze School of Advanced International Studies, John Hopkins University, 21 July 1997, www.sais-jhu.edu/pubs/speeches/talbott.html.

33. These included promoting the rule of law in an effort to combat crime and corruption; creating a stable environment for energy exports (as part of a broader US interest in diversifying energy supplies); reducing regional threats (non-proliferation, terrorism); and encouraging regional cooperation between Central Asian states. US White House, A National Security Strategy for a New Century, Washington DC, December 1999 (released on 5 January 2000), http://cgsc.leavenworth.army.mil. Referred to by Elisabeth Wishnick, *Growing US Security Interests in Central Asia*, Strategic Studies Institute, US Army War College, October 2002.

34. *RFE/RL Newsline*, 31 May 2002; *RFE/RL Newsline*, Vol. 6, No. 198, Part I, 21 October 2002.

35. BBC, *Inside Central Asia*, 13 April 2003.

36. 'US Cooperating with Russia, Central Asia on Global Energy Security: April 30 Senate Testimony of DOE's Leonard L Coburn', US State Department Press Releases and Documents, Federal Information and News Dispatch, Inc. 1 May 2003.

37. Elisabeth Wishnick, *Growing US Security Interests in Central Asia*, Strategic Studies Institute, US Army War College, October 2002.

38. US Department of Defense, *Quadrennial Defense Review Report*, 30 September 2001, p.2.

39. Lena Jonson, *Russia and Central Asia in a New Web of Relations*, London: Royal Institute of International

Affairs, 1999.

40. Lena Jonson, *Central Asia and Russian Foreign Policy Revision* (forthcoming).

41. Dov Lynch, *Russia Faces Europe*, Chaillot Papers No. 60, Paris: EU Institute for Security Studies, May 2003, pp. 25–26.

42. 'Sessiya Soveta kollektivnoi bezopasnosti gosudarstv-uchastnikov Dogovora o kollektivnoi bezopasnosti', *Diplomaticheskii vestnik*, No. 6, June 2002, pp.76–78. See also Lena Jonson, 'Russia and Central Asia: Post-September, 2001', *Central Asia and the Caucasus*, No. 1 (19), 2003.

43. S Z Zhiznin and P I Rodionov, 'Energicheskaya Diplomatiya v Kaspiisko-Chernomorskom regione (gazovye aspekty)', *Diplomaticheskii vestnik*, No. 6, June 2000, pp.79–87.

44. *Jamestown Fortnight in Review*, 26 May 2000.

45. BBC, *Inside Central Asia*, No. 444, September 2002.

46. Russia would now buy about 6 billion cubic metres of Turkmen gas in 2004, and this figure could increase to 80 billion cubic metres per year by 2009. BBC, *Inside Central Asia*, 13 April 2003.

47. However, since 50 per cent of the price is payable in kind, actual export revenues will be half the notional amount. After 2006 things get better, as the cost will be determined by world market prices. Arkady Dubnov, 'Turkmenbashi Boosted by Moscow Deal', RCA, 199, 17 April 2003.

48. Serbei Blagov, 'Efforts to Produce "Eurasian OPEC" falls short at CIS summit', *Eurasianet*, 1 March 2002.

49. 'Russia's alliance with Central Asian gas could serve Europe', UzReport.com, 6 November 2002. Document uzrepe0020021106dyb60005m.

50. Turkmen, R U Internet newspaper website, 17 July 2002/BBC, *Inside Central Asia*, 435 (2002).

51. BBC, *Inside Central Asia*, Issue 449, 21–27 October 2002,

'Draft agreement drawn up on Afghan–Pakistan–Turkmen gas pipeline'.

52.*Asia Plus*, 28 April 2003.

53. Kaana Aoidarkul and Mels Omarov, 'Cooperation Between Russia, the US and Kyrgyzstan in new Geopolitical Context', *Central Asia and the Caucasus*, No. 1 (19), 2003, p.119.

54. Charles William Maynes, 'America Discovers Central Asia', *Foreign Affairs*, Vol. 82, No. 2, March–April, pp.120–132.

55. Martin C Spechler, 'Economy and Security in Central Asia since 9/11: A Sceptical Look', *Central Asia and the Caucasus*, No. 1 (19), 2003.

# Chapter XI

# REGIONAL POLITICS IN CENTRAL ASIA: THE CHANGING ROLES OF IRAN, TURKEY, PAKISTAN AND CHINA

Svante E Cornell

## Introduction

11 September 2001 affected no region in the world as much as it affected Central Asia.[1] Afghanistan, of course, was the state most affected, as its erstwhile isolated and estranged Taliban government was overthrown and the country opened up to the world. Afghanistan received great amount of political and economic aid as well as American military presence, and a token international security force in Kabul. Twenty-three years of almost constant war had now come to an end, giving way to the gruesome reconstruction of this war-ravaged country. The five post-Soviet states of Central Asia, on the other hand, saw a greatly changed regional political scene emerge out of Operation Enduring Freedom (OEF). For one, the main threat to their security – terrorism originating from Afghanistan, especially the Islamic Movement of Uzbekistan – had been done away with. Moreover, aid provided by Western donors to Central Asia greatly increased, and American and allied military presence meant closer relations with the United States for Tajikistan, Kyrgyzstan and especially Uzbekistan, which

was singled out as a strategic ally of the United States. The biggest change, on a broader level, was that Central Asia no longer remained an isolated region. Indeed, before 11 September 2001, Western interest in the region had gradually waned. But America's advent on the scene restored a certain freedom of movement to Central Asian states that were increasingly becoming constrained in an environment dominated by Russian and Chinese influence. The ever evolving and shifting distribution of power and influence among the states surrounding Central Asia was fundamentally altered by the serious commitment of the United States to a military and security engagement in the region, even though the length of this commitment was not announced.[2]

American involvement hence redrew the geopolitical map of Central Asia and beyond, before redrawing the political map of the Middle East a year and a half later through the invasion of Iraq. This involvement greatly increased America's leverage in the region, with profound impact on the respective roles not only of Russia, but also of the other major powers involved in the region: Iran, Turkey, Pakistan and China. Now, two years after 11 September some repositioning of these major actors can be discerned. How have their interests been affected by American presence in the region? How have they responded to this development?

## Iran: The Politics of Encirclement

The independence of Central Asian states was welcomed with trepidation in Tehran. Traditionally oriented, primarily towards the Persian Gulf in its foreign policy, the Islamic Republic had only three years earlier emerged from the devastating Eight-Year War with Iraq. The dramatic developments in the Caucasus, especially the Armenia-

Azerbaijan conflict, threatened to spill over into Iranian territory and did so at least on one occasion. Moreover, the rise of nationalism in Turkmenistan and Azerbaijan worried Iran, home to a significant Turkmen minority and an Azerbaijani one at least twice larger than the population of the Republic of Azerbaijan. Relations with Azerbaijan have been tense for most of the past decade, whereas Iran's relations with Armenia have been the closest with any former Soviet Republic.[3]

After the collapse of the USSR, American and other Western actors voiced strong concern that Iran would seek to pursue a subversive and adventurist policy to export its brand of Islamic government to Central Asia and the Caucasus. In retrospect, these fears seem to have been highly exaggerated – partly due to the pragmatic character of Iranian foreign policy towards this region and partly due to the fact that Central Asian states are Sunni and not Shi'a. However, Iran has supported Shi'a activist groups on a low and covert level in Azerbaijan, the only Shi'a majority state. In general, Iran followed a policy of 'incremental engagement' with the region.[4]

The direct impact of OEF was positive for Iran: it removed a vehemently anti-Iranian and anti-Shi'a government from neighbouring Afghanistan. In fact, Iran and the Taliban had had a tense standoff on their common border in 1998, after the Taliban conquered Mazar-e-Sharif, leading to the killing of several Iranian diplomats. The rise of the Taliban had been a cause of concern for Iran and Iranian representatives expressed their vulnerability by arguing that they were 'sandwiched between the Taliban and Saddam Hussein'. Thus, OEF removed a government that was also, on an ideological as well as practical level, a threat to Iran. This was true also with the American overthrow of Saddam Hussein in Iraq eighteen months later. In both conflicts, Iran showed an ambivalent position, expressing the fact that Tehran had little problem with the overthrow of either the Taliban or Saddam Hussein. However, Iran was worried about the results of American presence on its doorstep. Having been included in the 'Axis of Evil' by President George W Bush, Iran increasingly felt a direct threat of American military action against it that has only increased after US operations in Iraq and the ensuing soaring debate about Iran's nuclear programme. Secondly, Tehran is worried about the impact of the unrest and instability that would result if American intervention did not stabilise these countries – fears that continue to this day.

On the whole, the largest impact of the two American operations on the Islamic Republic of Iran has been a negative one, in the form of an acute feeling of encirclement. Prior to OEF, the American military was by no means far from Iranian shores or borders. The US Navy was omnipresent in the Persian Gulf; America also had military installations in Saudi Arabia and other Gulf states. Meanwhile, Turkey was a NATO country with a US air base on the Mediterranean. But the US military was not a factor to the East or North of Iran. OEF changed this. Afghanistan became a de facto American protectorate; Pakistan hosted several, though minor, American troops, including in the province of Baluchistan neighbouring Iran; Uzbekistan and Kyrgyzstan became areas of permanent US bases; in the Caucasus, Azerbaijan saw increased American military assistance while US training forces were deployed in Georgia. With Operation Iraqi Freedom, the encirclement of Iran was completed: American forces now effectively surrounded the Islamic Republic.

This new situation is the one under which Tehran operates, and in which Iranian policy in Central Asia is being formulated. Consequently, Tehran has followed a policy that is best described as a combination of defensive caution and limited containment of the United States on its borders.

Caution and realism has always been a major determinant of the foreign policy of the Islamic Republic towards its neighbours. It never launched the much-feared campaign of Islamisation in Central Asia in 1991, nor is there evidence that Tehran ever planned to do so. Instead, Iran has been continuing its relations with Central Asian states in the economic, political and cultural spheres, with little major change since 11 September. In a sense, Iran has never been a major external actor in post-Soviet Central Asia on the political sphere, and if anything, this trend has consolidated since Operation Enduring Freedom.

This is in turn related partly to Iran's close relationship with Russia, which has meant the enlisting of Russian diplomatic support for Iran and crucially important nuclear technology and other weaponry.[5] This Moscow link has gained increasing importance in Tehran as the regime is apparently frantically seeking to achieve nuclear weapons capability, feeling that only such capability would give it a measure of security in an increasingly hostile environment. The cost of this policy has however been in the realm of Iranian policy in the former Soviet sphere. Indeed, it seems to be an unwritten rule that Iran's role in the Caucasus and Central Asia is circumscribed by its deference to Russian domination. In other words, Iran's policy seldom interferes with or contradicts Russian policy in these regions. Its policy of supporting Armenia and counteracting the development of a strong and wealthy Azerbaijan is in tandem with Moscow's interests, though for clearly different reasons. Moscow seeks to dominate the South Caucasus and secure a monopoly over energy resources there, while Iran is mainly afraid of the possible effect of a wealthy and American-allied Azerbaijan on its sizeable and increasingly restive Azeri population. Increasingly close relations between Baku and Washington, however, have aggravated tensions between the two. In fact, rumours in summer 2003 that Azerbaijan would be used as a launching pad for an American invasion of Iran and that Baku had already consented to this led to thinly veiled Iranian threats of military action and violations of Azerbaijani air space by Iranian jets.

With regard to Afghanistan, Iran has played a much more prominent role. Iran, like Russia, has supported the Northern Alliance to grab power in Kabul, which has created a government with little legitimacy as a broad-based national government capable of reining in the provincial warlords who still wield much power in the country. Concomitantly, Tehran has extended full support to Ismail Khan, the warlord controlling the north-western part of Afghanistan centred around the historic city of Herat. By extending military supplies and cooperating in keeping a trade flow generating over US $1 million in duties levied by Ismail Khan (none of which is sent to the Central government), Iran effectively undermines the emergence of a strong Central government in Afghanistan.[6] The reasons for this policy are clear: given American preponderance in Afghanistan, a strong Afghan government would mean, from the perspective of Tehran, a strong American presence in the region. Tehran would prefer to prop up the warlords whom it can influence rather than face the prospect of competing with the US in influencing a Central government in Kabul. Therefore, Tehran is following a policy of mild containment of the US on its eastern border. Tehran's policy towards Azerbaijan is also along similar lines and it has sent clear warnings to Baku regarding a larger American military presence there. Finally, in Iraq, the Iranian policy remains to be determined. Iran allowed some Iran-based groups that are opposed to Saddam Hussein to engage with the United States. But this was aimed at influencing the post-Saddam processes in Iraq rather than pleasing the US.

Iran is at present in a defensive position. With regard to former Soviet Central Asia, its policies have changed little and its influence remains relatively circumscribed; in Afghanistan, Iran keeps being an influential actor, especially at a regional level, clearly in contradiction with the stated interests of the United States.

## Turkey: Domestic Preoccupations

Turkey's policy towards Central Asia has gone through several phases since the fall of the Soviet Union. Immediately following the collapse of the USSR, at a time when Turkey felt rejected by Europe, it was suggested that Turkey should take advantage of the creation of five new Turkic states in the Caucasus and Central Asia, and at least seek to forge closer ties with these countries. However, it did not take Turkey long to realise that this policy had slim chances of success. Russia had not abandoned its ambitions in these regions and thwarted Turkish ambitions, especially in the Nagorno-Karabakh conflict. Moreover, Turkey's economy was heavily oriented towards Europe, and it was not in a position to take on the task of supporting the process of economic reform in the former Soviet states. Turkey's internal troubles, especially the PKK rebellion, also cast doubts on its ability to exert influence so far away. In addition, pronouncements of a Turkic twenty-first century scared Russia and Iran, while the Central Asian states were put off by some Turkish representatives' big-brotherly behaviour. By the late 1990s, Turkey had developed a more pragmatic policy, focusing security relations on the South Caucasus, specifically Azerbaijan and Georgia, while entertaining economic, political and cultural interactions with Central Asian states. Hence, Turkey gradually downscaled its ambitions in the region. It allowed its private sector to take the lead, with state support, in forging closer ties with Central Asia. Much like Iran, Turkey had not, during the 1990s, managed to achieve a position as a major player in the political scene of Central Asia.[7]

In the Caucasus, on the other hand, the Turkish economic and political role has become increasingly clear. Here the main vehicle of Turkish foreign policy has been the military establishment, which considers both Azerbaijan and Georgia to be of strategic importance. Turkey spent most of the 1990s building up the Azerbaijani military, in fact, developing its military forces from scratch after their debacle in the war with Armenia. Following this, Turkey established a military academy in Georgia as well, and relations with that country by the late 1990s reached the level of strategic partnership. This reflected a generally more activist trend in Turkish foreign policy, especially in areas close to home. The military alliance with Israel, Turkey's active participation in peacekeeping in the Balkans, and taking responsibility for the security of Azerbaijan are examples of a more activist Turkey. Yet it has stayed away from Central Asia.

11 September allowed Turkey the opportunity to capitalise on its role as a secular, American-allied Muslim country. Immediately after 11 September, Turkey took part in the International Security Force in Afghanistan (ISAF) which it also headed for more than six months. Turkish commandos also took part in OEF, supporting American forces especially in the Uzbek-populated north of Afghanistan. Turkey also upgraded its security relations with Uzbekistan, and launched anti-terrorism training programmes in that country.[8]

However, Turkey was plunged into a domestic crisis, first with the economic crisis in February and later as a result of Prime Minister Bülent Ecevit's failing health in spring 2002. Its fragile coalition of three parties with diverging platforms (a social democratic, a liberal and a nationalist party) collapsed, prompting early elections in November 2002. These elections fundamentally reshaped the Turkish political scene, leading to the expulsion from Parliament of most parties that had formed the core of Turkey's political scene for a decade. In their place, the AK Party (AKP), a moderate Islamic-oriented party grabbed 36 per cent of the votes and a two-thirds majority in Parliament. This development seemed to augur well, as it gave Turkey a consistent government with a clear political orientation as well as a manifestly business-friendly one. The leader of the AKP, Recep Tayyip Erdogan, visited Azerbaijan, Turkmenistan and Kazakhstan in January 2003, with a specific economy-oriented agenda – increasing trade with the Caucasus and Central Asia.[9] Unfortunately, Ankara did not sustain a political interest in Central Asia. The AKP government was by no means experienced, with much of its leadership and parliamentary group consisting of newly elected provincial politicians new to the national scene, as well as the core leadership of the city administration of Istanbul that Erdogan had chaired previously. Shortly after coming to power, the AKP was confronted with the need to kick-start Turkey's economy, while passing relevant judicial and political reforms to be accepted as a candidate country to the European Union. At this point, the US war in Iraq began to loom large over the horizon, leading up to the 3 March 2003 vote in the Turkish Parliament that did not produce a sufficient majority for allowing US use of Turkish territory for the war in Iraq. As this implied that a large chunk of the AKP parliamentary group had voted against the wishes of its own government, it plunged Turkey into a period of political as well as economic instability, as the US aid that had been tied to the passing of the resolution did not come through.[10]

In other words, Turkey started off on a positive note in its relations with Central Asia after 11 September, especially in the security sphere but also, to some extent, in the economic field. However, the war in Iraq prohibited a greater attention to this region and forced Turkey to focus on domestic concerns to a greater extent.

## Pakistan: Coping With The Aftershock

Much like Turkey, Pakistan initiated its relationship with Central Asia in the early 1990s with great hopes. While Turkey put its ethno-linguistic affinities with the region as well as its relationship with the West as a base for its relationship, Pakistan took advantage of the fact that it is the only neighbouring power sharing the Sunni Islamic faith with Central Asia. More importantly, Pakistan portrayed itself, logically, as the natural trade route for Central Asian states to reach world markets and break out of their trade and economic dependence on Russia. The second government of Benazir Bhutto in the early 1990s made the greatest effort to translate this policy into practice, as it mapped the mountain passes on its northern border to identify the most suitable trade routes. Out of this, partially, was born the idea of creating a major trade route from Central Asia through Herat and Kandahar to Quetta and down to the port of Gwadar in Baluchistan.

Pakistan's main problem in establishing a relationship with Central Asia was geographic: while only several miles away from Tajikistan across the Wakhan Corridor, it is separated from the region by Afghanistan. The break-up of the USSR coincided with the breakdown of law and order in Afghanistan, and the civil war between rival mujahideen factions that led to a collapse of the Central government authority in Kabul.[11] As a result, Afghanistan descended into lawlessness, making it a particularly unsuitable conduit for trade. Trade convoys were routinely robbed and drivers injured or killed; and rival mujahideen factions extorted money at numerous checkpoints across the country.

In fact, one of the main reasons for the Pakistani government's decision to sponsor the Taliban movement when it emerged in late 1994 was to clear the barriers to building a trade route. The first major raid conducted by the Taliban was aimed at setting free a test convoy that had been tasked to create a land trade route between Pakistan and Central Asia via Kandahar and Herat. The convoy, organised by the then Pakistani Minister of Interior Nasirullah Babar, was held hostage by a local commander, but was soon freed by a Taliban attack.[12] Within days, the Taliban captured Kandahar, beginning a series of conquests that eventually gave them control over close to 90 per cent of Afghanistan's territory. At this time, the Inter-Services Intelligence (ISI) and military establishment, both in conflict with the Bhutto government, were still supporting long-time Pakistani favourite Gulbuddin Hekmatyar. The bulk of the Pakistani state switched allegiance to the Taliban only after Hekmatyar was defeated and the Taliban were about to capture Kabul.

Pakistan's support for the Taliban has often been described in terms of a policy motivated by Islamic zeal. In fact, it served many pragmatic purposes. First, it helped in establishing a pro-Pakistani government in Afghanistan, whereas earlier governments had been hostile to Pakistan and friendly to India. This provided Pakistan with a certain strategic depth in its relation with India. Second, the Taliban emerged as a new force and the only one that seemed capable of stabilising Afghanistan after the civil war of the early 1990s. Last, but not the least, these two conditions, a stable and pro-Pakistan Afghanistan, were to provide the framework for a Pakistani role in Central Asia as the main artery for trade, and therefore, political influence resulting from increased economic interactions.

Unfortunately for Islamabad, this did not happen. For one, the Taliban movement did not take orders from Pakistan. In fact, Pakistan's ability to influence the Taliban has been widely overrated. As a result, Pakistan was unable to prevent the Taliban from pursuing its self-destructive policies towards women, minorities, and the population in general that brought it international ostracism, sanctions, and isolation. The Taliban was providing shelter to rebel Islamic groups from Central Asia such as the Islamic Movement of Uzbekistan and the neighbouring Central Asian states feared that they too would be affected by the 'spread of the Taliban' movement. This led Uzbekistan to close its borders with Afghanistan and Tajikistan to serve as the major conduit for military and political assistance to the Northern Alliance fighting the Taliban. Only Turkmenistan, itself increasingly isolated, kept working relations with the Taliban government. Though by 1998, the Taliban was controlling enough of Afghanistan to serve as trade conduit, it could not fulfil this role for political reasons. The regional backlash against the Taliban also reverberated against Pakistan. With the support of Russian policy and media, Pakistan increasingly became depicted in Central Asia as a country with an Islamic agenda, covertly supporting Taliban-style extremism to subvert the region. This generated large-scale resentment against Pakistan, and led to increasing suspicion against Pakistanis in general, making the task of Pakistani diplomats and businessmen very difficult.

Thus, Pakistan's Afghan policy proved immensely counterproductive. Far from making Pakistan a conduit of trade, it alienated Central Asian states from Pakistan and generated suspicion that may take a long time to undo. In retrospect, Pakistani support for the Taliban was a bad idea. It reflected a failure in Islamabad to assess the changes in international politics. In the 1980s, during the tenure of Zia ul-Haq, Pakistan and the United States had in tandem used radical political Islam to fight the Soviet Union in Afghanistan. For Pakistan, it made perfect sense: its closest links were with the Pashtun population in southern Afghanistan, but supporting nationalist Pashtun groups meant supporting groups that had inherent territorial claims on Pakistan's Pashtun areas. Islamic groups, however, would not necessarily have such claims and seemed to be better suited from Islamabad's vantage point. When the Soviet Union had been defeated in Afghanistan, the Pakistani elite supported the use of religious groups to meet political objectives. In the mid-1990s, Islamabad again felt that a religious grouping could fulfill a political purpose. But times had changed. Whereas Islamic fighters in Afghanistan had been the heroes of the West in the 1980s, Islamic fighters in the post-Cold War era had, by a twist, come to be depicted as a threat to peace and stability and potential terrorists. The same policy that had worked with the West in the 1980s hence became an international debacle in the 1990s. By 11 September, the Taliban had clearly become a failure and an embarrassment for Islamabad. Pakistan's change of policy towards the Taliban on 12 September was hence in line not only with international necessities but also with the domestic realisation that the policy was counterproductive.

Operation Enduring Freedom led to both positive and negative consequences for Pakistan. On the positive side, the collapse of the Taliban regime and the presence of American forces in Afghanistan impeded most problems related with the Taliban government, such as the sheltering of radical sectarian Sunni groups banned in Pakistan. A significant irritant in Pakistan's relations with the Taliban was the refusal by Taliban authorities to hand over members of the Lashkar-i-Jhangvi (including its leader Riaz Basra)[13], Sipah-i-Sahaba, and Tehrik-i-Nafaz-i-Shariat-i-

Mohammadi, wanted for sectarian terrorism in Pakistan.[14] The collapse of the Taliban helped Musharraf to reinvigorate his own 'war against terror' and crackdown on the sectarian groups. The death toll in sectarian violence decreased by half from 2001 to 2002, while over 50 leading members of Lashkar-i-Jhangvi were either killed or apprehended, and the Tehrik-i-Nafaz-i-Shariat-i-Mohammadi decimated.[15] It also, on a larger scale, allowed Pakistan to put the Taliban episode behind it and begin a new phase in its relationship with Central Asia. The renewed international attention to Afghanistan and to the reconstruction of the infrastructure of that country also seemed to increase the feasibility of finally realising Pakistan's role as a conduit for Central Asian trade to and from the Arabian Sea. Along with this, Pakistan's international standing benefited greatly from allying with the US, with very tangible benefits to the macro-economic situation in the country – the economy is now stabilising. Within four months of 11 September, Pakistan secured pledges of $1.5 billion in direct assistance or grants, signed debt rescheduling agreements with fifteen countries, and secured a number of new loans from International Financial Institutions.[16] There has been a complete turnaround in the macro-economic situation in the country, and Pakistan's previously bleeding economy is now stabilizing. In fact Pakistan is 'enjoying a measure of economic stability it hasn't seen for decades'.[17] Its growth rate has increased from 3.6 per cent to 4.5 per cent for the fiscal year ending June 2003; textile exports increased by 19 per cent in the same period; and foreign exchange reserves have jumped from $3.2 billion in July 2001 to 10.2 billon in March 2003.[18]

On the other hand, Pakistan faced serious consequences from the events in Afghanistan. First, it no longer had a pro-Pakistan government in Kabul. On the contrary, the vehemently anti-Pakistani Shura-i-Nazar, the dominant

Panjsheri Tajik faction of the Northern Alliance, came to dominate the Afghan government heavily after the fall of the Taliban. Over a very short period of time, Islamabad had gone from being the main external influence on Afghanistan's rulers (though its influence over the erratic Taliban was limited) to a position where most regional players including Russia, Iran and even India probably exerted a larger influence on Kabul than it did. New Delhi's relations with Kabul developed rapidly in all fields, including the opening of two Indian consulates near Pakistan's borders (in Jalalabad and Kandahar) which were perceived in Pakistan as threatening its security.

The war in Afghanistan also carried implications for Pakistan. The US war on the Taliban and American occupation of Afghanistan was highly unpopular in the Pashtun-populated border region of the North-West Frontier Province and northern Baluchistan. This was partly due to the fact that it led to the demise of the Pashtun-dominated government. The other reason was that a significant section of the population of the border areas of Pakistan was heavily dependent on cross-border trade and smuggling, which saw a severe downturn with the increased military presence on both sides of the border. These factors contributed to the victory of the Islamic-minded Muttahida Majlis-e-Amal in the elections in the NWFP.

In sum, these factors made it difficult for Pakistan to formulate, let alone implement, a strategy towards Central Asia. Its focus has been on its domestic situation, its relations with the United States and India, given the renewed tensions with India in the aftermath of the 13 December 2001 suicide attack on the Indian Parliament. As of mid-2003, Pakistan has not made significant efforts to lower its tariffs and boost trade with Afghanistan and Central Asia. On the other hand, with Chinese help, Pakistan has made significant progress in building the deep-water port at Gwadar in Baluchistan, which is now to be linked with Pakistan's rail and road network as well as with Afghanistan and Central Asia.[19] Likewise, important steps have been made at the inter-governmental level to develop the project of building a gas pipeline from the Daulatabad gas fields of Turkmenistan to Multan via Afghanistan.[20] The pipeline project nevertheless has doubtful economic feasibility, at least as long as India is unwilling to have Pakistan as a transit country for its energy resources.

Pakistan remains the logical trade corridor for Central Asia, and has a great potential to become an important actor in the region. This will nevertheless require a stable Afghanistan, and a strategy on the part of Islamabad to build relations with its northern neighbour.

## China: Aiming for the Long Haul

Of the countries bordering Central Asia, it is safe to say that the People's Republic of China is the only power that has considerably increased its influence in both political and economic terms since the collapse of the Soviet Union. Discussions of Central Asian regional politics in the early and mid-1990s often completely ignored China's policy and interests, focusing instead on a purported rivalry between Turkey and Iran. This rivalry never happened, as the would-be contenders had neither the means nor the intention, eventually, to pursue it. China never made large pronouncements of its interests and policy in Central Asia, instead pursuing its policies in the quiet and, undoubtedly, with a considerably longer-term strategy than most players involved.

Chinese interests in the region are manifold. The most acute relates to Xinjiang, which is, in fact, the Chinese part of Central Asia.[21] Populated mainly by Uighurs (people closely related to the Uzbeks), Kazakhs and Kyrgyz, the nominally autonomous province of Xinjiang has been a restive area that is only reluctantly being incorporated into the political and economical structures of the People's Republic. Uighurs, forming half of Xinjiang's population today, are in general resentful of Chinese domination, especially given the large-scale migration of Han Chinese into Xinjiang. Only half a century ago, Uighurs formed 90 per cent of the population of the region, whereas an active colonisation programme led by the Beijing authorities has sought a 'Signification' of Xinjiang. Today Han Chinese and Uighurs are approximately equal in number in Xinjiang.

The independence of the five states of Central Asia hence served as a reminder to both China and Uighur political groups that the status of Xinjiang as a constituent part of China was by no means a foregone conclusion. A main vector of Chinese policy has hence been to ensure that former Soviet Central Asian states and Afghanistan do not become safe havens for Uighur separatists to operate and agitate for the independence of Xinjiang.[22]

While the collapse of the USSR has therefore added an element of unease for Beijing – in the light of the threat to the security of China's borders – it also provided notable opportunities. The two most significant developments were the removal of control over the region exercised by a hostile power, the USSR; and increasing Chinese access to the natural resources of Central Asia.[23] China has been worried about the region opening up to international presence and the increasing activities of the United States and NATO in Central Asia, including the Partnership for Peace exercises in Kazakhstan in 1997. These worries, as well as an increasing realisation of a common interest with Moscow to minimise Western influence in Central Asia, led China to take the lead in turning the Shanghai 5 group. The group, which had been created in the early 1990s to solve border issues between former Soviet states and China, developed into a full-fledged regional organisation, the Shanghai Cooperation Organisation (SCO). This organisation was intended to institutionalise security cooperation with Central Asia before the United States was able to do so, hence pre-empting what Beijing feared could at some point turn out to be American encirclement of China. By the summer of 2001, China and Russia had effectively managed to include even the most independent-minded Central Asian country – Uzbekistan – in this cooperative mechanism. In fact, the dramatic threat created by the IMU insurgencies in Kyrgyzstan and Uzbekistan in the summers of 1999 and 2000 had challenged the militaries of these countries, forcing the governments to seek outside assistance to deal with the problem. As the United States was less than forthcoming in providing military assistance, Russia and China were able to benefit from disillusionment in the region with the US to create an embryonic collective security mechanism within the SCO.

China's most substantial success in Central Asia, however, lies in the sphere of economy and trade. To date, more than $500 million have been invested, and China has become a major trading partner and investor especially in Kyrgyzstan and Kazakhstan. Cross-border trade has also boomed, and low-cost Chinese goods have flooded into the region. Beijing has announced plans to increase trade by a factor of fifty in the next ten years. Although this may be utopian, it is clear that the Chinese government sees trade as its chief vehicle of gaining influence in Central Asia. In terms of energy, China has taken an especially strong interest in Kazakhstan, recently pledging to invest the equivalent of US $4 billion in the energy sector of that country.[24]

China's policy towards Afghanistan was also characterised by a larger dose of caution than Russia and most Central Asian states. It never actively took part in the regional efforts to oppose the Taliban militarily, perhaps feeling, somewhat correctly, that if the Taliban could not be defeated by the joint efforts of Russia, China, India and Central Asian states, China's contribution would make little difference other than angering the Taliban. Instead, China followed a two-pronged policy. First, it sought informal contact with the Taliban and initiated trade and infrastructure projects in Afghanistan. Second, it applied pressure on its close ally, Pakistan, to use its influence with the Taliban to prevent the latter from hosting anti-Chinese Uighur groups. This two-pronged policy in retrospect seems to have been relatively successful. Only a handful of ethnic Uighurs seem to have been trained on an individual basis in the terrorist camps of the IMU and Al Qaeda in Afghanistan, whereas no Uighur militant group per se was given sanctuary in Taliban-controlled Afghanistan.

11 September did alleviate some of Beijing's fears that Afghanistan would serve as a safe haven for Uighur militants but it worsened China's economic and political standing in the region. Economically, the increase of Western and American aid and investments put China at a disadvantage. More importantly, America's military presence in the region was accepted only grudgingly by Beijing in the framework of the war against Al Qaeda and the Taliban. While China understood the deployment of US military in Uzbekistan on Afghanistan's border, the choice of Kyrgyzstan, a country not bordering Afghanistan but bordering China, for the location of the largest American base in Central Asia did not go down well. In fact, China seems to view American involvement in Central Asia in the context of American presence in South Korea and its support for Taiwan, i.e. in terms of a fear of encirclement by the US. Thus, China has lost its influence considerably.[25] The SCO failed to lure the Central Asian states, especially Uzbekistan, into an exclusive alliance with the Russian and Chinese. As

soon as the opportunity arose, Tashkent, followed by Bishkek and even Dushanbe, developed strategic relations with the United States and granted America basing rights, in spite of clear Chinese and Russian disapproval.

Clearly, the American military presence so close to its own backyard is a cause for great discomfort for China. The fact that the People's Liberation Army conducted its first military exercises outside China in the PRC's history in Kyrgyzstan clearly indicates this. Yet, China's proximity to the region, its gradually developing economic strength and trade advantages, and not least its long-term approach to its relations with Central Asia are all factors that suggest China is a key actor in the region and will shape future regional security relations in Central Asia.

## Relations among the Powers and with Greater Powers

The present dynamics of the security environment in Central Asia involves the United States, Russia and China as the chief external actors. Though Turkey, Iran, Pakistan, and India all play complementary roles, that cannot be compared with the influence of the key powers. The dynamics of the interactions among these players is in constant flux. Few relationships can be categorised as clear-cut alliances or as exclusively antagonistic.

Alliances are primarily the Turkish-American, the Russian-Iranian, and the Sino-Pakistani relationships. However, neither of these is active to a considerable degree in Central Asia. Turkey and the United States have had military consultations on Central Asia and the Caucasus, and these meetings do provide for a mechanism to coordinate policy. They do share a common vision for Central Asian Republics to develop into Western-oriented, democratic societies and polities with market economies.

However, America and Turkey often follow separate policies to safeguard their respective interests independently from one another in Central Asia. These separate interests often do coincide, and mutually reinforce each other. However, it is unclear whether the congregation of the roles of Turkey and the United States is larger than the sum of its parts. In practice, the two states coordinate policies towards security in the Caucasus, involving security cooperation with Georgia and Azerbaijan as well as the building of the east-west pipeline corridor. In Central Asia, both powers tended in the late 1990s to distance themselves from close involvement with security issues in the region. 11 September catapulted America into a central role in the security of the region, while Turkey's engagement with Central Asia has not changed significantly. In the Caucasus, Turkey and America need each other's support, while America seems to see less of a crucial role for Turkey in Central Asia.

As for the Russian-Iranian alliance, it is also based on common geopolitical interests: containing the spread of American military, political, economic, and not least cultural influence in the region. However, in practice, the alliance is mainly focused on certain sectors, such as armaments cooperation and trade, and containment of Turkey and to some extent western interests in the Caucasus. The level to which there is bilateral coordination of policies with respect to Central Asia is probably low. Russia is content with the present situation allowing a limited and predictable role for Iran in the region, and Iran too sees enough benefits from its relationship with Russia. The two also have points of disagreement, such as on the sectoral division of the Caspian Sea, where Russia abandoned Tehran's position of a condominium several years ago. Iran's increasing encirclement also prevents Tehran from playing too active a role in the region.

Finally, the Sino-Pakistani alliance seems to involve Central Asia mainly in the framework of trade. China is financing the bulk of the building of the Gwadar port, a $260 million project. Plans to connect some of the trade between eastern parts of Central Asia (eastern Kazakhstan and Kyrgyzstan) to Pakistan through Xinjiang are progressing, though the difficulties in expanding the Karakoram Highway may prove to be a major obstacle. In political and security terms, the two countries, however, follow independent policies towards Central Asia.

In sum, America, Russia, and China play such a large role in the security of Central Asia that their need to coordinate policies with, respectively, Turkey, Iran and Pakistan is limited. To qualify these three relationships as patron-vassal relationships would also be inadequate. The three lesser powers do occasionally play a complementary role to their respective larger ally. However, they are regional powers in their own right and pursue policies that occasionally clash with their would-be 'patrons'.

As for antagonistic relationships, the US-Iranian and Indo-Pakistani relationships stand out, and affect the interests of the respective powers in Central Asia. Iran is clearly the most affected, with American presence further circumscribing Tehran's freedom of movement in the region. America's greater influence over regional governments often translates explicitly and directly into a diminishing influence for Tehran. In a less obvious way, American interests are also affected by Iranian antagonism. In Central Asia, the lack of Iranian cooperation in dealing with the increasingly erratic nature of Turkmenistan's leadership is a case in point. So is the role of Iran in sponsoring Ismail Khan in Herat. India and Pakistan also affect each other's interests in Central Asia. In fact, the deadlock in relations between New Delhi and Islamabad prevents both parties from realising their respective interests in the region.

Pakistan's ambitions to become a trade corridor to and from Central Asia would be much more attractive if such trade could reach India as well. But the Trans-Afghan Pipeline is unlikely to be realised as long as the logical destination for Turkmen gas, India, is not willing to accept a pipeline through Pakistan. Conversely, India's ambitions to play a larger role in the region will continue to be thwarted unless it can have geographic access to the region, which means access through Pakistan. India is unlikely to be able to satisfy its growing energy requirements through Central Asian resources without transiting Pakistan's territory, the only economically feasible transit route. Attempts to circumvent Pakistan through the prohibitively expensive underwater gas pipeline project from Iran, or the abortive idea to build a Russia-China-India pipeline over Tibet, all carry major economic, technical and security problems.[26] Relations with Central Asia are an area where India and Pakistan have a need for one another, and their continuing conflict is going to impede the possibilities of both in the region.

The remaining bilateral relations are all characterised by a mixture of cooperation and rivalry. Turkey and Iran, and Iran and Pakistan, are examples: the three states have been driving forces behind the attempt to build multilateral cooperation among themselves and with Central Asia through the ECO (Economic Cooperation Organisation), though at times they have differed strongly on security issues. Turkey and Iran have been since 1979 following completely divergent policies regarding their domestic state structure, with Turkey espousing a secular state and Iran an Islamic republic. Their policies have clashed in the Caucasus, with Turkey supporting Azerbaijan and Georgia, and Iran supporting Armenia; the two have never clashed openly, though Turkey responded strongly to Iranian threats of use of military force against Azerbaijan in the

Summer of 2001 over a dispute in the Caspian Sea. The two states maintain, as they have for two centuries, a relationship of rivalry, but not enmity.

Iran and Pakistan have a history of close and uneventful relations, yet divergent policies on Afghanistan in the 1990s created mutual suspicion and a downturn in relations. Since the early 1990s, and after the advent of the Taliban and Pakistan's open support for the Taliban movement, Iran and Pakistan have been in a state approximating a cold war with one another. From 1995 to 2001, they were actively arming opposing sides in the Afghan civil war. Yet the overthrow of the Taliban and the change in Pakistan's policy allowed them to have a rapprochement of sorts, though Iran's developing ties with India are a major concern in Islamabad.[27] Pakistan's relations with Russia and the United States also deserve mention. With Russia, Pakistan has a history of hostility, partly due to the conflict in Afghanistan and Pakistan's leading role in supporting the Afghan resistance in the 1980s. However, hostility has continued through the 1990s, again with Afghanistan being the major point of contention. The aftermath of 11 September nevertheless allowed some improvement in relations, which both Islamabad and Moscow seem to desire.[28] Pakistan's relations with the United States are a broad and complicated topic. Pakistan's policy towards Afghanistan has been considerably affected by America's military presence there. From having been extremely active in Afghan affairs for twenty years following the Soviet invasion, Pakistan has, since 11 September, kept a very low profile in Afghanistan. Accusations of support for the Taliban and Hekmatyar in the post-11 September period have been voiced. The ethnic linkages across the border, however, imply a large concern among Pakistani Pashtuns with the conditions of Pashtuns across the border in Afghanistan. As the Pashtuns remain sidelined in the politics of Afghanistan and as resentment with this grows in the Pashtun belt, this naturally also affects the Pakistani border areas.[29] Given that Pashtun resentment is being channelled into support for Hekmatyar and Taliban remnants, support for these forces also grows in Pakistan. Tensions between Islamabad and the Northern Alliance government, including the ransacking of the Pakistani Embassy in Kabul in July 2003 shows the volatility of this problem. On the whole, the Musharraf government has clearly delineated a policy of non-interference in Afghanistan, very much due to the debacle of the pro-Taliban policy and America's dominant position in Afghanistan, which leaves little role for Pakistan unless it challenges America's policies there, something Islamabad is clearly unwilling to do. Non-state actors in Pakistan, including radical religious parties, clearly have an agenda that differs from that of the government, posing significant trouble for the government, which has been unable to effectively constrain these elements. Still, Musharraf's government has taken the unprecedented step to deploy the Pakistani military in the semi-independent Federally Administered Tribal Areas, in order to ensure that the situation there does not spiral out of control.

## Conclusions

The unstable nature of regional politics in Central Asia is caused partly by the dynamics of the region itself, and the multitude of internal challenges facing the region. These include disputed borders, a slow and stagnant economic transition, widespread poverty, the soaring problem of narcotics production and trafficking, the growth of political and religious extremism and terrorism, corruption and mismanagement. But a major factor in the security of the region is the diverging and fluid policies of regional and external powers towards the region. The number of regional powers with an interest in Central Asia is large, and their policies towards one another are often ambiguous and contradictory. This does not provide a framework for stable regional development, especially as there is a remarkable absence of mechanisms or institutions for regional cooperation in the region. While intra-regional mechanisms exist, and some institutions led by one or two regional powers have been created (such as the SCO), there is no mechanism or institution bringing together, even as a forum for discussion, all interested parties. These clearly include the six Central Asian states, but also at least seven foreign powers: the United States, Russia, China, Turkey, India, Iran, and Pakistan. While such a mechanism is difficult to envisage due to the occasional hostility among several of these powers, its absence allows for unwarranted fears and threat perceptions to go unchecked as little discussion takes place between many of the interested parties.

The roles played by powers such as China, Iran, Turkey and Pakistan in Central Asia will continue to depend, as they do today, partly on their domestic dynamics and problems; and partly on their relationships with one another and the great powers. Given the number of parties involved, the intricate puzzle that is the regional politics of Central Asia is likely to remain for the foreseeable future a web of complex, intricate, and sometimes contradictory relations.

# Notes

1. Central Asia is here defined as including the five post-Soviet states of Kazakhstan, Kyrgyzstan, Tajikistan, Turkmenistan and Uzbekistan as well as Afghanistan.
2. Svante E Cornell, 'Entrenched in the Steppes: The US Redraws the Map', *Foreign Service Journal*, April 2003; 'America in Eurasia: One Year After', *Current History*, October 2002; Charles William Maynes, 'America Discovers Central Asia', *Foreign Affairs*, March–April 2003.
3. Seyed Kazem Sajjadpour, 'Iran, the Caucasus, and Central Asia', in Ali Banuazizi and Myron Weiner (eds.), *The New Geopolitics of Central Asia and Its Borderlands*, Bloomington: Indiana University Press, 1994, pp.197–215.
4. Anoushiravan Ehteshami, 'Iran and Central Asia: Responding to Regional Change', in Mehdi Mozaffari (ed.), *Security Politics in the Commonwealth of Independent States*, Basingstoke: MacMillan, 1997.
5. Robert E Freedman, 'Russian-Iranian Relations in the 1990s', *Middle East Review of International Affairs*, Vol. 4, No. 2, June 2000.
6. *See* e.g. 'Afghan Fears as Iran Arms Warlord', *Daily Telegraph*, 24 January 2002.
7. Mustafa Aydin, 'Turkey and Central Asia: Challenges of Change', *Central Asian Survey*, Vol. 15, No. 2, June 1996, pp.157–178.
8. *See* Kemal Kaya, 'Turkey's New Challenges in the Caucasus and Central Asia', *Central Asia-Caucasus Analyst*, 7 November 2001.
9. Antoine Blua, 'Turkey: Erdogan Begins Tour Of Turkic-Speaking Countries Of The Former Soviet Union', RFE/RL, 7 January 2003.
10. Cornell Caspian Consulting, 'The Turkish Parliament Rejects War Plans: Causes and Implications', Policy

Brief, 4 March 2003.

11. Anthony Hyman, 'Afghanistan and Central Asia', in Mehdi Mozaffari (ed.), *Security Politics in the Commonwealth of Independent States*, Basingstoke: MacMillan, 1997.

12. Ahmed Rashid, *Taliban*, New Haven: Yale University Press, 2000, p.28. *See also* Imtiaz Gul, *The Unholy Nexus: Pak-Afghan Relations under the Taliban*, Lahore: Vanguard Books, 2002.

13. Rory McCarthy, 'Death by Design', *The Guardian*, 17 May 2002.

14. *See* e.g. Ali Abbas, 'Taliban Refuses to Hand over Wahabi Terrorists to Pakistan', Shianews.com, 25 April 2001.

15. *See* Kanchan Lakshman, 'Deep Roots to Pakistan's Sectarian Terror', *Asia Times*, 9 July 2003.

16. Moinuddin Ahmed, 'Assistance, Loans and Rescheduling Pacts after 9/11', *Dawn*, 11 September 2002.

17. Naween A Mangi, 'Pakistan: It Pays to be Uncle Sam's Pal', *Business Week*, 7 April 2003.

18. Ibid., also Ashfaque Hasan Khan, *Economic Performance during 1999–2002*, Government of Pakistan, Finance Division, 30 October 2002, http://209.71.203.116/summary/main.htm.

19. *Pakistan Economist*, No. 27, 2003, 7–13 July 2003; 'Development of Gwadar port discussed', *Dawn*, 2 April 2003; 'Gwadar port to change fate of region: PM', *Dawn*, 21 May 2003.

20. Aftab Kazi and Tariq Saeedi, 'India and the Politics of the Trans-Afghan Gas Pipeline', *Central Asia-Caucasus Analyst*, 28 August 2002.

21. Michael Dillon, 'Central Asia: The View from Beijing, Urumqi and Kashghar', in Mehdi Mozaffari, (ed.), *Security Politics in the Commonwealth of Independent States*, Basingstoke: MacMillan, 1997, pp.133–150.

22. Phunchok Stobdan, 'China's Central Asia Dilemma', *Strategic Analysis*, Vol. 22, No. 3, June 1998, pp.399–408.

23. The concept of China's three ancient categories of

interests in Central Asia was articulated by David Finkelstein at a conference on 'China's Emergence in Central Asia', Centre for Strategic and International Studies, Washington DC, 5 February 2003. *See* event summary available at http://www.csis.org/china/index.htm.

24. Niklas Swanström, 'Chinese Business Interests in Central Asia: A Quest for Dominance', *Central Asia-Caucasus Analyst*, 18 June 2003.

25. Stephen Blank, 'China's Defeats in Central Asia', *Central Asia-Caucasus Analyst*, 14 August 2002.

26. Aftab Kazi, 'Is the Proposed Russia-China-India Pipeline Feasible?', *Central Asia-Caucasus Analyst*, 3 July 2002.

27. Rizwan Zeb, 'The Emerging Indo-Iranian Strategic Alliance and Pakistan', *Central Asia-Caucasus Analyst*, 12 February 2003.

28. Zahid Anwar, 'Identifying the Irritant in Pakistan-Russian Relations', *Central Asia-Caucasus Analyst*, 6 December 2002.

29. Awamdost Pakhtunkhel, 'Gulbuddin Hekmatyar: A Magnet of Discontent in Afghanistan', *Central Asia-Caucasus Analyst*, 12 March 2003.

# Chapter XII

# THE POST-9/11 REALIGNMENT OF REGIONAL SECURITY IN CENTRAL ASIA

Dr Anita Sengupta

## The Importance of Eurasian Regional Fora

It is inevitable that the 'war against terrorism' will restructure regional alignments in Eurasia and reconfigure the international security environment. While the extent of this realignment still remains unclear, certain developments point to the fact that a watershed is in sight. In the first week of October 2001, NATO Secretary General George Robertson requested the Central Asian states to balance their relationship with Russia and the West. This statement, which nearly went unnoticed in an eventful month, is significant for a number of reasons.

The first and most obvious point is that NATO has preferred to deal with the Central Asian states through a Russian-led forum such as the CIS, rather than individually. The second and more significant factor is that there seems to be a recognition of the fact that there are likely to be certain realignments that could change the balance of power in Eurasia over the coming months. It also points to a realignment of security arrangements in the region and the emergence of alternative global arrangements to deal with new challenges, a preferred theme in most analytical writings about the impact of 9/11 on the region. The consensus seems to be that in terms of security arrangements, the emerging choices are reminiscent of those exercised during the Cold War by the two worlds. With the end of the Cold War, local and regional dynamics have played a greater role in shaping Asian security practices and consequently there has been a trend towards the development of an independent stance towards security, rather than a regional-forum-based system. However, analysts perceive a distinct reversal of this trend in the post-11 September scenario, particularly in Afghanistan's immediate neighbourhood.

It is felt that the 'war against terrorism' would demonstrate the significance of global security alignments, particularly in the context of the Central Asian region. Many feel that the security environment has changed dramatically and there are new types of threat perceptions – particularly in the context of the perception of threat among non-state actors, including terrorist networks that are beyond the control of international law and law enforcement agencies. While it is assumed that dealing with such perceptions of threat would remain within the internal jurisdiction of each state, tackling international terrorism and the threat that it poses not just to the state where it has emanated but to others as well calls for a cooperative approach.

There has also been an increase in non-traditional security threats, such as drug smuggling, arms trafficking, international crime, international disputes caused by environmental deterioration and the scramble for water and energy resources that affects more than one state. As a result, regional fora have a role to play in such a scenario. There is also the threat posed by groups and states where the forces of modernisation, globalisation and economic reform have not resulted in any substantial changes. The ability to deal with these threats would depend on the success of international coalitions.

But are such alignments an outcome of the events of 11 September 2001? This paper argues that viable regional security alignments have been in place during the last decade, and that post-11 September events merely highlighted these arrangements. The paper also argues that to deal with complex, multiple security issues, a multiplicity of security arrangements is necessary rather than agreements under a single global system. While older security arrangements remain in place, newer ones are being forged to deal with emerging security issues.

Several factors – including compulsions of regional powers as well as requirements of the new states – have led to such initiatives. Some of these initiatives have been necessitated by border disputes, the presence of minorities across the borders of the states and the need to prevent secessionism by coming to some understanding about borders. The Shanghai Cooperation Organisation is an outcome of an effort to tackle these contentious issues. Others recognise that strategic borders of states extend well beyond the boundaries of individual nations and hence a multinational system is required to guard them. The Collective Security Agreements of the CIS are an effort to address this need. Still others feel the need for global linkages to enhance internal security as well as undertake various tasks including, peacekeeping, management of crisis, etc. The Partnership for Peace initiative is the outcome of such an understanding. The common factor here is the presence of one or more global and/or regional power as part of the initiative. However, before examining the linkages, let's consider the significance of regional initiatives in the global scenario.

A regional initiative as a concept is not new. The 1960s witnessed a spate of such initiatives worldwide. Attempts to create common markets and free trade associations proliferated in the Middle East, Africa, the Pacific, Western Europe and the Americas. Most of these projects failed, and except in Western Europe and South-East Asia, regionalist policies did not lead to major progress. Regionalism remained on the international agenda during the entire later period of the Cold War but had limited scope. Regionalist rhetoric reappeared in the late 1980s in many parts of the world and this time, unlike in the previous period, it translated into political reality. Cohesive efforts effectively institutionalised regionalist experiences and these were no longer confined to Western Europe.

A number of factors came into play here. The first was the legacy of borders determined in imperial times that inevitably left large minorities in most states. The multi-ethnic profile of nations posed risks of secessionism in all the states and therefore there was a strong reason for alliances. With possibilities of global rivalries receding, along with security guarantees that reduced the possibility of internal instability, the need to act in concert on particular issues increased. Common economic resources were another important reason for integrative tendencies. While Asian states have had a history of antagonistic relations, they also have a mutual interest in pursuing economic modernisation, which requires stability. This mutual interest gave rise to multilateral fora, which attempted to limit the use of force, provided for sanctity of contracts and arranged for assignment and recognition of property rights.

Other factors that provided an impetus to regional fora were the end of the Cold War which had subordinated all regional arrangements and the need to deal with foreign security concerns at a regional rather than at a global level. The rise of new trading blocs in the developed world, the decline in Western support for regional arrangements in the Third World, and the replacement of broad coalitions among Third World countries by more viable regional coalitions were some of the other factors. The end of the

Cold war, however, was assumed to contribute significantly towards rationalisation of international politics. It was also assumed that security in Europe, Asia, Middle East or Africa could now be evaluated independently of developments in other regions. During the Cold War, Asian regional security was closely linked to, and in many ways subordinated to, the Soviet-American confrontation and the associated Sino-Soviet conflict. Attempts by Asian nations to escape the dynamics of superpower competition through movements and strategies such as non-alignment, neutrality and peace zones were only partially successful.

With the disintegration of the Soviet Union and the emergence of the Central Asian states as independent republics, a similar examination of prospects of regional cooperation began. Indeed one of the first proposals, mooted by Kazakhstan President Nazarbayev, envisaged the formation of a Eurasian Union. This was visualised as a multinational model that would aim at creating a unified state through various stages of a confederation leading up to a union. While this failed to take off and a number of other options were put forward.

The Central Asian region currently has three options in terms of regional integration: first, a reinforcement of linkages with the CIS countries based on economic and institutional priorities; second, the formation of a community of Central Asian states; and third, the integration of neighbouring states. However, in the light of recent developments, a fourth alternative is available to the region: an alignment with the West, particularly one sponsored by NATO through the Partnership for Peace initiative.

Do regional fora in the Central Asian region actually reflect a reversal of trends in terms of seeking Cold War-type linkages with one global power in the post-'war on terrorism' period? It is necessary to acknowledge that the nature of such a global linkage will be significantly different.

In fact with changes in perceptions of threat, there is a greater emphasis on the need for internal security and national integrity. Also a multiplicity of arrangements has emerged with both bilateral and multilateral linkages being simultaneously maintained in various regional initiatives. This paper examines the extent to which Russian linkages will be transformed in the light of a new security environment. It also examines the new initiatives that are being taken by Russia and China in the region and concludes with an analysis of the extent to which NATO's influence will be effective in balancing traditional security arrangements in the region.

## Commonwealth of Independent States

The Alma Ata Declaration described the CIS as a community of independent and sovereign states. The agreement explicitly stated that the Commonwealth did not constitute a political union, federation or confederation. The overarching goal of the CIS was to maintain coordination of the CIS countries' policies by taking into account the individual features of these countries. On 15 May 1992, at the fifth summit meeting of the CIS states held in Tashkent, Russia, Kazakhstan, Kyrgyzstan, Uzbekistan, Tajikistan and Armenia signed the Treaty on Collective Security.

The signatory countries agreed that their security was indivisible. If one party to the agreement was subject to aggression, that would be regarded as aggression against all parties to the Treaty. Therefore, immediate assistance to the nation including military assistance would be provided. The signatory countries also agreed to the principle of sharing responsibility for maintaining security, non-interference in internal affairs, collective defence and safeguarding collective security through consultation. The agreement stipulated that some specific military bases and facilities of one member state could be stationed or deployed in other member states with the consent of the states concerned.

The signing of such a collective security agreement among the CIS states at the time was only natural, as the Central Asian states' military capabilities were extremely weak. It would take some time for them to establish their own comprehensive military forces. Signing such a collective security agreement with Russia certainly enhanced the security of these countries. The agreement also stipulated that the parties to the agreement would not use force to settle disputes among themselves. This also reduced any possibility of Russia using force against the signatory countries. From the Russian point of view, the signing of such an agreement gave the CIS its raison d'être. It also reduced political pressures to withdraw Russian troops from CIS states. At the same time it helped secure Russia's special interests in Central Asia. However, the agreement was signed by only six member states and concluded without identifying any clearly perceived external military threat. It has therefore been perceived as a defensive mechanism to manage potential conflicts among the CIS states.

Russia's current engagement in Central Asia is broadly based on its Military Doctrine on Commonwealth of Independent States of November 1993. The broad outline of this doctrine argues:

- Russia as a great power has both regional and global responsibilities.
- The territory of the former Soviet Union is a geostrategic area in which Moscow has special interests.
- Russia has extra-territorial responsibilities when it comes to the well-being of ethnic Russians, Russian citizens and Russian-speaking communities throughout the CIS.

From the very beginning, however, differences arose on the nature of collective defence. In May 1995, an agreement on protecting the external borders of the CIS was signed by seven states. However, Ukraine, Turkmenistan, Moldova, Azerbaijan and Uzbekistan declined to sign. Earlier in February 1995, at a joint meeting of the Council of Heads of Governments and Council of Heads of States, a proposal of joint defence of the external borders of the CIS countries was seriously debated. However, Azerbaijan and Ukraine categorically opposed it. Many other of the CIS countries states noted that mutual cooperation on defence and borders was more acceptable than a joint defence external borders of the CIS countries.

Meanwhile, the signing of the Collective Security Treaty paved the way for the abolition of the Soviet-era Turkestan Military District on 30 June 1992. However, even as the Soviet military was being disbanded, there was confrontation between groups in Tajikistan. It ended with a UN-brokered negotiated settlement in June 1997 where the two sides involved in the conflict agreed to share power. The conflict itself affected the nature of security arrangements in the region. Uzbekistan, as the country most affected by disorder in Tajikistan, sought to increasingly align itself in security relationships that gave it more flexibility than an alliance with Russia. In 1996, Uzbekistan announced its intention to join the Partnership for Peace initiative. In 1997, Centrasbat '97 created a 500-strong battalion of Kazakh, Kyrgyz and Uzbek troops under the aegis of the UN.

Such developments meant that the CIS was not particularly successful in forging a partnership among countries in the region. This was partly due to the fact that the CIS was formed at a time when Russia's priorities did not include a strongly integrated Eurasian commonwealth. Russia, therefore, failed to halt NATO's eastward expansion or to mobilise opposition to this project among the CIS members. With the exception of Belarus, no member of the CIS accepted Russia's 'counter block' rhetoric in 1995. The creation of a new security environment in Russia's western borders did not have any direct consequences for the security interests of the states in Central Asia or the Trans-Caucasus. Russia had apparently underestimated the extent to which the CIS members would be able to dissociate their own security interests from that of Russia. As fears of a Soviet revival faded and new dangers of extremism, terrorism, drug trafficking and separatism emerged, there was renewed enthusiasm for forging strategic partnerships with Russia in the region. However, with the exception of the Russian-Tajik partnership, these arrangements have mostly remained tactical agreements.

One of the reasons for the failure of the security arrangements under the CIS banner is that they translated into Russian hegemony over the areas where its troops were stationed. For example, critics point to Russia's 201$^{st}$ Motorised Infantry Division, which has been stationed in Tajikistan since 1993, under a security arrangement that included efforts to fight drugs and weapons smuggling across the Afghan border. Until recently, the soldiers worked under a CIS mandate as part of the Commonwealth's peacekeeping troops. The mandate has since been lifted, but the troops remain as part of the bilateral agreement between Moscow and Dushanbe. Similarly, Vladimir Romanenko, the deputy director of the CIS Institute think tank notes that of the 400 agreements adopted by the CIS within a military cooperation framework, in practice only one or two really work. And these are the ones that have been signed on a bilateral basis. Another factor weakening the collective security of the CIS, Romanenko adds, is that the agreements are often not 'collective'. Tashkent, for instance, abandoned the Collective Security Treaty in favour of drafting a bilateral military agreement with Russia to exchange weapons for natural gas. Georgia, Azerbaijan and Moldova have also dropped out of the Treaty while

Turkmenistan never signed it.

While most observers tend to blame the CIS for its failures, they do not appreciate its very real contribution in terms of an easy and hassle-free dismantling of the Soviet Union. The CIS has been, and continues to be, a facilitator in the transition process of the unitary Soviet superstate to national statehood. The most visible aspect of the CIS is the regular summit meeting of the leaders of the new states. The summit is instrumental in keeping the lines of communication open and averting crisis. The CIS's major contribution has been in the facilitation of the 'divorce proceedings' among the Soviet successor states.

The CIS has provided these states with a political forum in which to discuss issues linked either to their internal sovereignty or to their external sovereignty. Given this mandate, a proposal has been initiated by CIS member states Russia, Kyrgyzstan, Tajikistan and Kazakhstan to create a rapid action force to combat the growing regional threat of Islamic militant groups. Supporters of the plan feel that it is a move towards an effective defence partnership. But some Russian analysts, looking at other joint military agreements of the CIS, are doubtful of its success.

Recently there have been moves by Russia to reassert its influence over the post-Soviet space on the basis of the Collective Security Treaty. Using anti-terrorism as a catch phrase, Russia is pushing to create a full-fledged regional military bloc. Russia and five other CIS states have formalised a security alliance that could help boost Russia's strategic presence in Central Asia. At a summit meeting on 28 April 2003, Russia, Armenia, Belarus, Kazakhstan, Kyrgyzstan and Tajikistan formally created the Collective Security Treaty Organisation which will attempt to provide a more efficient response to strategic problems confronting member states.

## Shanghai Cooperation Organisation

The Shanghai Forum was essentially formed to give a boost to confidence-building measures along the common borders of the states. Over the years as the Shanghai 5 was transformed into the Shanghai 6, it developed as a multi-lateral cooperative mechanism. The fields of cooperation have extended to politics, foreign affairs, trade and economic sectors and culture. As noted by a scholar from the Shanghai Institute of International Studies, the SCO strengthens mutual trust and cooperation among the five states. It enables the five countries to strike in close coordination at various kinds of forces sabotaging peace and development in the region and defend their own stability and development. Further, it initiates peaceful settlement of disputes and checks destabilising factors.

The Shanghai 5 also emphasises commonality of Sino-Russian interests in the Central Asian region. The Chinese stake in the forum is dependent on the way it views Islam and treats its Muslim population. Beijing's participation in the Shanghai 5 is based on fears of Islamic secessionism in Xinjiang and its concern that it should not be branded as an anti-Muslim state. The Russian initiative in the Shanghai 5 is seen as a direct outcome of its domestic political environment.

The collapse of the Soviet Union has not only resulted in a 'permanent arc of crisis along the northern and southern Caucasus' but also has wider ramifications. Although, largely confined to the North Caucasus, the breakdown of law and order and the gradual loss of state authority and power are felt throughout Central Asia. As the principal successor state to the Soviet Union, Russia has claimed responsibility for containment of all intra-regional conflicts. Moscow's current disposition towards the region includes its economic, security and great power interests.

Also since Russia continues to follow its traditional interests in the Caucasian and Central Asian region, it feels threatened by US incursions in the region.

As a formal multilateral forum, the Shanghai 5 owes its origin to the 26 April 1996 joint border agreement between China, Kazakhstan, Kyrgyzstan, Tajikistan and Russia. In the beginning the aims and objectives of the grouping were rather vague. The document formalised the commitment of the states to establish collectively a range of confidence-building measures in the field of military cooperation along their common borders. Although there was no specific reference to it, the initiative was undertaken primarily to protect trans-border trade among the states, which had increasingly come under attack. The agreement also entrusted the members to 'stand against stirring up ethno-religious nationalism'.

Under the Shanghai Agreement the military forces of both sides stationed along the border areas promise not to attack each other. The agreement rules out conducting military exercises aimed against each other. It also specifies that limits will be imposed on the scale, scope and number of military exercises on both sides of the border areas. The concerned sides should inform each other of any major military activities taking place in any area within 100 kilometres of the border. It further stipulates that the relevant countries will invite each other to observe military exercises and will prevent any dangerous military activities. It proposes friendly exchanges between the military forces and frontier guards of both sides.

Since its inception, the organisation has focused its attention on the regional security situation and the unrest in Kazakhstan, Kyrgyzstan and Tajikistan. In fact in recent years, the member nations have unanimously stated that non-traditional threats to their national interests and internal security could destabilise the existing ethno-religious harmony within their borders and endanger their territorial sovereignty. Indeed the fear of secessionism is the main reason for the Shanghai Forum's objective of regional cooperation in the military sphere. The initial Shanghai 5 Agreement on strengthening confidence-building measures in 1996 resulted in reduction of tension and initiated demilitarisation along the borders.

While the Central Asian states' efforts for cooperation in the economic and political spheres have been largely unsuccessful, they have found common cause in seeking a solution to the Afghan crisis and the expanding array of sub-national security threats. This has pushed them towards new forms of alliance. In 1993 China, Russia, Kazakhstan, Kyrgyzstan and Tajikistan commenced a diplomatic dialogue concerning their common borders. On 26 April 1996, the presidents of the five border states met in Shanghai to sign a package of fourteen agreements on border issues. The Shanghai Accord constituted a breakthrough in establishing a framework for border normalisation. More importantly, the Shanghai 5 or the Shanghai Forum evolved into a region wide united front to address the challenges to political normalisation of the Central Asian region. Meeting in July 2000, the heads of states of Russia, China, Kazakhstan, Kyrgyzstan and Tajikistan (with the Uzbek president as an observer) agreed to deepen inter-state cooperation in diplomatic, commercial, military, technological and other areas with the purpose of reinforcing regional security and stability. The leaders pledged new cooperative initiatives in combating trafficking in drugs and weapons, terrorism, political extremism and separatism, and in resolving disputes over trans-boundary resources such as water, energy and transport infrastructure.

After Uzbekistan joined the Shanghai 5 on 14 June 2001, the six countries declared that the Shanghai 5 mechanism would be upgraded as the Shanghai Cooperation Organisation, the first regional multilateral cooperative organisation. Subsequently, the six leaders signed the Shanghai Convention against terrorism, separatism, and extremism on 15 June 2001. The establishment of the Bishkek Anti-terrorism Centre is an important initiative that will be taken up in the near future. Economic and commercial cooperation, however, will be in the forefront.

## Partnership for Peace

The Russian tendency has been to view American engagement in the Central Asian region as a zero-sum game, whereby any gains for the US automatically means a loss for Russia. As a result, considerable efforts were made to block or limit American political, economic and military involvement in Central Asia. Russian foreign and security policy experts expressed the fear that American involvement in the region, particularly in the development of energy resources, was aimed at creating an enabling environment for the US to establish its military presence. American corporations may lead the process, but Pentagon would quickly follow.

On the other hand Russia's own security concerns have changed and the focus is now on controlling the flows of weapons, drugs, refugees, radicalism and terrorism. The Russian elite, increasingly concerned about the dangers of nuclear proliferation and terrorist groups' access to biological and chemical weapons, welcomed American efforts to remove nuclear warheads from the successor states that possessed them, including Ukraine and Kazakhstan. They also supported American efforts to remove stocks of fissile materials from Kazakhstan. More recently, the threat of biological terrorism has become an area of increasing concern. The US is also involved in efforts to neutralise this threat in the region. There is thus clearly a trade-off between costs and benefits. While there is disquiet about the prospects of a major American presence in the region, it has also been argued that American presence would reinforce stability in the region and in Russia's southern borders. This could be of considerable benefit at a time when Russia alone is not capable of managing the new threats in the region.

The Central Asian states began to develop closer ties with the US in the post-1991 period, when the Clinton administration moved to create diplomatic, political and economic ties with countries. The US also committed itself to promoting and protecting the security and sovereignty of these new states. Under the leadership of Defence Secretary William Perry, the Partnership for Peace programme was launched to tackle the delicate issue of NATO expansion and develop broader ties with the Central Asian states. This programme laid the framework for a growing network of cooperative, political and military ties, with Uzbekistan in particular. These ties eventually helped in facilitating joint efforts after 11 September.

The Partnership for Peace (PFP) programme is a significant instrument for the expansion of USA's role in the region. It was launched as a programme to transform relations between NATO and participating countries at the ministerial meeting of the North Atlantic Cooperation Council (NACC) in Brussels in January 1994. NACC and other CSCE (Commission on Security and Cooperation in Europe) countries able and willing to contribute to the programme were invited to join. The PFP would operate under the authority of the North Atlantic Corporation Council and forge new security relationships between the North Atlantic Alliance and its Partners for Peace. The partnership was expected to expand and intensify political and military cooperation across Europe, increase stability, diminish threats to peace and build stronger relations by promoting the spirit of practical cooperation and commitment to democratic principles.

It was agreed that NATO would consult with any active participant in the Partnership if that partner perceived a direct threat to its territorial integrity, political independence or security. It was envisaged that concrete steps would be taken in the areas of transparency in defence budgeting, promoting democratic control of defence ministries, joint planning, joint military exercises and creating capacities to operate with NATO forces in peacekeeping, search and rescue, and humanitarian operations. The capacity and desire of individual participating states would determine the pace and scope of the partnership. To promote closer military cooperation and inter-operability within the Partnership framework, it was proposed that peacekeeping field exercises be held from 1994.

The NATO-PFP initiative has been in force for a decade now. The North Atlantic Cooperation Council first met in December 1991. It was established to help break down east-west divisions and build mutual trust in the wake of the end of the Cold War by bringing together NATO allies and former Warsaw Pact countries in a forum for security dialogue and cooperation. Three years later the Partnership for Peace was launched to enable partner countries to develop individual programmes of practical cooperation with NATO and complement the opportunities for multilateral political dialogue afforded by the NACC. The Euro-Atlantic Partnership Council was created in 1997 to replace the NACC and build on its achievements.

Over the past decade strategies built around partnership and cooperation rather than political confrontation and military competition have dramatically altered the Euro-Atlantic Security environment. NATO and partner countries consult regularly on security issues, their forces interact frequently and conduct joint exercises and their soldiers are deployed alongside each other in NATO-led peace support operations in the Balkans.

Aimed at promoting transparency and generating mutual confidence, the Euro-Atlantic Partnership Council (EAPC) brings together twenty-seven partners and nineteen Allies for regular consultation on issues encompassing all aspects of security and all regions of the Euro-Atlantic area. Meetings take place regularly at the level of ambassadors, foreign and defence ministers and chiefs of defence. A two-year EAPC Action Plan provides for longer-term consultation and cooperation on a range of political and security-related matters, including regional issues, arms control, peacekeeping, defence and economic issues, civil emergency planning and scientific and environmental issues. In the wake of the terrorist attacks on the US in September 2001 combating international terrorism has become a priority. EAPC and ad hoc working groups focus on other areas of interest such as regional cooperation in south eastern Europe and the Caucasus or global humanitarian action and preventing the spread of small arms and weapons. While the EAPC is a multilateral forum, it also serves as the political framework of the PFP.

Individual partnership programmes are drawn up between NATO and partner countries from an extensive menu of activities – the PFP work programme – according to each country's specific interests and needs. The biennial programme contains more than 2,000 activities ranging from large military exercises to defence-related cooperation in crisis management, peacekeeping, civil emergency planning, air traffic management and armaments cooperation.

## Conclusion

It has been pointed out that unlike in Western Europe where economic and political integration processes went hand in hand with the build-up of the NATO as a powerful security organisation, the CIS failed to complete the process of taking over the military forces of the former Soviet Union. This is said to have resulted in the strengthening of Western security arrangements in the territory of the former Soviet Union. What remains to be seen is whether the strengthening of the Western security organisations on Russia's southern flank and the aspirations of several Central Asian and Caucasian countries for greater Western involvement in their region will lead to an effective Western hegemony over security arrangements in Eurasia.

It also remains to be seen whether such a presence could lead to a new opportunity for the settlement of ethnic conflicts and greater efficiency of regional integration projects. Another possible scenario is based on the assumption that the West acknowledges the stabilising potential of the CIS, specially in regions on its far periphery such as the Caucasus and Central Asia, but simultaneously succeeds in establishing Western hegemony in the whole of the former Soviet Union. In all three scenarios, the decline of Russian influence and the rise of Western clout in Eurasia are taken for granted.

This paper calls for the recognition of a new reality: the multiple security arrangements that are now in place in the region are significant in determining the future direction of regional security. These arrangements are vastly different from the Cold War-type arrangements. These initiatives reflect a new reality where multiple arrangements will be needed to deal with a myriad security concerns.

## Notes

1. *See* for instance Gail Lapidus 'Central Asia in Russian and American Foreign Policy After September 11, 2001', Presentation from Central Asia and Russia: Responses to the War on Terrorism, a panel discussion held at the University of California, Berkeley, on 29 October 2001 *see also*, Svante E Cornell, 'Introduction', *Nordic Newsletter of Asian Studies*, No. 3, 2002.

2. For writings that stress on the inevitability of change in geopolitical alignments around Central Asia, *see* Cornell, 'Introduction'.

3. *See* for instance, A Menteshashvili, 'Security and Foreign Policy in the Central Asian and the Caucasian Republics', www.nato.int/acad/fellow97-99/menteshashvili.pdf, where she notes, 'In geopolitical aspect Washington considers Uzbekistan as a serious counterweight to Russian influence in Central Asia.'

4. Muthiah Alagappa, *Asian Security Practice: Material and Ideational Influences*, Stanford: Stanford University Press, 1998, p.4.

5. For details of this argument *see* Yu Xintian, 'September 11 Incident and Change in Security Concept', *SIIA Journal*, Vol. 9, No. 2, May 2002.

6. Bruno Coppieters 'Conclusions: The Failure of Regionalism in Eurasia and the Western Ascendancy over Russia's Near Abroad', in Bruno Coppieters, Alexei Zverev and Dmitri Trenin (eds.), *Commonwealth and Independence in Post Soviet Russia*, London and Portland: Frank Cass, 1998.

7. *See* for instance Paul Kubicek, 'Regionalism, Nationalism and Realpolitik in Central Asia', *Europe-Asia Studies*, Vol. 49, No. 4, 1997.

8. For a detailed analysis of the nature of Central Asian

regional security initiatives *see* Anita Sengupta, 'Region, Rationalisation, Regionalism: The "Myth" of Tsentralnaya Azia Revisited', unpublished paper presented at a seminar on 'Central Asia: Ten Years of Independence', organised by the Maulana Abul Kalam Azad Institute of Asian Studies and the Central Asian Studies Division, Jawaharlal Nehru University, at the India International Centre (IIC), New Delhi, on 21–22 November 2001.

9. Gregory Gleason, 'Inter-State Cooperation in Central Asia from the CIS to the Shanghai Forum', *Europe-Asia Studies*, Vol. 53, No. 7, 2001.

10. *Nezavisimasti*, 6 July 1994, cited in Guangcheng Xing, 'Security issues in China's Relations with Central Asian States', in Yongjin Zhang and Rouben Azizian (eds.), *Ethnic Challenges beyond Borders: Chinese and Russian Perspectives of the Central Asian Conundrum*, Oxford: Macmillan (in association with St Antony's College, Oxford).

11. Ibid.

12. Michael R Lucas, 'Russia and Peacekeeping in the former USSR' *Aussenpolitik*, Vol. 46, No. 2, 1995, cited in Amalendu Misra, 'Shanghai Five and the Emerging Alliance in Central Asia: The Closed Society and its Enemies', *Central Asian Survey*, Vol. 20, No. 3, 2001.

13. Coppieters, 'Conclusions: The Failed Regionalism in Eurasia and the Western Ascendancy Over Russia's Near Abroad'.

14. For details *see* Anita Sengupta 'What is Central Asia to Russia? The Heartland Debates and Russia's Central Asian Policy', in Professor Shams-Ud-Din (ed.), *India and Russia Towards Strategic Partnership*, New Delhi: Lancers, 2001.

15. Sophie Lambroschini 'Central Asia: CIS Force Not Best Way to Combat Islamic Threat, Say Analysts', *Radio Free Europe-Radio Liberty*, 23 May 2001.

16. Ibid.

17. Dmitri Trenin, 'Introduction' in Coppieters, Zverev and Trenin (eds.), *Commonwealth and Independence in Post Soviet Russia*.
18. Lambroschini, 'Central Asia: CIS Force Not best way to Combat Islamic Threat'.
19. Igor Torbakov, 'Russia Moves to Reassert Influence in Central Asia, Caucasus', *Eurasia Insight*, 18 December 2002.
20. Pan Guang, 'China-Central Asia-Russia Relations and the Role of the SCO in the War Against Terrorism', *SIIA Journal*, Vol. 9, No. 2, May 2002.
21. Guang, 'China-Central Asia–Russia Relations'.
22. Misra, 'Shanghai Five and the Emerging Alliance in Central Asia: The Closed Society and its Enemies'.
23. *Beijing Review*, 13–19 May, pp.6–8, cited in Misra, 'Shanghai Five: The Emerging Alliance'.
24. Xinhua News Agency, 26 April 1996.
25. Lapidus, 'Central Asia in Russian and American Foreign Policy After September 11, 2001'.
26. For details *see* Press Communiqué M-1 (94) 2, Issued by the Heads of state and government participating in the meeting of the North Atlantic Council, NATO Headquarters, Brussels, 10–11 June 1994.
27. For details *see* 'Partnership and Cooperation', NATO Fact Sheets, www.nato.int/docu/facts.htm.
28. The matters included within the ambit of the Partnership (for details *see* Partnership Work Programme for 2000–2001, NATO Partnership for Peace Documents) include:

    1. Air Defence Related Matters
    2. Airspace Management/Control
    3. Consultation, Command and Control, including Communications and Information Systems, Navigation and Identification systems, Inter-operatability Aspects, Procedures and Terminology

4. Civil Emergency Planning
5. Crisis management
6. Democratic Control of Defence Forces and Defence Structures
7. Defence Planning, Budgeting and Resource management
8. Planning, Organisation and Management of National Defence Procurement Programmes and International Cooperation in Armaments Field
9. Defence Policy and Strategy
10. Planning Organisation and Management of National Defence Research and Technology
11. Military Geography
12. Language Training
13. Consumer Logistics
14. Medical Services
15. Meteorological Support for NATO/Partner Forces
16. Military Infrastructure
17. Political and Defence Efforts
18. Conceptual, Planning and Operational Aspects of Peacekeeping
19. Operational, Material and Administrative Aspects of Peacekeeping
20. Operational, Material and Administrative Aspects of Standardisation
21. Military Exercises and Related Training Activities
22. Military Education, Training and Doctrine

29. Coppieters, 'Conclusions: The Failed Regionalism in Eurasia and the Western Ascendancy Over Russia's Near Abroad'.

# Chapter XIII

# CENTRAL ASIA: NEW ERA, NEW REALITIES, NEW CHALLENGES

Dr Sanjay Deshpande

## Introduction

The death of the Soviet Union gave birth to fifteen sovereign and independent countries. Prominent among them are the five Central Asian Republics (CARs) – Kazakastan, Kyrgyzstan, Tajikistan, Turkmenistan and Uzbekistan. Due to their remote location, landlocked status, geopolitical situation and dependence on Russia, the CA Republics remained isolated in the initial years after their independence. Moreover, the US and its allies had no history of any engagement with the CARs prior to the collapse of the former USSR. Post-1991, Central Asia became an important region of the eastern hemisphere, occupying areas adjacent to several nuclear powers such as Russia, China, Pakistan and Iran. The United States and the North Atlantic Treaty Organisation (NATO) have now established a bridgehead in Central Asia and have gradually expanded their military presence in this region. The terrorist attack of 11 September 2001 on the US also triggered a dramatic reconfiguration of American security priorities, particularly in the context of the Central Asian region. With the launch of the war on terrorism, the spotlight has shifted to Afghanistan. Inevitably, the countries of the region have had to grapple with the dynamics of new priorities and concerns in their inter-state relationships as well as new challenges presented by overall regional and global developments.

## New Allies and Equations are Emerging...

Since the beginning of the Afghan campaign in October 2001, the US acquired bases or transit points for its war planes and military supplies in many countries in Central Asia. The security concerns arising due to 9/11 have legitimised the military presence of Western powers in this strategically important region. American policy makers have argued that the CARs will increasingly rely on the US to ensure their security in a threatening and unstable geopolitical environment.

Uzbekistan is host to a permanent American base at Khanabad, housing 1,500 personnel. Manas near Bishkek in Kyrgyzstan is described as the future 'transportation hub' housing more than 3,000 soldiers, war planes and surveillance aircraft. More airfields are under US control in Kazakhstan, Tajikistan and Pakistan. The Pentagon has started regular replacement and rotation of troops. Clearly, what was meant to be a temporary deployment is developing into a long-term presence.

American military presence in Central Asia is also justified for reasons of economic development and sustaining reforms in this region. Elizabeth Jones, assistant secretary of State, advocated this argument before the Foreign Affairs Committee in December 2001. The US Secretary of State General Colin Powell declared in Tashkent that US interests in Central Asia stretch 'beyond the crisis in Afghanistan'. The American media has reported that the US is considering abrogating the law that restricts US trade relations with a number of CARs due to their poor human rights track record. During the US visit of Uzbek President

Islam Karimov in March 2002, the US made it amply clear that it was keen on engaging with the region by signing a Declaration of Strategic Partnership with Uzbekistan. For the first time, no mention was made of human rights. Bilateral military relations and joint exercises have clearly translated into support of the CARs for the US campaign in Afghanistan. The authoritarian regimes of the CARs claim that US military presence has had a positive effect on the economy of the region.

On the economic front, Russia continues to be of importance to the CARs. 'Most of Central Asia's economic problems are tied in one way or the other to its relations with Russia,' writes Martha Olcott. Though the leaders in several Central Asian countries are keen to sever ties with Russia, it is proving to be extremely difficult. This is due to the fact that there is a strong Russian presence in all spheres of economic activity despite the dismantling of the Soviet infrastructure. Central Asia has so far been Russia's underbelly and a strategic hot spot, where security and strategic concerns have traditionally overshadowed economic ones. However, the situation in this regard is fast changing. All the major economic powers in the world are hoping to set up facilities to access the vast untapped energy resources and consumer markets in this region.

## ...But Will the Old Order Change?

The collapse of the Soviet Union has forced the Central Asian countries to renegotiate their relations with each other, with Russia, as well as with a host of other countries. Although they share a common set of domestic concerns, they have pursued increasingly divergent foreign and security policies. They have all sought to maintain their political, economic and cultural ties with Russia. This has led to the constant fear of the revival of Russian imperialism, which in turn drives these countries to counter Russian dominance at every opportunity. This schism has been further widened in recent times.

Russian policy towards the Central Asian countries has seen a dramatic shift after September 2001. Moscow has begun to realise that its security environment is changing and the major threats to Russian security arise from the instability, turmoil and the volatile nature of politics across Russia's southern borders. Initially, Russia supported the US-led war against terrorism as sources close to President Putin and Russian foreign ministry (MID) felt that Kremlin would get a free hand in dealing with religious extremism and secessionism in Chechnya. However, the Russian elite fears that the American war against terrorism is aimed at promoting American geopolitical interests and traditional foreign policy objectives in Central Asia and the Caucasus region. Russian leaders are also unhappy with the CARs and their decision to permit US military bases. This was perceived to be a violation of the Collective Security Treaty signed by Central Asian countries. Russia also does not wish to see permanent US bases appear in this region. Not surprisingly, there is deep concern in Moscow over these developments. Many of Russia's high-security military, nuclear and space infrastructure are located in the north of Kazakhstan and western Siberia, once the farthest points on the globe for any US military facility, but now easily approachable by short-range US aircraft.

The Central Asian leaders have turned a deaf ear to Russian concerns about American military intrusion in the region. However, Moscow is trying to consolidate its relations with Kazakhstan, Tajikistan and Turkmenistan. This shows that it has reconciled itself to a long-term US presence in Central Asia. The Russian response to these geopolitical changes is quite confused and contradictory. In a meeting with the leading staff of the defence ministry in end-2002, President Putin emphasised that Russia should promptly react to these serious geopolitical changes including those arising from the concerns of the armed forces. But Putin's address to the federal assembly did not reflect any concern on these serious changes. He said, 'To attain these goals we are taking part in the creation of a general system of security, maintaining dialogue with USA and working to change the quality of our relations with NATO.' At a conference in Moscow, deputy chairman of the State Duma's Defence Committee expressed concern over the United States' unilateral activities on a range of issues in recent years and proposed a conference on international anti-terrorism.

In contrast, the first deputy chief of the general staff, Lt General Yuri Baluyevsky said, 'American military presence in Central Asia is connected with anti-terrorist operations in Afghanistan and US troops were deployed with the consent of concerned countries and found a full understanding on part of Russia.' The General also complimented the US and its allies for a successful anti-terrorist operation in Afghanistan. Participants at a seminar held on 14 March 2002, however, remarked that Russia made a strategic mistake when it voluntarily withdrew from its zone of influence in Central Asia. Konstantin Zalutin, director of the Russian Institute of CIS, pointed out that Russia encountered a new US geopolitical challenge in Central Asia and American military presence posed a threat to both the CIS and the Collective Security Treaty. Many speakers were of the view that Kazakhstan and Uzbekistan were the two key states in Central Asia and Russia should concentrate on these two by evolving a new policy towards them.

In this rapidly changing political scenario, Turkmenistan is the only country that has refused to open its airfields to US war planes during the anti-Taliban military campaign in

Afghanistan in accordance with its policy of 'positive neutrality'. Turkmenistan is not a member of the CIS Collective Security Treaty. President Saparmurad Niyazov has attended very few CIS summits since 1992. In January 2002, Niyazov rejected a German request for use of Turkmen airfields by military aircraft to provide support to the UN-mandated International Security Assistance Force. Niyazov's stand is that Turkmenistan's participation in the international efforts in Afghanistan will only be in terms of humanitarian assistance. However, Turkmenistan has shifted from its old neutral foreign policy to a new pro-Russian policy after the war on terrorism in Afghanistan. During President Niyazov's visit to Moscow in January 2002, a joint Russian-Turkmen communiqué reiterated the two countries' support for the resolution of the Afghan conflict under the aegis of the UN and the Security Council. Both the presidents stressed that an all-embracing settlement of the internal conflict was needed to remove the threat to stability in Central Asia. They also confirmed their efforts to determine a new legal status of the Caspian Sea by taking into account the interests of all Caspian states.

American military presence in Kazakhstan and Uzbekistan has provoked Russia not only to work towards a new legal status of the Caspian Sea, which is acceptable to all, but also to launch a fresh initiative to establish a Eurasian Alliance of Gas Producers comprising Russia, Kazakhstan, Turkmenistan and Uzbekistan. Stephen Cohen, a leading American political scientist, admits that the United States has more enduring goals to achieve, including military hegemony, widening its sphere of influence at the cost of Russia and China and access to the rich oil and gas resources which are not under OPEC control. These goals seem to have been largely realised in view of Putin's attitude as reflected in the agreements signed at the Moscow and Rome summits in May 2002. The allure of economic cooperation with the

European Union and the US has led Kremlin to turn its back to Eurasianism in Central Asia. Historically, this region had been a strong component of its foreign policy. The key issue is: how will Russia redress the balance in a new geopolitical alignment?

## Soviet Legacy in Central Asia

During the first decades of Soviet rule, Central Asia went through a process of national delimitation. The political boundaries of the region were redrawn in an effort to incorporate the major nationalities of the region into their own Republics or Autonomous Republics. At the same time, these institutions were instrumental in further developing a national classificatory grid within the region through Soviet-orchestrated language development programmes, codification of national histories and creation of national symbols. In the case of Central Asia, it was a mixture of Soviet ideology along with realpolitik considerations that resulted in a policy of divide and rule whereby the region was configured into five national republics. Immediately after the Russian Revolution and Civil War, the Bolsheviks' objective was to create a new historical community of Soviet people (*Sovetski Narod*). However, the emergence of nationalism meant that the Soviet state would have to fulfil the desires of various nationalities that had come to the fore during the Civil War. A 'federal compromise' was reached with the creation of a federation with each state possessing the purported right to secession. According to Stalin, a federation should be a historically evolved stable community arising on the foundations of a common language, territory, economic life and psychological make-up and be manifested in a community of culture.

The Bolshevik concept of federalism, therefore,

institutionalised two forms of nationhood so that the titular nations were defined simultaneously in territorial terms (as national republics) and in extra-territorial terms (as nationalities). The Anglo-American media has argued that nationalism was severely repressed during the Soviet period. The establishment of natural republics designed to subdue political movements actually led to the representation of such nationalities within the federation at both institutional and cultural levels.

After acquiring independence, the leaders of Central Asia reaffirmed their common historical ties by renaming the region Central Asia (*Tsentralnaya Azia*), thereby refusing to recognise the Soviet-imposed separation of Kazakhstan from the other four republics which were grouped together and known collectively as Middle Asia (*Srednyaya Azia*). Even before the break-up of the Soviet Union, a cultural renaissance had begun with calls for the re-establishment of the primacy of the national language and the reinterpretation of the 'blank spots' of Central Asian history so that the key figures of the Alash and Jadid movements could be rehabilitated. This renaissance has continued apace with all the national languages being given the status of 'official language of state communication'. National ones have replaced Soviet appellations of various streets and places and historic figures have been elevated to national hero status.

The Soviet system brought about a considerable degree of homogeneity in Central Asian societies, pushing aside local characteristics in favour of uniform national features. Two of the attributes that had provided the basis for their national existence during the Soviet period – language and territory – assumed critical importance. The United Nations Human Development Report, though critical of many past Soviet policies, nevertheless recognised the importance of those policies in building Central Asian nations. The report says that the Soviet legacy also bestowed a collective identity that has contributed to some degree of unity.

The cohesion of a nation state depends upon the ability to surpass the traditional historical identities of a particular society in the presence of industrialisation and modernisation. Soviet authorities claimed that they had destroyed the traditional structures of nomadism and tribalism prevalent in Central Asia. However, it was evident that the impact of modernisation and industrialisation was not evenly distributed as they were carried out only around the urban centres of Central Asia. Some regions and pockets were not touched and remained under the influence of traditional structures. Strong family bonds are an important trait of this society. The collectivised agricultural activity of the Soviet acted as a medium for family units to regenerate themselves in more tangible economic terms. A majority of state-run farms were based on extended family units.

Representatives of the old ruling elite, which was formed during the Soviet period, are now enjoying power in all the Central Asian Republics. The Central Asian elite managed to leverage existing bureaucratic institutions to ensure a transition towards economic and political independence. The population is hardly aware of political events and there is an enormous gap between the ruling elite and the masses.

The kind of nationalism that the ruling elite seeks to build in their respective countries is 'cultural nationalism', based on the majority ethnic group. Such attempts at building mono-ethnic states in multi-ethnic societies by the ruling elite not only affects inter-ethnic relations in the CARs, but also the stability of the Eurasian region as a whole. Joane Nagel called this process 'political construction of ethnicity'. The recognition of ethnicity as a legitimate basis for political organisation by the government renders prior ethnic divisions more permanent, increases solidarity, and also promotes new mobilisation by formerly unrecognised groups lest they be excluded from an ethnically defined polity. In a region where all groups share a common history, the building of non-ethnic states has dangerous implications. The effective way to tackle this problem is to build 'civic nationalism' based on institutions and a set of broader values. Such nationalism normally appears in well institutionalised democracies. Ethnic nationalism, which depends on culture rather than on institutions, appears spontaneously when an institutional vacuum occurs. It dominates when institutions collapse or existing institutions fail to fulfil the basic needs of people and when satisfactory alternative structures are not readily available. This situation applies to the CARs.

Industrial development in this region has lagged far behind the rest of the former Soviet Union, to the extent that per capita industrial output has been less than half of the levels prevailing in the Russian federation. The economy of this region has been overwhelmingly dominated by the extraction of raw materials and the production of agricultural goods and livestock, a phenomenon epitomised by the cotton monoculture of Uzbekistan, where production of the 'white gold' led to environmental devastation of the land. The region initially lacked an industrially skilled workforce. The industrialised areas of Central Asia have a dominant Slav (predominantly Russian) population, which had migrated to the area in order to fill many of the job vacancies. The traditional preponderance of Slavs within industry continued throughout the Soviet period despite affirmative action to reverse the trend. Several reasons have been put forward to explain this: the preponderance of Slavs made industry an unappealing prospect for Central Asians; the existence of a 'second (shadow) economy' especially in the agricultural and service industries meant that it was far more beneficial to remain employed in these sectors; Central Asian culture regarded industrial work as lowly and denigrating. Large number of Central Asians remaining in agricultural production has led to a low rate of migration from rural to urban centres. Some of the Central Asian economists and historians blame the Soviet socialist system and the Russians for the destruction of their society.

However, M S Asimovs has rightly pointed out:

> It is unacceptable to wipe out everything that was done in Soviet days. We should by no means pretend to be blind and deny that it was during the Soviet regime, the universities and a highly elaborate network of schools were opened, industry and agriculture started to develop, archaeologists discovered important monuments of the past, physicians successfully fought endemic local diseases, engineers constructed hydropower stations and illiteracy was overcome. All this and much more permits me to insist in a very modest way that it is quiet impossible to accept a unilateral negative position to the recent past of Central Asia.

It is argued that the Soviet disintegration has damaged the economy. Virtually all skilled specialists have left the region. In terms of net material product services, the rational economy has shrunk by almost 70 per cent in the first decade of independence. In the first five years (1991–1996), inflation raged at rates sometimes in excess of 1,000 per cent per annum. However, it is gradually coming down. Economic reforms resulted in the emergence of a small, prosperous new Central Asian elite. Nevertheless, it has been overshadowed by the rapid expansion of poverty at the other end.

## Central Asia and Religious Extremism

The influence of Islam in the region has not diminished despite Soviet attempts to impose secular rule in Central

Asia. Heavy-handedness of Soviet-era bestowed a heritage of authoritarianism, corruption and disrespect for human rights. Things are not too different today. The Bush administration too is prepared to turn a blind eye to human rights abuses in the CARs in return for their loyalty. Islamic religious revivalism in this region received a new impetus when these republics gained independence. During the Soviet era, Islam had continued to flourish underground even as several mosques and religious educational institutions were closed down. The Ferghana Valley straddling three countries – Uzbekistan, Tajikistan and Kyrgyzstan – has emerged as the centre for resurgent Islam. The cities of Bukhara, Samarkhand, Khiva and Namangani are the centres of Islamic studies. Islam appears to have a lot to do with the two conflicts in this region – civil war in Tajikistan and fratricidal war in Afghanistan.

Tajik President Emamoli Rakhmonov of the Peoples Front, whose political platform was hostile to Islamic fundamentalism, soon found opposition to his rule assuming the character of a civil war. Tajikistan and Afghanistan share a 1,500-km border, which has always been porous. Once the Taliban captured power in Kabul in 1996, the Tajik Opposition received full support and military aid from them. In order to oppose the danger posed by these elements, President Rakhmonov sought the help of Russia under the Collective Security Treaty. Since then, a CIS peacekeeping force has been guarding the Tajik-Afghan border. In 1997, peace was instituted under the auspices of the United Nations and since then a coalition government has been ruling Tajikistan.

Uzbekistan too has clamped down on radical Islam. The secular government in 1991 banned political parties from espousing the cause of religious extremism. However, these measures did not attain the desired results. The Ferghana Valley, the heart of Central Asia, is divided between

Uzbekistan, Tajikistan and Kyrgyzstan. Ferghana exhibits the most vivid example of Islamic evolution taking place throughout the region and reflects the impact Afghanistan's Islamic ideology has had on Central Asia.

After the Taliban came into power, religious extremism in Uzbekistan increased. Although the Adolat Freedom Party and the Unity Popular Movement were banned, some underground extremist organisations continued to operate in the country. The Islamic Movement of Uzbekistan (IMU), instituted by Juma Namangani and Tahir Yuldash, was a reincarnation of the Adolat Party and drew support from the Taliban. Namangani began to work to replace the government's rule in the valley with laws based on his political interpretations of the Koran. Members of this organisation assassinated corrupt regional Uzbek officials and as a symbol of their crude justice one of the beheaded official's head was left at the gates of the chief of Namangani internal affairs office. In 1999, Uzbekistan was rocked by a series of bomb blasts. The Islamic rebels also made an attempt on the life of President Karimov.

The IMU worked – and continues to work – for the specific objective of overthrowing the president and instituting a Caliphate in Central Asia. After 1999, armed IMU squads made incursions into Kyrgyzstan, vowing to replace the governments in both Tajikistan and Kyrgyzstan with a Unitary Ferghana Valley Caliphate. In his speech to a joint session of the Congress on 20 September 2001 US President George Bush identified the IMU as a terrorist organisation. This prompted Uzbekistan to support the US campaign against Osama bin Laden and the Taliban that sheltered Namangani. However, after the fall of the Taliban, the whereabouts of Namangani and Yudash are unknown. Another organisation, Hizb-ul-Tahir, that has a wide network in the region, has been working for the creation of an Islamic Caliphate expanding from Mongolia to the Caspian Sea. It was established during the Soviet era in the early 1950s by Sheikh Jakitdin Nabahony.

Kyrgyzstan also faces the dangers of religious extremism, especially in its southern part. While in Kazakhstan and Turkmenistan there has been a revival of Islam, especially of Islamic traditions and values, they are not yet confronted with radical Islam. Despite the fact that the CARs have a shared perception of challenges posed by religious extremism to their regimes, their concerns are not the same. After the Taliban came into power and espoused the concept of 'Greater Afghanistan', the countries faced with the prospect of destabilisation were Uzbekistan and Tajikistan. This idea provided a platform for the Opposition forces in these countries to launch an offensive against their respective governments. It also led to drug trafficking, smuggling of small arms and transnational crimes.

The process of democratisation and modernisation is very slow in the region. But Central Asian leaders feel that this process should be gradual, or else chaos will follow. Uzbek President Karimov asserted that 'social harmony and stability are essential conditions for reforms and not merely its consequences'. Hence Islamic fundamentalism and religious extremism are the main threats to the stability of Central Asia.

## Oil Politics in Central Asia

Several analysts are of the opinion that the real reason behind American intervention in Afghanistan is to secure access to energy sources. The discovery of huge hydrocarbon deposits in the Caspian Sea basin is expected to transform this region into the Kuwait of the twenty-first century. The competition for influence is most visible in the sphere of oil transportation routes. The country that controls the transportation routes will be the real master of the region.

The principal energy resources in the Caspian region are to be found in Azerbaijan, Kazakhstan and Turkmenistan. All these countries are landlocked which has led to international competition for the exploitation and transport of these resources to global markets. While plans have already been made to build a major US-controlled oil pipeline from Kazakhstan and Azerbaijan to Ceyhan in Turkey, the US is championing another plan to evacuate gas from Turkmenistan through Afghanistan and Pakistan. It is widely reported that the Bush administration is making the pipeline issue the centrepiece of rebuilding Afghanistan. *Forbes* writes, 'With the collapse of the Taliban, oil executives are suddenly talking about nation building.'

Bush's hidden agenda is to exploit the oil and gas reserves in the Caspian basin. Six US oil giants – Unocal, Amoco, Chevron, Exxon, Pennzoil and Total – have made heavy investments in the enormous hydrocarbon potential of the CARs and the Caspian basin. Immediately after the Taliban took over Afghanistan, Unocal executives started negotiations with them regarding building of pipelines. Hence, the US administration was slow to condemn the Taliban regime for their excesses. From the US point of view, the Taliban could have helped weaken Russian monopoly over oil and gas in the region. However, the terrorist attacks of 11 September forced President Bush to declare military action against the Taliban.

Bush authorised his National Security Advisor Condoleeza Rice to take all necessary decisions and actions to safeguard and promote American interests. The assignment did not come as a surprise to Rice who is a former director of the US oil company, Cheveron Texaco. Soon after assuming charge of her new assignment Rice assured Russian leaders that the United States had no designs and ambitions on Russia's traditional hegemony over Central Asian oil reserves. According to Russian oil experts, Karzai's pro-

American regime in Kabul will support US plans to build an Afghan pipeline for Caspian oil. On 11 December 2001 Moscow's state-owned news agency TASS reported that Russia had signed a long-term cooperation accord with Turkmenistan covering natural gas exploration, production, processing, transport and marketing. The deal was announced just ten days after Gazprom (Gazovaya Promyschlenost – Gas Industry, Russia's leading private oil and gas company) announced that it had reached a similar agreement with Kazakhstan. These deals did not come as a surprise to Condoleeza Rice. It was during her tenure as director of Cheveron Texaco, that the company had, as part of a consortium including Russia, Kazakhstan, Oman and Exxon Mobil, contracted to complete the work of the pipeline carrying oil from the Tengiz oil field in Kazakhstan to the Russian port of Novorossisk. Cheveron was so grateful to Condoleeza Rice for her services that it named an oil tanker after her.

Afghanistan is expected to play a crucial role in this strategic game of control over the region's oil wealth. The US hopes to strike a deal to build a two-billion-dollar pipeline through the country to carry gas from Turkmenistan to Pakistan and India. President Hamid Karzai has already held talks with US officials during his visit to Washington in September 2002. After getting the green signal from Washington he is expected to hold talks with his Turkmen and Pakistani counterparts. According to Alam Razim, Afghan minister for mines and industries, 'The work on the project will start after finalising an agreement in the coming summit.' The minister told the BBC that Unocal is the leading company which would build the pipeline. This project would bring thirty billion cubic metres of Turkmen gas to the market annually. Afghanistan also plans to construct a road parallel to the pipeline, which will link Turkmenistan with Pakistan. This will benefit nearby villages and Afghanistan will be capable of exporting gas to the international market. The government hopes to earn revenue by exporting oil and gas and also hopes to take over the ownership of the pipeline after a few years. The Asian Development Bank (ADB) is surveying the routes to transport local gas from areas in northern Afghanistan to Kabul and to the iron ore mines at the Haji Gak Pass in west Afghanistan. The pipeline network is expected to be completed with funds from ADB and donor countries. In short, the Western countries will exercise a combination of economic and political influence to secure its interests in Central Asia. This cannot, but, be a worrisome development for Moscow. A section of the Russian media and political leadership is of the opinion that Western countries cannot, however, accomplish all their economic and political objectives without the support of the ethnic and political groups, most of which continue to be anti-West. This could well upset Western plans in the region.

## The New 'Great Game' in Central Asia

R Kipling originally coined the term 'Great Game' to describe the nineteenth-century Anglo-Russian rivalry for hegemony in Central Asia. After the demise of the USSR, analysts and observers of the region are liberally using the term to describe the endeavours of the great powers in their competition for strategic superiority, energy resources and political one-upmanship. The New Great Game is replete with intrigue as the new powers battle it out for the fabulous oil and gas wealth of the region. The intimation of Islamist violence has added a further twist to the Central Asian Great Game.

The United States and NATO, which have now established a bridgehead in the CAR, continue to expand their military presence on former Soviet territory, despite

Moscow's protests. American military build-up in Central Asia is accelerating. A few thousand US soldiers are already stationed in Uzbekistan, while agreements have been signed allowing the use of Tajik and Kazakh airfields for military operations. Even neutral Turkmenistan has granted permission for military over-flights. Uzbekistan has agreed to deploy American troops at its Khanabad air base. In return, the USA has promised to provide aid of US $160 million to Uzbekistan in the year 2002, which is an increase of $100 million over the previous year.

US and NATO military installations in the CARs are instrumental in providing logistics support to operations in Afghanistan. This apart, ranger units, AWACS-type aircraft, psychological warfare and reconnaissance planes are also being deployed. The Pentagon has plans of converting some of the former Soviet military bases into full-fledged Western outposts.

While the US has treated the region primarily as a convenient staging base for its own interests, the political leadership of the CARs too have used the situation to their advantage. They all have felt confident enough to use the threat of Islamic fundamentalism and religious extremism to extend their tenure in power. There has been no change in the leadership in the Central Asian Republics since their independence. These leaders have retreated from their initial pursuit of democracy and economic reform and today argue that stability is the need of the hour. This has often translated into authoritarianism and crackdown on political dissent. The establishment of US military installations in the region has emboldened these regional leaders to bolster their personal authority in their respective countries. The rapid increase in Western military and economic aid to the CARs since September 2001 has led to a spurt in corrupt practices as competing regional interest groups scramble for a share of the new income.

## Russia and Its Role in Independent Central Asia

Russia's relations with the CARs continues to remain a significant factor in the region. Despite the collapse of the USSR, its inter-regional economic links, though weak, are still intact. Due to several geographical, demographic, economic and military factors, the Russian presence in the region is immense. The fact that these republics need Russia economically suggests that the CIS grouping holds much promise. Kazakhstan, Kyrgyzstan and Tajikistan have already moved towards greater integration with Russia in a wide range of areas. Events in Afghanistan, particularly the growth of fundamentalism and extremism, have pushed Uzbekistan to renew its ties with Russia. Turkmen President Niyazov's visit to Moscow in January 2001 helped improve the Russian-Turkmen relationship.

The leadership of the CARs is aware that their national self-interest requires them to foster a special relationship with Russia. As far as security and strategic cooperation is concerned, the CARs currently have little choice but to turn to Russia. Nearly twelve million Russians from the CARs have provided much needed technical capability for economic development. Seven decades of economic, military and strategic tie-ups with the former Soviet Union, and Russia in particular, have helped create a viable market for CAR goods and services. The CARs are dependent on Russia to export oil, gas and other goods through established rail roads to the West and to Far Eastern markets.

At the same time, the CAR leaders are keen to reduce their dependence on Russia by entering into defence agreements with other countries and by attracting Western capital and technology for developing their economies. They are concerned about Kremlin's meddling in their internal affairs under the pretext of safeguarding the interests of ethnic Russians in the region and the growing trend of Russian nationalism. While formulating their policies and developing relations with countries in their southern fringe, the CARs have had to maintain a delicate balance between them and Russia since interests of both the sides are closely intertwined – particularly in the context of Iran, Turkey and Pakistan. Hence Russia 'clearly sees the borders of the CARs as the outer limits of its own security frontier'. The volatile situation in Afghanistan after September 2001 has added a new twist to the already complex regional scenario.

After September 2001, American military presence in Central Asia has undoubtedly altered the geopolitical situation in the region. There is deep concern in the Russian national establishment over these developments. Many articles published in the Russian media have voiced this concern. According to some Russian scholars, Kremlin's influence has been debilitated, at least temporarily. In addition to this, the CARs have taken different and frequently conflicting routes towards national consolidation and forged new regional economic and political alliances. After September 2001, the CARs have engaged in a number of US-led political, economic, military and development programmes in the region, which is extremely worrisome for Russia.

President Putin's support of the deployment of American troops in Central Asia and his declaration of joining the allies in their war against international terrorism is being interpreted by Russian policy makers as a move aimed at winning support for Kremlin's initiatives against Chechen rebels. However, it has also evoked severe criticism as the Russian elite fears that the US and its allies may continue to stay in the region indefinitely. The US Secretary of State Colin Powell's remark in an address to journalists in December 2001 in Tashkent that 'US interests in the Central Asian region stretch beyond the current crisis in Afghanistan' has fuelled Russian fears. While some US leaders have tried to calm Russian apprehensions, Moscow lacks the military-economic leverage to influence the situation. So far Russia has been unable to clearly formulate a relevant political blueprint to counter expanded US and NATO influence on CIS countries. Its leaders merely say that they oppose the use of Central Asian airbases by the US.

The CARs nevertheless continue to voice pro-Russian sentiments. Kyrgyzstan's President Akayev remarked: 'Russia, as a great power, could become the main force in the formation of a system of stability and security in Central Asia.' At the back of the mind of the CAR leadership is the fear that the West's foray into the region could be temporary and instability could return. Russia is still seen as a guarantor of the last resort.

## Chinese Engagement in Central Asia

Another player vying for supremacy in the region is China. The Asian giant has taken steps to counter the threat posed to its security by US military presence close to its border in the Central Asian region. The foreign ministers of the Shanghai Cooperation Organisation (SCO) met in Beijing in January 2000, where they endorsed a call for a neutral Afghanistan and opposed arbitrary expansion of the global war on terrorism to Iraq, Iran and North Korea – countries described by President Bush as 'axis of evil states'. China along with Russia played an important role in establishing the regional organisation of the 'Shanghai Five' in 1996. The main purpose of constituting this organisation was to delimit and demilitarise the China-CIS border. The members – Russia, China, Kazakhstan, Kyrgyzstan, and Tajikistan – signed an agreement titled 'On Confidence Building in the Military Sphere in the Border Area'. A sixth member, Uzbekistan, joined the organisation later. The document proposed setting up of a 100-km 'Confidence

Zone' on either side of the border. A year later an agreement was signed in Moscow entitled 'On the Mutual Reduction of Armed Forces in the Border Area'. The organisation then shifted its focus to international terrorism and religious extremism.

China is facing a threat from terrorism in its Xinjiang province. In January 2002, while meeting with the foreign ministers of the Shanghai Six, Chinese President Jiang Zemin is reported to have said that the most urgent need is to set up a regional anti-terrorism outfit. China seems to be keen to carry Russia along in its struggle to prevent US global hegemony in the region. This problem was discussed by Russia and China during President Putin's visit to Beijing in December 2002. Both sides criticised unilateral US military actions. They advocated the strengthening of the UN, which they felt should play a key role in ensuring international security and cooperation in a multipolar world. Both countries highlighted their collaboration on issues of strategic stability with the aim of strengthening international security, global and regional stability.

Thus, China is joining Russia to fight US hegemony not only in the Central Asian region but also all over the world. China is using its geographical advantage to move towards a leading position in the struggle for influence in post-Soviet Central Asia. It has far fewer limitations than its Middle Eastern rivals. China's major strengths are its regulated economy and available financial resources. China offers the CARs use of its territory to gain direct access to the Pacific, the Far East and South-East Asia.

## The Regional Players

Besides the US and its allies, Russia, China, Turkey, Iran and Pakistan, all are trying to play key roles in post-Soviet Central Asia. The Central Asian Republics are equally keen on fostering stronger ties with countries lying on their southern fringes.

## TURKEY

After the disintegration of the Soviet Union, the CARs initially turned towards Turkey for several reasons. Turkey offered support to help the CARs replicate its successful experience with economic and political reforms. Like the Central Asian Republics, Turkey is a moderate Muslim nation with a state-controlled economy. The Turkish model looked attractive, especially in comparison to the ideological Islamic states in the region. However, due to a lack of initiative within the region and other problems, this model could not be implemented. Nevertheless, Turkey was the first country to make a successful move towards establishing a new relationship with Central Asia. A great advantage was the centuries-old ethno-linguistic and cultural ties with Central Asia. With its Western orientation, the US and Europe also perceived Turkey as the right kind of player, which would help further their objectives in Central Asia. Initially, Turkey was handicapped by its adversarial orientation as a member of NATO. However, with NATO propagating the idea of Partnership for Peace with all Central Asian Republics, initial reservations against Turkey disappeared. Hence, Turkey has had greater success in Central Asia than any of the CARs' other immediate neighbours.

## IRAN

Iran has been an economic and political heavyweight in post-Soviet Central Asian politics. It was active in backing different political groups in the Tajik-Afghan imbroglio. Iran also played a crucial role in spreading Islamic fundamentalism to Central Asia. It later moderated this approach and started cultivating the CAR governments to develop bilateral relations. The geo-strategic location of Iran between the Persian Gulf and Caspian Sea is not lost on the CARs – Iran's proximity to the Persian Gulf makes it a perfect strategic and transport ally for landlocked CARs. Iran, along with Russia, helped the Northern Alliance troops against Taliban. At the same time, Iran is trying to counter American presence in the region. Although Iran has successfully established relations with all Central Asian Republics, it has failed to cultivate cordial relations with Uzbekistan. Consequently, Iran-Uzbek relations have at best remained lukewarm.

## PAKISTAN

Pakistan's entry into independent Central Asia is not a coincidence. Pakistan has long recognised the importance of this region. Pakistan has tried to emerge as a key economic and geopolitical player in the region. It has jointly mooted several strategic projects, including one with Uzbekistan. The proposed Uzbek-Afghan-Pakistan rail project involving a 13-km rail link via the Wakhan Corridor will give Uzbekistan access to Karachi port. For Pakistan, Central Asia could offer a lucrative market for its textile industry. The other reason for Pakistan's entry into the region is international security arrangements jointly planned by the US and Pakistan. It is believed that American policy makers propose to use Pakistan as a partner for its activities in Central Asia. The only problem is the tremendous influence of rogue non-state and state players in the relationship. The widespread activities of drug barons and narcotics trafficking continue to be a major problem. Many Pakistani traders and top military officials are reported to be engaged in this lucrative business and consequently bilateral agreements have failed to make any dent on drug trafficking. Despite these hurdles, Pakistan has been trying to expand its political, economic and cultural ties with this 'Islamic heartland'.

INDIA

Despite favourable signs in Indo-Central Asian relations, Indian investment in the region continues to be insignificant. Lack of transportation facilities, perceived investment risks stemming from political uncertainties, civil war, low profit margins, high competitiveness and lack of infrastructure for business are some of the reasons for the Indian business community's cautious approach towards Central Asia's emerging markets. Thus, India is of secondary importance to the CARs. From the Indian perspective, the objective is to cultivate relations with the CARs for security and strategic reasons and for promotion of trade. After the Afghanistan war both Russia and China seem to be keen on carrying India along with them in their struggle to prevent the establishment of US hegemony in this region. The possible alliance between India, Russia and China was discussed during Russian President Putin's recent visits to Beijing and New Delhi. Some leaders of Central Asia have also expressed support for India's participation in the Shanghai Cooperation Organisation. The CARs and Russia have expressed the belief that India's membership in the SCO would add to the strength of the organisation.

## Conclusion

Central Asia is a vast region with five independent republics. It has a territory equal to half of the US. Its population is nearly 51 million. With twenty billion barrels of proven oil reserves and seven trillion cubic metres of natural gas the region's importance to the global economy cannot but be significant. After the decline of the USSR, the region's vast energy resources has attracted new players. The nineteenth century 'Great Game' played for hegemony over the region by Russia and Britain is being played out in a new context and the key elements of the new Great Game are ethnicity and religion. The US along with its allies have until recently engaged in the region by proxy with the help of Turkey and Pakistan. The situation has changed dramatically after September 2001 and the projection of US military power in the region. This is perhaps the single most significant development after the collapse of the Soviet Union.

Whether Washington manages to achieve its political, economic and strategic objectives in the region will hinge on several factors. For one, Russia will not withdraw entirely from Central Asia in the near future. Second, China is yet another major power, which is destined to play an increasing role in the region. India is not among the top three players in Central Asia but has nevertheless managed to secure a significant presence there. India desperately wants to ensure that these republics do not fall prey to militant Islam of the kind represented by the Taliban. At the same time, India also wishes to take a piece of the action in the areas of oil and gas. This it cannot do alone. The kind of partnerships it builds in the months and years to come will determine whether India can succeed in establishing a long-term foothold in Central Asia.

For the CARs, post-9/11 events have brought significant opportunities along with greater international attention as well. On the one hand, the CARs have gained support for the modernisation of their technological and economic infrastructure. On the other hand, threats from terrorism and religious revivalism have also brought them under great pressure to democratise their political structure and change over to a market economy. For the first time, the CARs are also seeking to establish their individual identity, moving away from the Russian zone of influence as well as the contemporary framework under which external powers treat the Central Asian region as a single entity.

## Notes

1. Gail Lapidus, Central Asia in American and Russian foreign policy after September 11, presentation – Central Asia and Russia: Responses to the war on terrorism (a panel discussion at the University of California, Berkley 29 October 2001) http://list-Socrates.Bekley.Edu/bsp/caucasus/articles/lapidus.2001-1029pdf.

2. Patrick Martin, US bases pave the way for long-term intervention in Central Asia, World Socialist website, January 2002, http://www.Wsws.Org/articles/2002/Jan.2002/base-J11.shtml.

3. *Izvestia*, Moscow, 16 May 2002.

4. Jean Christopher Peauch, 'Central Asia: US-Military Build-up Shifts Sphere of Influence', *REFRL*, Prague, 11 January 2002.

5. *The Times of Central Asia*, 13 January 2002.

6. *The New York Times*, 8 January 2002.

7. *The Washington Post*, 8 January 2002.

8. Yuri Chernogaev, *Kommersant*, Moscow, 14 March 2002.

9. Martha B Olcott, Central Asia, the calculus of independence, *Current History*, October 1995, p.338.

10. Fiona Hill 'Contribution of Central Asian Nations to the Campaign against Terrorism', Senate Committee on Foreign Relations, Sub-Committee on Central Asia and South Caucasus, The Brookings Institution, 13 December 2001, http://www.Brook.Edu/dybdocroot/views/testimony/hill/2001.1213.htm.

11. Bruce Pannier, 'Central Asia: Tajikistan, Kyrgyzstan: Balancing Relations with the West, Russia', *RFERL* Prague: 7 December 2001.

12. Igor Torbakov, 'Russia's Rivalry in Afghanistan with the Western Powers' *The Times of Central Asia*, 13 December 2001.

13. Ibid.
14. *News from Russia*, Vol. V, No. 12, 22 March 2002, p.1.
15. *News from Russia*, Vol. V, No. 16, 19 April 2002, p.4.
16. *News from Russia*, No. 13, 29 March 2002, pp.11–12.
17. *News from Russia*, No. 11, 15 March 2002, pp.7–8.
18. *News from Russia*, No. 3, 18 January 2002, p.16.
19. *News from Russia*, No. 12, 22 March 2002, p.10.
20. *News from Russia*, No. 3, 18 January 2002 p.13.
21. *News from Russia*, No. 4, 25 January 2002 p.13.
22. *Komsomolskaya Pravda*, Moscow, 30 January 2002.
23. V I Lenin, 'The Socialist Revolution and the Right of Nations to Self-Determination' *Lenin on the National and Colonial Questions*, Beijing: Foreign Languages Press, 1975, p.2.
24. Richard Pipes, *The formation of the Soviet Union*, Massachusetts: Harvard University Press, 1964, p.38–39.
25. Rogers Brubaker, *Nationalism Reframed*, Cambridge, Cambridge University Press, 1996, p.36.
26. UNDP, National Human Development Report of Tajikistan, http://www.undp.Org/rbec/nhdr/1996/Tajikistan/htm.
27. Joane Nagel and Susan Olzak, 'Ethnic mobilisation in new and old states: An extension of the Competition Model', *Social Problems*, Vol. 30, 1982, p.127–145.
28. A S Asimov, 'Rewriting Tajik History' *Tajikistan update*, http://www.angelfire.Com/sd/tajikistanuuupdate/art/html.
29. *The Times of Central Asia*, 01 November 2001.
30. Islam Karimov, *Uzbekistan on the threshold of the twenty-first century*, Cambridge, Mass, 1998, p.xv.
31. Daniel Fisher, Oil Companies Have Dreamt of a Trans-Afghan Pipeline. Are They Crazy Enough to Pull it Off Now?, *Forbes*, 2 April 2002.
32. Thomas Valasek, Terror and Oil in Central Asia, *CDI Weekly Defence Monitor*, Vol. 6, No. 18, 13 June 2002.
33. Gail Lapidus: op. cit.

34. Rashid Ahmed, 'Central Asian Elites Suddenly Shift into Revolt', *Eurasia Light*, 26 June 2002.
35. Igor Torbakov, Trends Towards Political Confrontation in Central Asian States Accelerating Since September 11, *Central Asian Perspectives*, 26 March 2002. http://www. Asiasource.Org/americacrisis/centralasia/torbakov.cfm.
36. Herbert Ellison and Bruce Acker, 'The New Russia and Asia 1991–1995', *Analysis*, Vol. 7, No. 1, June 1996, p.29.
37. *The Times of Central Asia*, 13 December 2001.
38. *Nezavisimaya Gazeta*, 23 August 2000.
39. Radio Free Europe/Radio Liberty, 15 June 2001, http://www.rferl.org/bd/ta/magazine/default.asp.
40. *Nezavisimaya Gazeta*, 4 July 1998.
41. Irina Zvyagelskaya, 'Central Asia and the Caucasus': New Geopolitics in Vitaly Naumkin (ed.), *Central Asia and Transcaucasia: Ethnicity and Conflict*, Westport: C T Greenwood Publishing Group, 1994, p.133.
42. Asoke Banerjee, Ethnicity, Geo-political Entity, *World Focus*, New Delhi, March–April 1993, p.5.
43. Iftikar Malik, 'Pakistan's National Security and Regional Issues: Politics of Mutualities with Muslim World', *Asian Survey*, Vol. XXXIV, No. 12, December 1994, p.1089–90.
44. Stephen Blank, Central Asia, South Asia and Asian Security, *Eurasian Studies*, Vol. II, No. 3, Fall 1995, p.12.
45. *The Times of India*, 28 September 2002.

# Chapter XIV

# ENERGY POLITICS IN THE CASPIAN REGION

Prof. Nirmala Joshi

## Introduction

Ensuring energy security is fast becoming one of the key concerns of the international community, particularly for the industrialised countries of the West. As the joint statement on the New US-Russian Energy Dialogue, May 2002, stressed: 'Successful development of the global economy depends on timely and reliable energy delivery.'[1] All economic activity hinges on access to energy and consequently securing this vital resource provides a powerful stimulus to a nation's policy and conduct. A case in point is the struggle to secure the energy resources of Central Asia and the Trans-Caucasus. Located around the Caspian Sea, Kazakhstan, Turkmenistan, Uzbekistan (not a Caspian Sea littoral) and Azerbaijan have enormous energy resources including oil, natural gas and hydrocarbons. The Caspian Sea basin too has vast, unexploited energy reserves.

The oil rush in the Caspian region began in the mid-1990s and since then the region has witnessed intense competition among the major powers to control this resource and influence the states. Not surprisingly, the race to control the energy resources of the region is being dubbed by many analysts as the twenty-first century's Great Game. What is interesting though, is the fact that the energy resources of the region have yet to reach the markets. Politics, rather than economic considerations, seems to be at the heart of the oil rush.

Central Asia's location is of enormous strategic significance: adjoining Russia in the north and China in the east, the Trans-Caucasus is the gateway to the Russian Federation from Europe. Turkey, a member of the North Atlantic Treaty Organisation (NATO), Iraq and Iran are its neighbours. Given the growing significance of Asia in international politics, and the region's geopolitical proximity to Afghanistan – the hub of international terrorism – the geopolitical significance of Central Asia is enormous. In the prevailing after the Iraq conflict scenario, new developments in the Persian Gulf region are expected to have an impact on Central Asia as well, which in turn will influence global policies towards the region. Energy is the key to the region's political and economic status and to understand the dynamics that are at play, an overview of the estimated energy wealth of the region is essential.

## Estimates of Energy Resources

Various studies offer different estimates of the total energy reserves in the Caspian region. According to Ariel Cohen, a well-known scholar at the Heritage Foundation, the region has possible deposits of 170.5 billion barrels while gas is estimated at 15.3 trillion cubic metre.[2] The Scottish firm, Wood Mackenzie, estimates the proven reserves at 26.01 billion barrels and 58.64 billion barrels of possible oil reserves[3] (see table). It has also been reported that the Caspian Sea basin could also contain energy deposits further enhancing the potential energy reserves of the zone. Though the reserves are not comparable to that of the Persian Gulf, estimated to be between 450 and 530 billion barrels, the region's energy resources constitute a significant source of good-quality oil and gas.

| Country | Billion Barrels | | | Trillion Cubic Feet | | |
|---|---|---|---|---|---|---|
| | Proven Oil | Possible Oil | Total Oil | Proven Gas | Possible Gas | Total Gas |
| Azerbaijan | 3.6–11 | 27 | 31–38 | 11 | 35 | 46 |
| Kazakhstan | 10–16 | 85 | 95–101 | 53–83 | 88 | 141–171 |
| Russia | 0.2 | 5 | 5.2 | NA | NA | NA |
| Turkmenistan | 1.5 | 32 | 33.5 | 98–155 | 159 | 257–314 |
| Uzbekistan | 0.2–0.3 | 1 | 1.2–1.3 | 74–78 | 35 | 109–123 |
| Iran | 0 | 12 | 12 | 0 | 11 | 11 |

*Note*: The energy wealth of Russia and Iran depicted in the table covers only their Caspian zones.
*Source*: Rajan Menon, 'Treacherous Terrain: The Political and Security Dimensions of Energy Development in the Caspian Sea Zone', *NBR Analysis*, Vol. 9, No. 1, February 1998, p.11.

Among the countries of the Caspian region, Azerbaijan and Kazakhstan are extremely rich in oil. Both countries also have sizeable deposits of natural gas. Medieval travellers have written about Azerbaijan's abundant supply of oil since the ninth century. Referred to as the Oil Capital of the region, Azerbaijan drilled its first oil well in 1846 in Bibi-Heyat.[4] Despite its long history of oil production, Azerbaijan has not prospected for new oil fields. Experts believe that there could be many unexplored oil fields in Azerbaijan's sector of the Caspian Sea. Its proven oil resources are 1.1 billion tonnes which translates into one million barrels per day (b/d). Potential oil resources are estimated at 3.5 billion tonnes.[5]

There are two major oil companies in Azerbaijan, the State Oil Company of the Azerbaijan Republic (SOCAR) and the Azerbaijan International Operating Company (AIOC), a joint venture led by British Petroleum (BP). However, Azerbaijan's oil sector has stagnated rather than progressed when compared to the development of oil production in neighbouring Kazakhstan. In Azerbaijan, total oil production for 2001 was 299,000 b/d while in Kazakhstan, it was expected to be 922,000 b/d by end-2002. Azerbaijan has only recently started developing its offshore gas deposits. The slow implementation of structural reforms is responsible for the country's tardy development in the oil sector.[6]

In contrast, Kazakhstan's proven oil reserves are ten billion barrels and potential reserves are estimated at a whopping eighty-five billion barrels. The country also has enormous reserves of gas: confirmed deposits are estimated at 2.5 trillion cubic metre while potential reserves are estimated to be in the region of four trillion cubic metre.[7] The Tengiz-Chevroli, a joint venture between American oil companies Chevron and Texaco, produced 250,000 b/d in 2001 at the Tengiz oil field in western Kazakhstan. Besides, Kazakhstan has three oil refineries. Despite the strides made by Kazakhstan in oil production, former prime minister, A Kazhegin, has stated that it would take another 10–12 years for the country to emerge as a major oil producer.

Turkmenistan also boasts of rich energy resources, particularly gas. With proven oil resources at 1.5 billion barrels and possible resources estimated at 32 billion barrels, Turkmenistan is expected to emerge as a significant player in the energy market. Gas resources, including proven and potential deposits, are estimated at 8.9 trillion cubic metre.[8] The country has ambitious plans for developing new gas deposits. A great deal of uncertainty, however, shrouds these plans as the business environment in Turkmenistan is not conducive to foreign investment.[9] In 2002, the country's oil and gas exports stood at 2.3 billion tonnes (46,000 b/d) and 37.2 billion cubic metres (3.6 billion cubic feet per day). A large chunk of these were exported to Russia and Ukraine while a limited quantity was exported to Iran through pipelines built during the Soviet regime. (*Source*: US Embassy in Ashgabat, Turkmenistan, quoting Turkmen government reports.)

Uzbekistan, though not a Caspian Sea littoral state, is considered to be a part of the Caspian Sea region. With confirmed oil deposits of 0.2 billion barrels and potential deposits estimated at 1 billion barrels, the country's energy wealth is modest. Natural gas deposits, both proven and possible, are estimated at 3.1 trillion cubic metre. The state-owned company, Uzbekneftgaz, handles the production of both oil and gas as well as their export. Since Uzbekistan's reserves are not substantial, its market comprises energy-resources-deficient neighbours, including Kyrgyzstan and Tajikistan. Uzbekistan's energy sector is plagued with problems of low pricing and defaulting customers. Russia and Ukraine are exploring investment opportunities in Uzbekistan's energy sector. However, the lack of currency convertibility and an unfavourable business climate have deterred Western investors from entering this sector.[10]

The Russian sector of the Caspian Sea is believed to be devoid of energy resources. However, recent geological surveys in the northern part of the Caspian which is rich in sturgeon fish – from which world-class caviare is obtained – have revealed modest quantities of oil. Siberia and the Russian Far East, in contrast, are rich in energy resources.

## The Pipeline Network

Transporting the energy from the region to the markets is the biggest challenge for the Central Asian countries. Since the region is landlocked and not located on major sea routes, the energy resources can only be transported through a network of pipelines that run across several countries. During the Soviet regime, the northern route was the only pipeline network that brought oil to the port city of Novorossisk on the Black Sea. In 1979, the Soviet Union started exploration of the massive Tengiz oil field. After gaining independence, the newly emergent independent states were keen to exploit their energy resources. Due to insufficient funds and lack of independent infrastructure facilities, the CIS states began inviting foreign investment to explore, exploit, develop and transport energy. This marked the entry of Western oil companies in the region.

In charting out the transport routes, four options were available to players in the energy sector:

- Rely on the old northern route via Russia up to Novorossisk and then carry the oil in tankers through the Black Sea and the Straits of Bosphorous to European markets. This would mean upgrading and modernising the Russian pipeline so that it could handle increased oil exports. This option would further give Russia tremendous leverage over the new republics.

- Create a new transport corridor in the west that would carry oil from Azerbaijan to Georgia by railway or to Turkey by a new pipeline. Western oil companies, supported by their governments, preferred this route as it sought to bypass Russia.

- Open up a southern channel from Turkmenistan to the Pakistani port of Gwadar via Afghanistan. This route would meet the demands of the Southeast Asian countries. The southern route could further be extended up to India.

- Create an eastern route to service the markets of China, Japan and South Korea. This project is being pursued quietly and without fanfare.

THE NORTHERN ROUTE

While the best option would be to use the Iranian corridor, as this would provide access to the Persian Gulf, this route is not favoured by the United States. Currently, only the northern route is functional. The Caspian Pipeline Consortium

(CPC), formed by Russia, Kazakhstan and Oman, in which American oil company Chevron-Texaco also has a stake, is operating successfully. Initially, Chevron exported Kazakh oil via barges in the Caspian Sea to Baku and from there by rail to the Georgian port of Batumi on the Black Sea. Tankers would then carry the oil to Turkey via the Black Sea route. Another alternative explored was a swap deal with Iran, whereby Kazakhstan would send oil to the northern part of Iran through the Caspian Sea, and in turn Iran would export an equivalent quantity of oil from its southern ports on the Persian Gulf.[11]

Subsequently, the CPC opted for the northern route, perhaps due to the strategic considerations of the main players, Kazakhstan and Russia. As is well known, Kazakhstan has a large population of Russians (approximately 34 per cent of its 16.74 million population) and it also shares a long border with Russia. Therefore, it would not be in Kazakhstan's interests to alienate Russia. The prospect of earning substantial transit revenues helped in winning Russian consent. The 1,580-km CPC network connects the Tengiz oil fields in Kazakhstan to Novorossisk on the Black Sea. Facilities at the port have also been expanded and modernised. Inaugurated in November 2001, the pipeline is equipped to transport 565,000 b/d.

THE WESTERN ROUTE

On 20 September 1994, SOCAR and a consortium of companies led by BP, signed a whopping three-billion-dollar contract for a thirty-year period which was popularly termed the 'contract of the century'. The plan was to build a transport route that would begin at Baku and go up to Ceyhan, a Turkish port on the Mediterranean Sea via Tbilisi, the capital city of Georgia (BTC). From Ceyhan, the oil would be transported to the European market. The projected export pipeline would be 1,750 km in length and its initial capacity would be 360,000 b/d which would later be expanded to one million b/d. The Russians applied pressure on Azerbaijan who agreed to transport oil to Novorossisk. The pipeline, formally launched in 1997, had its share of problems. The 140-km long Chechen sector of the pipeline is the most vulnerable due to unstable political conditions and high transit fees. The second pipeline from Baku to the Georgian port of Supsa on the Black Sea is relatively trouble-free. The 700-km long pipeline's capacity is 145,000 b/d.

Azerbaijan is pinning its hopes on the success of the BTC pipeline. After a lot of delay, the construction of the pipeline eventually began in September 2002 in Baku. President Geidar Aliyev of Azerbaijan hailed it as the 'triumph of independent Azerbaijan's oil strategy'. Transportation is expected to begin in 2005. The BTC will not only bypass Russia but will also avoid the tanker traffic congestion in the Straits of Bosphorous. The major challenge that the BTC is likely to face is the prospect of inadequate oil exports. This could be overcome if Kazakhstan and Russia join the BTC pipeline network to raise the volume of energy exports. The other problem is the pipeline's passage through the troubled Kurdish territory in Turkey.

## THE SOUTHERN ROUTE

The third route under consideration is the Trans-Afghan Pipeline (TAP). The two companies involved in this project are the US multinational Unocal and Delta of Saudi Arabia. Turkmenistan is eager to begin the project as it would reduce its dependence on Russia. The 1,270-km pipeline would transport Turkmen gas to Pakistan via Afghanistan. The pipeline could also be extended to India. But with political instability in Afghanistan, the project was put on the back burner. After the defeat of the Taliban, Turkmenistan has again revived the project and is seeking to involve

UNOCAL of the US and the World Bank. Turkmen President Saparmurat Niyazov has suggested that power and road networks be developed alongside the gas pipeline. The road network would lead to new job opportunities for unemployed Afghan youth and contribute to economic progress in that country. A framework agreement on the gas pipeline was signed by the heads of governments of Turkmenistan, Afghanistan and Pakistan in Ashgabat in the last week of December 2002. Turkmenistan hopes that American oil companies would once again come forward to invest in the pipeline project. India has also been invited to join the pipeline project. In fact, one of the priority items on President Hamid Karzai's agenda during his visit to India in March 2003 was to persuade India to join and support the gas pipeline project. So far, the Indian response has been lukewarm. However, on the question of building the Afghan road network, India has extended cooperation in terms of providing both material and expertise. Whether President Niyazov succeeds in fulfilling his aspirations is another question.

## Energy Politics

Despite the grandiose plans, progress on the pipeline network has been slow. The high cost of building such a network and the inability of the CAR governments to raise the requisite fund are the main reasons for the slow development of the region's energy sector. The intense competition among the Western countries – led by the US and the UK – and Russia for control of the region's energy resources has further slowed progress. Each group is competing to develop the route that would be the most beneficial to its own political and commercial interests. Besides, ethnic strife in South Caucasus and the spread of religious extremism in Central Asia have further complicated efforts to exploit the energy resources of the region. Perhaps the most significant barrier to the development of this sector is that there is no immediate urgency for Caspian Oil. American oil companies estimate that the need to exploit new reserves of energy would arise only after 10–15 years. This has also affected the progress of the Central Asian pipeline networks.

The political rivalry between Russia and the West has also led to the slow development of the CARs' energy sector. The origin of the rivalry dates back to 1993, when the Russian Federation enunciated its military doctrine. The doctrine highlighted that the threat to Russia emanated from local wars and regional conflicts due to the rise of nationalistic feelings based on ethnic and religious considerations. South Caucasus and Central Asia, on the Russian periphery, were identified as the main sources of tension. Historically, the border dividing South Caucasus and Russia has always been porous and border demarcation between Central Asia and Russia has always been nebulous. All through the Soviet period, its southern flank was perceived to be vulnerable and, therefore, protected at a great cost. With the break-up of the USSR, new borders came into existence. Given the volatile nature of politics on its southern perimeter, Russia perceived that the arc of instability in the region had the potential to destabilise Russia. Russian apprehensions were proved correct when the Chechen crisis erupted in 1994. The Chechen issue brought into sharp focus the issue of Russia's territorial integrity. In response to these developments, Russia proposed the idea of creating a belt of stability and security and extending goodwill among its neighbours. This clearly indicated that in the post-Soviet period, Russia was keen on retaining its century-old economic, political and cultural influence in its immediate neighbourhood. Also, it signified Russia's intention of being the sole guarantor of peace and stability in the region and an arbitrator in regional conflicts.

These developments were perceived in the West, particularly the United States, as Russian attempts to reintegrate the post-Soviet space into a Union or a Confederation. American analysts have often classified Russia as an unstable state. Some have even labelled it as a 'messy' and 'confused' state. Prof. Z Brzezinski, a reputed scholar, predicted further break-up of Russia in his book *The Grand Chessboard*. For such a state to aspire to greater power would spell chaos and conflict, analysts cautioned. To counter the Russian proposal, the US put forth the concept of 'geopolitical pluralism and multi-centrism'. In other words, the West also considered the post-Soviet space to be its area of special interest. The then deputy secretary of state Strobe Talbott spelt out the American view. According to Talbott, the countries of Caucasus and Central Asia should be independent, prosperous and secure. This would widen the area of stability in a strategically vital region that borders China, Turkey, Iran and Afghanistan. 'We believe that our presence and influence in the region can itself be a force for the right kind of integration,' declared Talbott.[12] The long-term objective of American policy was to bolster the position of Turkey as its regional ally. Perhaps, the US was trying to compensate the loss of its long-term ally Iran. The US sought to make the point that Russian policy vis-à-vis the region could not be exclusive but had to be inclusive.

The divergent approaches, reminiscent of Cold War attitudes, marked Russian and American policies towards the Caspian region during the mid-1990s. Russia, which no longer had the economic resources to support its policy, began to apply political pressure to gain influence in the region. In contrast, the US and its allies used economic resources to win new friends. It is in this context that the proposal of laying oil pipelines that bypass Russia to export oil out of the region assumes significance. As a result, for nearly a decade, the countries were under tremendous political pressure from the two rivals.

A virtual scramble ensued among Western oil companies, aided by their respective governments, to secure contracts and plan a network of pipelines that would bypass Russia. As Russian commentator Kondrashov pointed out: 'A pipeline across Turkey means not only financial losses, but a speedy drafting of a number of post-Soviet states away from Moscow to Ankara.' This would affect the stability of the regions within the Russian Federation.[13]

Unfortunately for Russia, the effort to reduce Russian influence in the region by the West found support among some post-Soviet states including Georgia, Azerbaijan and Uzbekistan, who were keen to distance themselves from Russia. Russia has had an uneasy relationship with these countries, which have been encouraged by the West to assert their independence. Although Georgia is not a producer of oil, it is a potential transport corridor that could help Western oil companies bypass Russian territory. Azerbaijan offered military base facilities to the US, primarily to protect the pipeline, but the offer was not taken up by the Americans.

The deal of the century, the Baku-Tbilisi-Ceyhan pipeline project, commenced in 1994 and the BTC was touted as the key driver of economic development in the Central Asian region, the Caucasus and Turkey. It was also a significant development, given the West's intention of limiting Russia's sphere of influence. As Ambassador Richard Morningstar, special advisor to the president and the Secretary of State for Caspian Basin Energy Diplomacy, remarked: 'Baku-Ceyhan will ensure that Turkey remains an integral player in the development of the Caspian energy resources. Turkey can play a stabilising role in the volatile regions of the Caucasus and Central Asia. Encouraging

Turkey is important not only from the US foreign policy perspective, but also to securing the immense investments now under consideration by private companies.'[14]

Russia has used the leverage it has in the region to prevent these countries from forging independent and close ties with the West. For instance, Georgian President Eduard Shevardnadze has charged Russia of periodically stoking the fire of ethnic conflict and causing trouble in Abkhazia. In September 2002, in his customary broadcast to the nation, President Shevardnadze said, 'The military tension between Georgia and Russia was not due to Russian concern about the Pankisi Gorge (where Chechen rebels take refuge), but due to Russian displeasure over the start of the construction of the BTC pipeline.'[15]

Similarly, the Azerbaijani leadership feels that the Nagorno-Karabakh conflict is kept simmering because of Russia's wholehearted support to Armenia. However, due to Russian pressure Azerbaijan agreed to export 'early oil' via the Baku-Novorossisk pipeline that became operational in 1997. In the initial stages of the CPC planning, Russia refused to allow Kazakhstan to use its existing network of pipelines. It was only after the offer of a higher transit revenue that Russia allowed the CPC to pass through its territory. Russia has objected to the CPC plan of constructing underwater pipelines in the Caspian Sea to provide adequate oil to the BTC pipeline. The Federal Energy Commission (FEC) of Russia wants to bring the CPC within its regulatory regime. This would allow the Russian government to set tariffs for oil firms wanting to use the pipeline. Many analysts feel that Russia has exaggerated the rise of Islamic extremism in Central Asia in order to keep its hold on the Central Asian countries. Thus, the Caspian region has witnessed an intense competition for control and influence. Well-known author Ahmed Rashid says:

Were the Americans supporting the Taliban either directly or indirectly through Unocal or their allies Pakistan and Saudi Arabia? And what was prompting this massive regional polarization between the USA, Saudi Arabia, Pakistan and the Taliban on one side and Iran, Russia, the Central Asian states and the anti-Taliban alliance on the other?... It became apparent to me that the strategy over the pipeline had become the driving force behind Washington's interest in the Taliban, which in turn was prompting counter reaction from Russia and Iran.[16]

## Energy Politics in the Post-9/11 Scenario

A decade after the end of the Cold War, a new trend has emerged in international relations. One of the characteristic features of this trend is the stress on greater cooperation among nations. It is a change from the earlier Cold War mindset of a zero-sum game and non-cooperation to further one's own national interests. Nations have chosen to cooperate because issues confronting mankind are global in nature. One such issue is international terrorism. The events of 9/11 have thrust terrorism on to the centre stage of international politics and national governments acknowledge that the phenomenon can only be fought globally. This paradigm shift in international relations and the fight against terrorism have accelerated the process. This is not to suggest that traditional rivalries or the importance of geopolitics are no longer relevant. Differences among nations do exist but they are not viewed in terms of a zero-sum game. Nor are they highlighted as was the case earlier. The characteristic feature of the present times is cooperation among rival nations.

In the post-9/11 scenario, cooperative spirit has come to the fore. This has brought about a radical shift in the nature of energy politics. Russia's willingness to extend full cooperation to the international coalition forces against terrorism has brought a sea change in the relations among major powers. Despite the disquiet in certain influential circles in Russia, the Russian leadership has permitted the Central Asian states to extend full cooperation, including military, to the coalition forces. Foreign Minister Igor Ivanov's remark that 'it is normal for CIS states to diversify their international ties and to seek out new trade and economic partners' suggests that Russia has adopted a new approach to the post-Soviet space. He adds, 'However, Russia will not tolerate attempts by third party states to act within the CIS in a way that undermines Russian interests, excludes Russia from participating or in any way weakens Russia's position.'[17]

The Western military presence in Afghanistan and Central Asia has, nevertheless, fundamentally altered the geopolitical situation in the region. Many analysts feel that the hidden agenda of American forces in Central Asia is to control the energy resources of the region and gradually reduce Russian influence. A report in the *Times of Central Asia* has referred to an allegation that the US has set up military bases in Central Asia only to push through the Afghanistan pipeline route. Once the pipeline is built, it would provide political as well as economic leverage for the US.

On its part, the US has realised that cooperation with Russia is essential in a region that is already turbulent. Clearly, Russia's century-old presence, clout and understanding of the region would be beneficial to the US in its campaign against terrorism. Moreover, the states of South Caucasus and Central Asia would need time to grow out of the Soviet mindset.

Even after a decade of independence, the region continues to be unstable. Poor governance and economic decline are among the major factors contributing to the instability. Religious extremism is the other major factor that has contributed to instability in Central Asia. Fortunately for the CARs, the region has traditionally preferred Sufism to radical Islam. Along with this, the traditional bent towards culture and learning, exposure to science and technology, education and women's emancipation during the Soviet era has inculcated a modern outlook among Central Asians. The large presence of Russians in the region has strengthened a secular view of society. Nevertheless, religious extremism continues to simmer below the surface.

The fears of a revival in militancy, in the scenario following the Iraq conflict, is another cause for worry. Militant groups, particularly those active in the Ferghana Valley, could get a new lease of life. Coupled with regional ethnic conflicts, this could further destabilise the region. Tensions between Russians and the local population have existed and the Nagorno-Karabakh conflict between Azerbaijan and Armenia often erupts in violent clashes. The Abkhazia and South Ossetia are troublesome ethnic issues for Georgia. In Central Asia, the traditional rivalry between Uzbeks and Tajiks continues to cause tensions.

The fight against terrorism promises to be a protracted one and US presence in the region is expected to be a long-term one. Coupled with regional instability, this could further exacerbate the situation. Russia has a major role to play in containing these tensions. In fact, the Russian decision to support the US campaign against terrorism is an obvious attempt by Russia to engage with the US on crucial issues such as resolving the Chechen problem and creating a conducive environment for economic cooperation. The US has acknowledged the positive role that Russia could play during US President George Bush's visit to Moscow in May 2002. Accepting Russia as a partner is in itself a huge change from the past when the US viewed Russia as a source of instability. The Joint Declaration on the New US-Russian Relationship stated, 'The era in which the

United States and Russia saw each other as an enemy or strategic threat has ended. We are partners and will cooperate to advance stability, security and economic integration.'[18] Further, the Declaration stated:

> In Central Asia and South Caucasus we recognize our common interest in promoting the stability, sovereignty and territorial integrity of all the nations of the region. The United States and Russia reject the failed model of 'Great Power' rivalry that can only increase the potential for conflict in those regions.[19]

The change in American perceptions about Russia has paved the way for a breakthrough agreement on energy security. The US is keen to get a steady supply of oil and reduce its dependence on the Middle East and therefore its vulnerability to price blackmail by the OPEC. The New US-Russian Energy Dialogue seeks to 'reduce volatility and enhance predictability of global energy markets and reliability of global energy supply'.[20] This would enable Russia to garner sizeable investment in its fuel and energy sectors and stabilize oil prices in the long-term while the US would be ensured of a steady supply of oil and non-fluctuating oil prices. American and Canadian companies have shown interest in setting up production and infrastructure capabilities. The Joint US-Russian Working Group on Cooperation in Energy has held two meetings so far. The new US-Russian Energy Dialogue is also likely to have an impact on the Caspian region with Russia emerging as the biggest competitor for the energy-rich countries of the Caspian region. President Haider Aliev welcomed the US-Russian summit meeting and said in Baku on 28 May 2002 that the various agreements signed during the US-Russian Moscow Summit would expedite significant positive changes in the global political situation. He particularly lauded the US-Russian Joint Statement on the South Caucasus and Central Asia.[21]

The Iraq conflict could however queer the pitch. The states of the Caspian region were hoping that the conflict could be averted and the issues at stake could be resolved peacefully so that they did not have to take hard decisions. The difficult choice was between Russia on the one hand and the US and its allies on the other. After the outbreak of the Iraq war, the positions of these states broadly reflected the regional alignments. Turkmenistan adhered to its foreign policy of neutrality and non-interference in military conflicts in foreign countries. It neither supported Saddam Hussein nor the anti-Iraq coalition. Turkmenistan's dilemma was understandable. During a visit to Iran, President Niyazov expressed hope that Iraq would be spared destruction, ruin and human tragedy that are natural consequences of a war. Meanwhile, reports suggest that President Niyazov is concerned about the increasing activity of radical Islamic groups along Turkmenistan's 600-km border with Afghanistan. At the same time, Turkmenistan fears that American financial support to the TAP would be disrupted.[22]

The conflict in Iraq also poses a dilemma for Kazakhstan. It has not expressed any opinion on the conflict, but is worried at the outcome of the conflict, as it could affect the Kazakh economy. The likely decline in oil prices from the existing US $19 per barrel is a cause for concern.[23] Uzbekistan has unambiguously declared its support to the US and the anti-Iraq coalition against Saddam Hussein. Azerbaijan and Georgia have extended support to the US and its allies as well.

In view of the US and British military superiority, the defeat of Saddam Hussein's forces was a foregone conclusion. Many analysts have opined that one of the objectives of the anti-Iraq coalition was to capture the Iraqi oil fields, ranked as the second largest producer of oil after Saudi Arabia. The states of the Caspian region are hoping that they will not be marginalised in the near future. Reports suggest that the BTC pipeline is likely to be affected because of the huge expenditure involved. There is a distinct possibility that the attention accorded to the region will decline. The main reasons for this would be the region's geographic location, the endemic ethnic strife and an expected rise in religious extremism. Nevertheless, the Caspian region would never go completely off Western radar screens as it constitutes a significant alternative for energy resources.

At another level, Russia is actively working to retain its influence over the region's economy. President Vladimir Putin has suggested the creation of an Eurasian Gas Alliance, modelled on the OPEC. The alliance could consist of gas-producing as well as gas-transporting countries, including Kazakhstan, Turkmenistan, Uzbekistan and Ukraine. Such an alliance would be able to effectively control gas production. President Putin's special envoy on Caspian issues, Viktor Kalyuzhny, pointed out that the 'gas alliance's objective is to derive mutual economic benefits. To this end, we must solve complex problems. We must choose basic gas fields for maintaining and building gas supplies, build new pipelines and repair those already in use and study the market.'[24] Turkmenistan has rejected the alliance because it fears that Russia could control its gas exports. Russia has also launched other multilateral initiatives. It has sought to institutionalise the Collective Security Treaty of 1992 into a regional organisation, the Collective Security Treaty Organisation.

As economies in transition, these countries realise that they cannot rely only on oil exports. In an attempt to diversify their sources of revenue, these states have sought to overcome the barriers that their landlocked geographical status pose, by constructing a network of transport corridors.

Two options are being pursued, albeit slowly. The first option is to open up a north-south corridor linking Kazakhstan via Turkmenistan with Iran. Russia is also interested in the north-south corridor as it would link western Siberia and adjoining regions with the outside world. The second option involves the Kyrgyz plan of reviving the old silk route. China is believed to be interested in this project. The transport corridor is expected to facilitate the task of upgrading and modernising the industries that the states have inherited from the Soviet Union. The region has an industrial infrastructure that caters to non-ferrous metals, mining, petro-chemicals, hydroelectricity, machinery, cotton-processing plants and food-packaging units. For the present, however, the Caspian countries would have to rely on energy exports for development. The desire to diversify the routes of transportation indicates their need for independence. It would also offer the Caspian countries space for manoeuvrability, vis-à-vis Russia.

## Options for India

Energy consumption in India is growing at 6 per cent annually. Oil imports account for nearly 60 per cent of India's total oil consumption and is projected to increase to nearly 70 per cent in the next five years. Presently, India's energy demands are met mostly by coal, which accounts for nearly 60 per cent of primary energy consumption. Oil is ranked second at 30 per cent and natural gas stands at 8 per cent. However, by 2010, the share of coal is expected to come down to nearly 50 per cent while that of natural gas is projected to increase to 12 per cent. The share of oil is expected to be around 40 per cent. By 2010, India will be a major importer of oil. Currently, India's energy needs are met primarily with imports from the Persian Gulf. Given the present uncertainty in the region, it is important for India to diversify its energy sources. Central Asia could emerge as a viable alternative for India. In this context, the TAP is perhaps the best option. India, however, is not favourably inclined towards the TAP. The hostility in India-Pakistan relations raises concerns about the viability of the TAP option. There are also doubts about Pakistan's ability to maintain law and order in its tribal areas through which the proposed pipeline would pass. The other big question mark is the political situation in Afghanistan. Recently, a new factor of uncertainty has been added, with Afghanistan raising the issue of the validity of the Durand Line between Pakistan and Afghanistan. According to press reports, Afghanistan President Hamid Karzai was in India during the first week of March 2003 to elicit support for the TAP project.

The other alternative would be to execute the tripartite agreement signed by Turkmenistan, Iran and India in February 1997. A pipeline network could be laid along this route. Later, Kazakhstan and Russia could utilise this route to export oil through barges to Iran or to construct a network from Russia to Turkmenistan via Kazakhstan. In January 2003, President Syed Khatami of Iran was in India to explore this project among other things. Reports suggest that a new transport corridor is being planned. India would help Iran develop a new port, Chah Bahar, on the Persian Gulf that would enable oil to be transported by rail through Afghanistan (Delaram) to Uzbekistan. This transport corridor when functional would give India access to Central Asia. In the present scenario, transporting Central Asian energy resources and other goods through Iran seems to be the best available option. Moreover, it would provide India some leverage in an area that is fast becoming crucial for the international community. Besides, Indian expertise in the development of infrastructure capabilities in the energy sector could be made available to the Central Asian countries.

## Conclusion

The energy-rich Caspian region has become the hub of international politics. Both the US and Russia are vying for political leverage in the region. The conflict in Iraq is putting a strain on the US-Russian partnership that was forged with the objective of fighting global terrorism and ensuring future energy security. While it is expected that Russia and the US will continue to collaborate against terrorism, the changed equations in the post-Iraq conflict could result in an inevitable winding down of interest in the Caspian region. Future political alignments and reality will determine how the players capitalise on the energy resources of the region.

## Notes

1. Bush-Putin Joint Statement on New US-Russian Energy Dialogue, 24 May 2002. Issued by the International Information Programmes of the US Department of State.
2. Ariel Cohen, PhD Testimony before the Subcommittee on Asia and Pacific, United States House of Representatives, 17 March 1999.
3. R Hrair Dekmejian and Hovann H Simonian, *Troubled Waters: The Geopolitics of the Caspian Region*, London: I B Tauris, 2001, p.32.
4. Quoted in R G Gdadhubli, 'Oil Politics in Central Asia', *Economic and Political Weekly*, 30 January 1999.
5. Economic Intelligence Unit, Country Reports for Azerbaijan, May 2002, p.29.
6. Ibid., p.76.
7. Ariel Cohen, PhD Testimony before the Subcommittee on Asia and Pacific, United States House of Representatives, 17 March 1999.
8. Ibid.
9. Economic Intelligence Unit, Country Reports for Turkmenistan, June 2002, p.25.
10. Economic Intelligence Unit, Country Reports for Uzbekistan, September 2002, p.28.
11. R G Gidhadhubli, 'Oil Politics in Central Asia', *Economic and Political Weekly*, 30 January 1999, p.262.
12. *Strategic Digest*, September 1997, pp.1378–1383.
13. S Kondrashov, *Izvestia*, 3 December 1997; Reproduced by *Daily Review*, Moscow, 15 December 1997.
14. Ambassador Richard Morningstar's address to CERA Conference, Washington DC, 7 December 1998.
15. *Current Digest of Post-Soviet Press*, Vol. 54, No. 38 (2002), pp.15–16.

16. Ahmed Rashid, *Taliban, Islam Oil and the New Great Game in Central Asia*, London, 2002, p.163.
17. Igor S Ivanov, *The New Russian Diplomacy*, Washington DC, 2002, p.87.
18. Bush-Putin Joint Declaration on New US-Russia Relationship, Moscow, 24 May 2002. Issued by the International Information Programs of the US Department of State.
19. Ibid.
20. Bush-Putin Joint Statement on New US-Russian Energy Dialogue. Issued by the International Information Programs of the US Department of State.
21. Radio Free Europe/Radio Liberty, 29 May 2002, www.rferl.org/newsline/2002/05/290502.asp.
22. *Times of Central Asia*, 27 March 2003.
23. Ibid.
24. Viktor Kalyuzhny, 'Caspian Oil and Gas and Russia's Interests', *Commersant*, No. 29, in *Daily Review*, 19 February 2002.

# SECTION FOUR
## India and Central Asia

# Chapter XV

# INDIA JOINS THE GREAT GAME: INDIAN STRATEGY IN CENTRAL ASIA

Dr Stephen Blank

## The Changing Indian Policy

Confounding earlier charges of a 'directionless' foreign policy in Central Asia, India has unquestionably joined the great game there.[1] Whereas other powers, in and around Central Asia, particularly Russia, had previously discerned India's hesitancy regarding Central Asia that is no longer the case.[2] India's regional strategy is active and utilises all the tools of classical and modern statecraft. Indeed, even by 2000 some media reports and foreign observers had begun to detect a greater focus and coherence to Indian strategies.[3] As India has developed a growing arsenal of economic, political, and military policy instruments for use in Central Asia, most observers maintain that Indian policies and relationships in and around Central Asia have become much more coherent.[4]

The war on terrorism clearly accelerated this pre-existing trend because India already confronted terrorism emanating from Afghanistan and Pakistan.[5] In other words, India's policies and overall strategy in Central Asia cannot be considered apart from its rivalry with Pakistan, and even to some degree China. But Indian policy is not exclusively based on those parameters of its strategy. For example, we must consider its relations with Moscow and Washington as well.

India's growing interest in Central Asia is not confined merely to the linked threats of terrorism, separatism, drug trading, and incitement to civil violence. It also has deep and long-standing strategic and economic roots. Central Asia has newly and definitively entered into the 'mental map' of India's sphere of interests.[6] During the 1990s India sought to reduce Pakistan's ability to deflect it from playing the broader Asian role India craved by reaching out to all its interlocutors, including Central Asia.[7] Retired Brigadier General V K Nair, a leading strategist, told the US National Defense University in 2001:

> India needs to evolve a broad-based strategy that would not only ensure the security of its vital interests but also provide policy options for effectively responding to developing situations in the area. India's geostrategic location dictates that the primary focus of its security policies must be its relationship with the neighbouring countries and the countries that form part of its 'extended security horizon' which in one official publication is defined as 'regions with economic, social, cultural, and environmental linkages [that] result in overlapping security interests.'[8]

Central Asia is explicitly and widely cited as part of this 'horizon'.[9] This policy, called the Gujral doctrine after the then Foreign Minister (and later prime minister) I K Gujral, maintained that India, as the dominant regional power, should unilaterally grant its neighbours trade and economic concessions without expecting strict reciprocity.[10] He expected that this would foster improved political and economic relations thereby strengthening the reach of Indian economic power and political influence. This major policy innovation grew out of the vacuum created by the Soviet Union's dissolution and the pressure of globalisation along with the so-called Washington consensus in liberalising much of India's quasi-socialist economy, particularly as China's rise became too palpable to ignore. As Kishore Dash recently wrote:

> Such a paradigmatic shift in India's regional policy can be explained by post-Cold War global political-economic developments. Indian leaders well know that the success of their country's [concurrent] economic liberalisation depends upon its ability to increase exports to new markets in developed and developing countries. Until recently, India has achieved only restricted access to the markets of Japan, North America, and Western Europe due to these countries' projectionist policies and various kinds of non-tariff barriers against Indian products. Additionally, with the collapse of the Soviet Union and the gradual incorporation of Eastern Europe with the West European economy, India has lost two if its privileged market links.[11]

India suffered a tremendous decline in its trade with Central Asia during 1991–94 that highlighted its faltering competitiveness with an already reformed China.[12] Indeed, observers of Chinese policy were quick to note China's exploding economic and political ties with Central, South, and South-East Asia.[13] Thus the appearance of Islamic terrorism abetted by the Taliban (and behind it Pakistan) strengthened a rising disposition to see in Central Asia an area where important interests were at stake. Simultaneously, India's official threat assessment long predated the new policy in Central Asia. Already in 1997 Russia's press reported that in private Indo-Russian diplomatic conversations, 'Russian and Indian diplomats willingly open the cards: both Moscow and New Delhi see a threat in the excessive strengthening of China and the Islamic extremists.'[14]

Not surprisingly, many Indians now view China as India's current and long-term main rival and threat and see Central Asia in terms of that rivalry too. US analysts in communication with Indian elites before 11 September 2001 observed that one of the major negative consequences of Russia's decline has galvanised Indian apprehensions about Central Asia. Specifically:

> Russian weakness in Central Asia compounds India's immediate and long-term problems there. In the short term, the chaos in Afghanistan and parts of Central Asia over which Russia might once have exerted a strong restraining influence is now free to spread, and most Indians believe – correctly it appears – that it will spread southward, infecting Pakistan and, eventually, possibly India's large northern Islamic population. In the longer term, Russian weakness in the core of Central Asia creates a vacuum, especially in energy-rich Kazakhstan, into which China will expand. Among Indian strategists, one frequently hears the term 'encirclement' by China, and they view Central Asia as a part of the top of a China-dominated circle of states that includes most of Southeast Asia, Burma, Bangladesh, and Pakistan. In this sense Indian national security specialists believe that Russia's weakness encourages India's encirclement.[15]

Central Asia's large gas and oil reserves and India's rising demand for energy sources also suggested a naturally complementary relationship. This concern is even more compelling because India, like other rising Asian economies, cannot accept excessive dependence on energy flows from the Persian Gulf which are subject to periodic and recurring crises and threats of oil cut-offs. Similarly, India's overland trade with Central Asia is subject to forcible interruptions. When crisis engulfed Indo-Pakistani relations in 2001–02, Pakistan closed its air space to Indian trade, holding India's Central Asian trade hostage to Pakistani policy.[16] Therefore, increased terrorism has economic as well as strategic consequences and could also force India to retract its broader economic-political ambitions and curtail its rising trade with Central Asia. Paradoxically, this threat sharpened India's focus on Central Asia and the identity of Indian economic and strategic interests there.

India's new policies also evoke British imperial perspectives when the great game referred to British apprehensions about Russia's seemingly inexorable advance through Central Asia. Great Britain then discerned the need to control the overland route through Central Asia and Afghanistan to the North-west Provinces (now Pakistan) or through Iran and the maritime approaches through the Indian Ocean.[17] India's contemporary Central Asian strategy demonstrates this lesson's abiding relevance since Indian planners believe they must influence terrestrial and maritime trends in and around Central Asia. Indeed, two key Indian objectives are to deny Pakistan and China, its key rivals and threats, opportunities to increase their strategic capability by gaining predominant influence in Central Asia or by threatening India's assets there. Enhancing Indian influence in the region equates to a strategy of strategic denial.

Instability in Central Asia and Afghanistan, often linked to the Taliban and behind it Pakistan's intelligence service, the Inter Services Intelligence Agency (ISI) became a potent source of recruits and resources for Pakistani-sponsored terrorism in Kashmir and even North-east India. This policy directly continues and grows out of Pakistan's support for the Afghan Mujahiddeen in the 1980s.[18] The foregoing considerations inevitably oblige India to play a major role in Afghanistan and beyond lest Indian influence throughout Central Asia be marginalised while others try to create their own spheres of influence there.[19] Since instability in Afghanistan is likely to engulf Central Asia and Kashmir, India seeks to stabilise the new Afghanistan, establish ties with the Pushtun majority so that it will not relapse into an anti-India stance, and help it find a modus vivendi with the new Karzai government. These objectives certainly explain the substantial aid that India provided to Hamid Karzai's government in Afghanistan and its efforts to help it find trade routes that avoided excessive dependence upon Pakistan.[20] Thus India's support for Afghanistan, albeit expressed in economic terms, is fundamentally strategic in conception, namely to deny Pakistan an Afghan 'strategic hinterland' from which to strike at its interests.

Indian strategists also openly invoke those old strategic and realpolitik perspectives in its quest for regional hegemony. In 1979, Admiral A K Chatterji (retired) wanted 'a force equal in size and competence to the naval forces of any one of the superpowers now formally operating in the area.'[21] Defence Minister George Fernandes said in 2000 that India having 'high stakes in the uninterrupted flow of commercial shipping, the Indian Navy has an interest in the ocean space extending from the north of the Arabian Sea to the South China Sea.'[22] Others talk of denying outside forces an autonomous capacity to act in the Indian Ocean.[23] Not surprisingly, observers discern a growing Indo-Chinese naval rivalry in South-East Asia and the Indian Ocean since China's growing maritime reach has aroused much Indian concern.[24] Indian naval building in and around Pakistan's port of Gwadar also certainly intends to counter Chinese interest in the Indian Ocean as China is investing heavily in Gwadar's development.[25] India also hopes to wage economic war on Pakistan by restricting the development of trade from Central Asia through that port.[26]

Similarly, America's recent success in projecting naval-based air power from the Indian Ocean to Afghanistan and now more recently to Iraq is not lost on Indian planners. India's naval programme and ambitions in the Indian Ocean apparently validate the long-standing recognition that India could increasingly project power beyond its borders.[27] Hence economic needs and the impetus for a big navy go together.

Critics also charge India with aspiring to regional hegemony, seeking other regional actors' acquiescence in this role, and inducing the great powers to tolerate it.[28] Therefore, India's policies in and towards Central Asia are inevitably linked to its rivalries with Pakistan and China. Since India sees itself as South Asia's rightful *hegemon* and regards ethnic violence and sub-state conflict in Kashmir and Central Asia as threats to its integrity and vital interests, these assessments are not wholly misplaced. Indian analysts in 1997 discerned four linked threats arising from the violence across Central Asia, including Afghanistan and Kashmir.

Instability in Afghanistan in the past two decades has produced a new set of challenges to India's security interests. The most obvious implications arise from the extension of the arc of instability to newer areas. The easy availability of sophisticated arms and a growing number of mercenaries available for destabilisation take on monstrous proportions. In Jammu and Kashmir there has been in the past few years a marked increase in the number of Afghan war veterans from different parts of the world. These veterans, who have become mercenaries, have now joined several Kashmiri militant outfits.

The second consequence of the Afghan situation has been the spread of the Kalashnikov culture and drug addiction into India.

The third implication for India arising from the Afghan situation is the question of people-to-people contact. These ties present a historic opportunity for India to improve its economic presence in Afghanistan whenever peace returns to the country.

The fourth implication that flows from the earlier one is that Afghanistan will always be a battleground for Pakistan in negating Indian influence. The quest for strategic depth as well as to deny India an entrepôt into Central Asia via Afghanistan will make the Indo-Pak rivalry for influence in

Afghanistan of paramount importance. But the logic of being uneasy neighbours because of the Pushtunistan problem and the landlocked character of the country was thought to have ensured Kabul's neutrality, at the very least in terms of Indo-Pak hostility. But with the opening up of the Central Asian Republics, any regime in Kabul now has greater options to get around the Pakistan embargo.[29]

Obviously, the Taliban were bitterly hostile to India but the validity of this interpretation is clear when one considers that almost the first act of the new Karzai regime in Afghanistan was to solicit economic assistance from India thereby cementing ties with it.[30]

The Gujral doctrine simultaneously softened and built upon Indira Gandhi's South Asian doctrine based on internal conflict in Sri Lanka, stating that while it would not intervene in foreign states' internal conflicts, it would not tolerate an outside power's intervention against Indian interests.[31] India's rising interest in Central Asia and in seeing it in ways linked to rivalry with Pakistan expand this tendency. After all if Central Asia is part of the 'extended neighbourhood', New Delhi must include it in what increasingly seems to resemble an Indian version of the Monroe Doctrine. Sub-state fighting in Afghanistan, Central Asia, much of it instigated by Pakistan's government or the ISI, likewise evokes a strong desire to prevent a critical strategic zone from being overrun by anti-Indian regimes who could then threaten India itself.[32]

## The Strategic Context

Violence in Central and South Asia dominates India's policy and strategy-making environment. Because these conflicts are inseparable from the possibility of interaction with either conventional theatre scenarios like the 1999 Kargil fighting or earlier Indo-Pakistani wars, or even escalation to nuclear war with Pakistan, these three levels of possible and even actual war represent the three basic levels of India's security concerns.[33] These military contingencies must be assessed within a framework of constantly evolving but system-defining relationships among India, Pakistan, China, and Russia at the regional level of South and Central Asian politics and Sino-Russo-American relations at the global level.[34] Similarly, India's growing military ties with the United States must also be seen as an effort to gain military skills and a lasting tie with Washington that may pay dividends beyond South Asia.

Thus, Central Asian security is fully implicated in South Asian and broader Asian security rivalries as well as in Russo-American, Iranian, and Turkish policies. As this author has written, Central Asia's security parameters include South Asia, the Middle East, and the Far East.[35] Obviously this fact magnifies the importance of India's interests in Central Asia. India has supported America's military presence there to the extent that the former foreign minister Mr Jaswant Singh said that now America could not give up its bases there and should even maintain its military presence in Pakistan indefinitely to sustain local stability.[36]

Indeed the connection between the former Soviet Union and South Asia also applies to Pakistan. Pakistan has already begun military collaboration with Azerbaijan, selling conventional arms abroad, and has proliferated WMD technology.[37] Like India, Pakistan links together economic and broader strategic objectives there. Although Pakistan's relative lack of economic competitiveness obliges it to rely more on the military instrument of power than on economics, Pakistan's media linked bilateral military agreements with Azerbaijan in 2001 with the growth of economic relationships with that country and other Caspian states. The Urdu language paper *al-Akhbar* observed:

The recent developments that have taken place between Azerbaijan and Pakistan indicate that relations among the region's countries are becoming more multidimensional. In particular, Pakistan's trade relations with the Central Asian states have witnessed new warmth. It is also important for Pakistan to access Central Asian states because of the fact that it (Pakistan) lies directly on the route that leads to Central Asia. Moreover, outside countries will have to get permission from Pakistan to access the corridor to the Central Asian states. Pakistan will certainly have more chances to improve its economic condition by providing this corridor facility. In this regard, not only for Azerbaijan, it will be beneficial for Pakistan to develop close relations with other Central Asian countries.[38]

Not surprisingly India has followed suit, offering economic deals, military assistance, and arms sales to Uzbekistan, Tajikistan, and Kazakhstan, even buying Ilyushin-78 flight refuelling aircraft from Uzbekistan, and obtaining a base in Tajikistan.[39] Hence Indian policies must also be understood in the context of its aspiration to dominate the Indian Ocean militarily and the need to assert its presence in Central Asia.[40]

The violence in and around Central and South Asia that predated 11 September 2001 provided India with compelling strategic reasons for expanding its influence in Central Asia. Since Kashmiri terrorism, insurgency in North-east India, and Islamic insurgencies in Central Asia stem from Pakistan's wager on Islamic self-assertion and self-projection as an Islamic state and torch-bearer, India obviously felt it had to present itself to Central Asian states as a provider of stability and security whose power is essential to maintaining those objectives.[41]

Local governments must accordingly assess the potential for conflicts in Central and South Asia to connect with each other and become a factor for possible escalation of those conflicts. Any of these conflicts – Indo-Pakistani hostilities, Tajikistan's barely terminated civil war, and the war on terrorism inside Afghanistan – could join with the others and/or trigger new conflicts, e.g. terrorism in Central Asian states and/or Indo-Pakistani proxy wars in Central Asia.[42] Therefore, it is unclear whether Central Asia could escape the actual or political fallout of a potential Indo-Pakistani conflict. Indeed, security actors in each side of the Central-South Asian relationship and foreign observers publicly postulate the reciprocal relationship of war and peace in both areas.[43] This consideration gives Central Asia's leaders excellent reasons for trying to persuade the major powers to sign a treaty making Central Asia a nuclear-free zone.[44]

India's threat perception is well founded. Just as India's ties with the Soviet Union were 'determined by the historic divide on the subcontinent between Hindus and Muslims, which led to the partition of British India', the break-up of the Soviet Union made that Hindu-Muslim divide a prime conditioning factor for Indo-Russian and Indo-Central Asian relations.[45] The ensuing endless conflicts there now appear as both state-sponsored and self-motivated terrorism, either of which could escalate to more classical forms of conventional war and perhaps even into nuclear war. Indian analysts have long worried that Pakistan, if successful in Central Asia, could organise those forces for a campaign to foment unrest and separatism in India.[46] K Subrahmanyam, former director of India's Institute of Defence Studies and Analysis and a leading Indian strategist, writes that since 1983 India and other states have faced covert external aggression that has eroded the distinction between external and internal security threats and made covert internal war a legitimate foreign policy instrument.[47]

Foreign interventions now use men including mercenaries, drugs, money, and weapons purchased from abroad or territorial sanctuary, as a weapon of war. Foreign regimes can and do deliberately incite restive ethnic minorities across the border to paralyse domestic security or organised crime can become an instrument of transnational subversion. Such covert war is a cost-effective way to subvert, fragment, and destabilise host countries. It permits those launching the war to maintain strong conventional defences against the target to prevent it (which may be a stronger conventional power) from retaliating and winning a quick, decisive victory.

High and low-tech capabilities accompany each other as part of an overall strategy of protracted war where information warfare and the revolution in military affairs also play very useful roles.[48] Alternatively, the launching state may be too weak to prevent transnational ethnic and/or criminal movements from using it as a base for prosecuting such strategies and conflicts. These elements penetrate the weak state, hide behind its conventional might, and obtain sanctuary for their activities. Pakistan exemplifies this case, making its own destabilisation a constant danger given its support for terrorism, the entrenchment of political Islam in its schools and society, and those groups' linkage with drug running that gives them an enduring financial stream to destabilise Pakistan and its neighbours.[49] Indeed, American diplomats recently had to admit that the ISI has been substantially involved in drug running for years. Likewise, elements in Pakistan's opposition are harbouring Al Qaeda elements, possibly including Osama bin Laden himself.[50]

## Other Factors of Indian Strategy

India's strategy for projecting its influence and power into Central Asia also derives from factors beyond its ongoing low-intensity war with Pakistan to include economic globalisation and the Soviet collapse. The former trend fosters technological diffusion that allows India and Pakistan to become producers of weapons for export. India has opened its defence plants to foreign investors and seeks joint production deals, and not only with Russia.[51] The Soviet collapse opened Central Asia to foreign penetration and created independent states that needed to reach out to others. Pakistan subsequently sought to capture preferential economic positions there and appeal to Central Asia on religious grounds but failed. It then deliberately sponsored the Taliban and various terrorist and drug-running groups, obliging India to counter the threats of a destabilisation of Central Asia and of rising Pakistani influence there.[52]

Since India had always enjoyed good relations with Afghanistan while Pakistani elites had viewed Afghanistan as a strategic hinterland for conducting the struggle with India, Afghanistan has always been and remains part of the general Indo-Pakistani rivalry in South Asia and a cockpit of great-power rivalry.[53] Therefore, New Delhi's newly improved good relations with and economic assistance to the Karzai government in Afghanistan represents another round in South and Central Asia's abiding game of inter-state relationships. Indeed, Pakistani media reports stated that America sent India a demarche to restrain its activities in the new Afghanistan.[54] Similarly, Central Asian states came to see India as a potential ally, supporter, investor, and bulwark against Pakistan or Pakistan-inspired Taliban and terrorist intrigues.[55]

The election of the nationalist BJP in 1998 confirmed and accelerated India's movement away from Nehruvian concepts of non-alignment and international moralism towards a hard-headed realism that proclaimed India's far-ranging strategic aspirations from Suez to Singapore and perhaps beyond. The pursuit of prestige and security were and remain integral elements of BJP policy as expressed in India's nuclear tests in 1998 and subsequent efforts to construct a full-fledged nuclear triad and a robust conventional force modernisation. This modernisation entails acquiring and developing a serious power projection capability and a close military-political relationship with Russia, India's leading foreign supplier, that is essential to both governments' Central Asian strategy.[56] This relationship lets Moscow shift some of its burdens in Central Asia to friendly India and balance China's well-known aspirations. It also subsidises Moscow's ailing defence industries and reconfirms an earlier strategic relationship whose rationale transcends fighting the common enemy of Islamic terrorism.[57] This relationship underscores an important feature of Russia's overall policy in Central Asia, the search for partners who would help it realise common objectives there while lightening its burden of trying to stabilise the region. India's participation in this aspect of Russian policy goes back to attempts to have India participate in mediating Tajikistan's civil war of 1992–97.[58]

Arms sales and technology transfers greatly strengthen India's regional position. India's indigenous arms industry can produce and export sophisticated weapons to amortise its costs of production and extend Indian influence. Here India emulates the basic trend of globalisation as it affects major arms producers and even secondary or new producers like Israel, Turkey and Pakistan.[59] Globalisation allows them to develop their indigenous military technology. As the arms business has become a buyers' market they can compel sellers with superior technologies and skills to build factories in their countries and transfer skills, technology and know-how to them. India has exploited that trend to diversify its arms imports.[60] Russia is no longer India's sole provider of weapons and technology. India has recently signed major arms deals with France, Israel and the United States and is negotiating new ones that will clearly enhance its capabilities for conventional war and power projection into Central Asia.[61]

Accordingly, India's rising economic and military power lets it improve relations with an amazing number of major regional players, even mutually hostile ones like Iran and Israel. This 'omnidirectional foreign policy' partly stems from India's rising power potential but also from its shared interests with Israel and Turkey in fighting Islamic terrorism, rivalry with Pakistan in Afghanistan, concern for the stability of Central Asia, and access to advanced arms sales from France, America, and Israel.[62]

India's economic and political attractiveness to China and its importance have risen because China has grown more concerned that the warm Indo-US relationship might foster a US-backed and Indian-supported encirclement of China that stifles Beijing's aspirations. Increasingly, China discerns an expansionist trend in Indian thinking and policy that it seeks to curtail lest India threaten its ambitions and join with Washington, militarily and politically.[63] Consequently, China has become more responsive to India, displayed its new appreciation of India's importance, sought an improved relationship with New Delhi, and shown increased apprehension over Pakistan's support for terrorism.[64] Perhaps most importantly, China agreed before 11 September 2001, and again in December 2002, to take seriously Russia's long-standing proposals for a strategic triangle with India against Islamic terrorism in Central Asia and US interventions abroad.[65] However, this has not stopped Chinese proliferation to Pakistan which rates high on India's grievances with China.[66]

India's strategic capability is also based on a rapidly growing economy with a significant and well-known high-tech component that seeks markets and guaranteed energy supplies to sustain this growth. India's energy deficit, rising domestic demand, and need to sustain high growth rates make securing reliable long-term sources of energy a vital strategic priority.[67] The pursuit of energy sufficiency and markets in Asia impels Indian leaders to look seriously at Central Asia, East Asia, and the Middle East and to attempt to influence trends there. Indian economic power also makes it an attractive economic partner. Russia seeks Indian investment in Russia and obtained India's help in investing in the Sakhalin oil project with Japan and the United States while expanding India's access to energy supplies.[68] This investment also shows India's determination to play a key role in East Asia, improve ties with Japan, gain expanded access to oil sources abroad, including Central Asia and the Gulf, and explore offshore options near India.[69]

Thus India also invests in energy-producing fields in Central Asia, especially Kazakhstan. It also holds the deciding voice as to whether the projected Turkmen-Afghan-Pakistani pipeline will materialise. Although it would greatly benefit all those states, offering Turkmenistan an alternative to Russia's pipeline system and offering Pakistan and Afghanistan energy and revenues from transit fees, there are considerable economic and political difficulties. Those difficulties are not solely connected to the many political imponderables in all three of those states and Pakistan's rivalry with India. Financing remains unsettled because political instability precludes a stable climate for investment by the Asian Development Bank and other interested institutions.[70] But while India would be the main consumer of gas flows from this pipeline, it was not invited to the 2002 meetings in Ashgabat that formulated the new proposal and has refused to tie its gas supply to a pipeline through Pakistan.[71] Clearly India's decision will materially affect economic and political outcomes in the other three states.[72]

Although economics and strategy come together in India's vision of influencing trends from Suez to Singapore, including Central Asia, when it invokes this vision India also sees the lengthening shadow of China's spectacular ascent. While rivalry with China animates much of India's overall Asian policy, in Central Asia it appears as the other side of Russia's continuing crisis.[73] In that context the Shanghai Cooperation Organisation (SCO) involving defence against terrorism in Central Asia is the first sign of China's willingness to project military power abroad.[74] Undoubtedly India noticed that aspect of the SCO and that may be one reason for India's interest in joining it and for discussing a strategic triangle with China and Russia.[75]

Since China's rise to power generated concern in Washington, the Clinton and Bush administrations have responded since 1998 by forging closer military-political cooperation with India. Washington now sells weapons to India and is upgrading bilateral military collaboration with India across the board.[76] It is also using Indian Ocean bases with active Indian support.[77] While Washington's allure has recently diminished because it has endeavoured to keep Pakistan as an ally in the war on terrorism, Indo-American relations are at their highest point in years.[78]

At the same time trends within Central Asia have encouraged those states to approach India themselves. Russia sought India's involvement in a solution to the Tajik civil war in 1994.[79] Russia and India also have set up joint working groups to deal with terrorism as a common threat to themselves. Simultaneously, Central Asian states see India as an essential market, investor, and security provider as they confront multiple local threats.[80] Hence some of them have announced support for India's membership in the SCO.[81]

## Instruments and Objectives

Economic power, diplomacy and improved military capabilities constitute India's three main instruments for projecting power into Central Asia. On a daily basis, economic power is perhaps the most important and not just because it is the indispensable prerequisite for advanced military capability and for offering other states inducements to cooperate with India. More importantly, as Indian analysts recognise, India's rising economic profile is transforming India and its neighbourhood, impelling Indian leaders to rethink India's strategic requirements and goals while presenting them with new problems, opportunities, and instruments for dealing with them.[82]

Gujral noted in 1997 that much of India's foreign policy revolves around economic and infrastructural needs.[83] He outlined a vision of regional economic development including Central Asia which he called 'our near abroad'. Gujral emphasised investment in infrastructure: railway, roads, power generation, telecommunications, ports and airports, informatics, cross-border investments, energy exchanges, up to and including 'Trans-Asian pipelines', strengthened regional organisations, tariff reductions and free trade, and meeting 'an exponential surge in energy demand' through the cooperative development of all forms of energy.[84] Indian businessmen are clearly eager to compete with China in the region and exploit opportunities for expanding overland commerce with Central Asia provided that the trade routes go through pacified countries. As S Frederick Starr, director of Johns Hopkins Central Asia Caucasus Institute observed:

> The opening of transport corridors to Iran, Pakistan and India will dramatically shift these dynamics (China's rising share of Central Asian trade-author). Indian and Pakistani businessmen and traders are quite blunt about their desire to supplant China as a source of goods for Central Asia. Both countries have assigned governmental commissions to explore the development of transport to bring this about.[85]

Obviously hopes for greater trade and Gujral's vision would collapse if Central Asia including Kashmir were engulfed in anti-Indian violence. Then sustaining India's economic development and internal security becomes much more problematic. Thus international trade factors are a compelling motive for resolving the Kashmir issue.

To realise Gujral's policy vision India must overcome its obstacles. Domestically, this requires continuing economic liberalisation and privatisation of former state-owned sectors of the economy. This also compensates for the loss of Soviet arms subsidies during 1955–91. Without those subsidies and facing China's competition, India had to liberalise its economy and develop major export markets among all its Asian partners and the United States.[86] Indian strategy also entails further exploration of India's interior and off-shore regions for energy, investment of domestic resources in them, and welcoming foreign investors, e.g. Russia's Gazprom.[87] India has developed a three-part foreign economic programme to materialise this vision. First, its state-owned Oil and Natural Gas Company (ONGC) now invests in foreign oil and gas fields across Central Asia to even include Sakhalin. India also aims to assert itself as a major player throughout Asia and cement political ties with key states.

This is the second component of its foreign economic policy and diplomacy. Indeed with respect to Uzbekistan, Russia, Kazakhstan, and Iran these two policy dimensions march together. For example, Indian and Russian policy makers both accept that the strong bilateral political relationship is insufficient without deeper economic and trade ties.[88] The third aspect is stabilising Afghanistan, a necessary condition for a revival of Central Asian trade with India which declined precipitously after the Soviet break-up. Instability in and around Afghanistan prevents India and Pakistan from fully realising potential economic gains from trade with Central Asia.[89] Indian businesses stand ready to expand their overland trade with Central Asia and Afghanistan once they can safely move cargoes through those areas but violence in Afghanistan and perhaps Pakistan too inhibits them.[90] Therefore, India has made a large effort to stabilise Afghanistan, providing financial assistance, aid in transport, education, health care. India was also among the first governments to accept the Karzai government there and has steadily intensified its connections with Afghanistan.

To realise these interests and goals India has recently improved ties with China, Russia, Iran, Israel, and the United States, and is also consolidating key partnerships with them either in military sales or in trade. This remarkable diplomatic achievement has not received sufficient recognition abroad. A key programme that connects Russia, Iran, India, and Central Asian states like Kazakhstan is the north-south trade corridor that originates in Russia, provides a corridor for trade, including energy, through Central Asia, and then proceeds through Iran to India.[91] Pakistan has been excluded from this trade because during the Taliban period it was estranged from Iran and Russia as well as India. This programme is central to Russian and Iranian aspirations in Asia because it counters the EU's east-west Silk road and US pipeline programmes that exclude those states. It also comports with Russia's grand design for being a hub for east-west and north-south trade tying Asia to Europe.[92]

India benefits by being the entrepôt and final port of embarkation for these goods, by securing reliable access to Russian, Iranian, and Central Asian goods, including energy, and by marginalising Pakistan. Pakistan has very great ambitions for its own trade routes through Central Asia which would eventually end up at Gwadar. Obviously, India has had no interest in helping realise these ambitions. Thus while Pakistan has striven mightily to get a pipeline from Central Asia through Afghanistan to its own territory and has even waived all obstacles to India's participation in it, India has gone its own way, mainly through cooperation with Iran that has brought Central Asian states into this corridor.[93] Obviously, the north-south corridor's value was enhanced when trade routes through Afghanistan and Pakistan were held hostage to Pakistan-backed terrorism after late 2001. The north-south corridor bypasses Afghanistan and Pakistan and is a centrepiece of India's political closeness with Iran, Russia, and Central Asian governments. More recently, India's overtures to Pakistan for a political negotiation process also come with attempts to ensure that in the event of war Pakistan will not get the gas from Turkmenistan. So the economic rivalry continues.[94]

The new ties with Iran relating both to trade and to strategic issues exemplify the linkages between strategic and economic issues in Indian policy. In early 2003, India signed what amounts to an alliance with Iran against Pakistan. The new treaty paves the way for an offshore gas pipeline through the Indian Ocean that will connect Iran to India and bypass Pakistan. Iran had earlier sought assistance in building an overland gas pipeline through Pakistan to India. Options included a pipeline along the shallow-water coastline of Pakistan, or on the seabed from the Persian Gulf to India's west coast, or a fourth option that is already in place, liquefied natural gas (LNG) which is most expensive. Now Tehran and New Delhi have decisively rejected Pakistani participation in the pipeline and shut it out of trade with Central Asia. Instead, Iran and India both will compete vigorously with Pakistan for trade through Afghanistan. Thus, this accord's second element provides for much of Afghanistan's overland trade to go through Iran whence it will either go through Iranian ports abroad or to India. Either way, Pakistan will be bypassed. Deprived of options for overland trade and pipelines, Pakistan's position must invariably suffer relative to those of India and Iran. This is a major blow to the Pakistan's post-11 September strategy for Afghanistan and Central Asia.[95]

In return Iran seeks Indian support for joining the WTO, G-17 and G-77 and greater business, and perhaps also defence ties with India. India's ties with Iran ensure reliable energy supplies, and the stability of the north-south corridor. By striking at Pakistan, India serves itself and its allies. Thus, Indian policy puts continued pressure on Pakistan and promises to augment India's capabilities and leverage in Central Asia.

## Indian Diplomacy and Political Ties

India's connection to Iran is perhaps the most remarkable aspect of the new policy. Whereas ties with Russia are long-standing and visibly saturated with strategic implications, Indo-Iranian relations were never so prominent or important. While this relationship substantiates India's claims to be a rising power and reflects Iran's awareness that cooperation with India benefits it in and around Central Asia, it also exemplifies the broader trend of Indian relations with key actors there. Indeed, some analysts see this relationship as opening the way to a new structure of regional relations including an Irano-American rapprochement mediated by India.[96]

Whereas Pakistan's strident Islamism and support for terrorism and drug running has strongly alienated Central Asian governments and estranged China and Iran, India's opposition to those policies and superior economic attainments enhanced its status and generated an alignment with Iran against Pakistan.[97] These new political ties enable India to project power and influence further afield, e.g. the north-south trade corridor with Russia and Iran which could only emerge on the basis of common political goals.

Yet, ties with Iran are not exclusively based on this fact or on the fact that India's main supplier of oil will continue to be the Gulf states, Iran among them.[98] Rather, energy is one key factor along with Central Asia, Afghanistan, and general trade, especially as Iran seeks to become a centre of the international energy trade and sees Central Asia as the biggest market for its goods and capital investment.[99]

Another key factor that brings Tehran and New Delhi together is that both states oppose Islamist takeovers in Central Asia where Iran has been a notably cautious actor.[100] Thus their bilateral military accords exemplify the classical realpolitik of old-fashioned alliances. India will provide repairs and maintenance for Iran's Russian-built weapons and training for its officers in return for the use of Iranian bases in any future war against Pakistan.[101]

This relationship also constitutes a throwback to a type of diplomacy that supposedly had disappeared in the sunshine of globalisation. Pakistan's belief that it could destabilise its neighbours and rivals with impunity using terrorists as its instrument or that it could then seem to switch sides to recoup a positive position in Central Asia have been rudely shattered. In Central Asia Pakistan is now isolated while a potent Indo-Iranian-Russian entente that disposes of formidable economic and military instruments of power is visibly taking shape. Having unsheathed the sword, Pakistan could soon be impaled upon it.

Meanwhile, the shared perspective on terrorism with Moscow and Washington has allowed India to form permanent relationships and working groups with those governments to combat terrorism. As the new exercises and potential arms purchases from Washington show, these groups enhance military-political-intelligence collaboration with both capitals and their discussions about Central Asia apparently now include India as a shared subject of discussion.[102] India's membership in the UN-sponsored

6+2 process to deal with Taliban-ruled Afghanistan and the favourable reaction to its interest in the SCO also demonstrate its growing weight and repute in Asia generally, including Central Asia. China's growing ambivalence since 1994–95 about Pakistani-sponsored incitement in Kashmir, Central Asia, and Xinjiang is well known.[103] Thus, India has substantially improved relations with major players in and around Central Asia. Special emphasis here belongs to Indo-Uzbek and Indo-Kazakh relations which comprise heightened economic exchange and a growing security relationship.

## The Military Instrument

India's policies also reflect the rising importance of military factors and instruments in its overall national security policy. The Russo-Indian negotiations of 2000–2001 are particularly instructive for they show that India's growing power enabled it to extract from Russia not just favourable prices, but also political concessions regarding Kashmir and major issues of Indian security.[104] While its conventional power projection capabilities have always been primarily intended for use against Pakistan, they are fungible and usable wherever applicable, e.g. against terrorist activities on the high seas or for aerial reconnaissance over Central Asia or Pakistan's interior through AWACS or satellite technology. These examples show what capabilities India is either developing improving, or seeking to acquire from its suppliers.[105] Simultaneously, India also projects military power into Central Asia in other forms.

First, responding to Pakistan's closing of its air space, India negotiated base rights with Tajikistan. While little is known about this air base, it is reportedly at an operational level and could therefore be used for operations against either Central Asian insurgents in support of a friendly government or Pakistan.[106] This base exemplifies how foreign powers like Russia, China, and the United States project military power into Central Asia and establish more durable lodgements in the form of bases there. Since most of these bases are air bases, ground forces to defend them will also eventually appear. This base also confirms the tendency to use foreign bases to signify support for Central Asia's beleaguered governments. The locations of these Russo-American-Indian bases in Tajikistan, Kyrgyzstan, and Uzbekistan, and China's recent manoeuvres with the Kyrgyz armed forces reliably suggest an assessment of where major powers think Central Asian governments are in trouble and how they will help them.[107] India's base may not be its last one or remain small. Nor is it inconceivable that it will be the spearhead of a deepening Indian involvement in Central Asian defence.

India's increased ability and willingness to sell weapons to Central Asian governments parallels Pakistan's similar capability as both are entering the international arms market to find new export markets and keep defence plants open.[108] Indian spokesmen frankly admit the drive to find export markets among former 'pariah' states like Israel and South Africa to achieve economies of scale for their domestic defence industry. Capturing those markets will then reduce Indian dependence upon foreign suppliers, especially as India can increasingly compel them to transfer technology and know-how as part of their sales.[109] Probably India will provide training and assistance to Central Asian militaries as do Turkey, Russia, China, and the United States, and also find in them willing buyers of its weapons, especially those made jointly with Russia.

But India has even broader objectives. Because it competes with China in the small arms market and also seeks to penetrate into South-East Asia and Central Asia where China seeks to expand its influence, India must compete with China on price and quality in the same categories of weapons. India sells small arms, ammunition, patrol ships, light field guns, trucks, and aircraft parts to Southeast Asia at reduced price and with better equipment.[110] Furthermore:

> Over the next decade, India intends to produce weapons system China cannot, including an indigenously designed air defence ship – basically a small aircraft carrier. Through subsidies, loans, and higher technology New Delhi hopes to supplant China as a major regional arms supplier. It also can take advantage of underlying concerns about China within Southeast Asia, touting Indian weapons systems as free from the risks of being swallowed by an aggressive China in the future.[111]

All this also applies to Central Asia which is already the target of an Indian arms sales offensive. India has sold Kazakhstan and Tajikistan Ilyushin-76 transports and helicopters respectively.[112]

Finally, India has built a burgeoning security relationship with Uzbekistan based on a common antipathy to Islamic terrorism. Indian scholars believe these two states are natural allies who confront the same threats – terrorism, insurgency, separatism, drugs, etc. Uzbekistan has steadily widened its security discussions with India to include intelligence sharing, military and paramilitary training and joint working groups against terrorism as India has done with Washington and Moscow.[113] Here again, New Delhi emulates Moscow, Washington, Ankara and Beijing. More importantly, it has only begun to display its military instruments of power locally. As long as security threats remain and Pakistan seeks to obstruct India or to use this area as a 'strategic hinterland' against it the projection of all forms of military power are likely to grow.

## Conclusions

India is here to stay in Central Asia. Moreover, its involvement will probably deepen as its capabilities grow.[114] Though terrorism galvanised its policies, its presence was already growing along with a coherent threat assessment by 2001. Since the Indo-Pakistani front is critical to the war on terrorism and America's ability to prosecute that war, India's ability to help stabilise Central Asia is an important policy question for Washington. More broadly, Indian writers and officials who favour close ties with America assert that Washington and New Delhi are 'natural allies'. They argue for a close alignment or even an alliance between both states regarding Central Asia.[115] As the former foreign minister Mr Jaswant Singh observed, America will be criticised for staying in Central Asia because that obviously troubles Moscow and Beijing. But he told the *Washington Post*, 'You won't be able to give it up. And you won't be able to leave Pakistan.'[116]

Neither can India give it up. For the foreseeable future Indo-American interests coincide in Central Asia. But if they should diverge, India has the means and skills to pursue its own interests resolutely. Indeed, as argued above, Central Asia has long since become a part of South Asia's broader security calculus and vice versa.[117] While few American or European writers have discerned this dimension of the new great game, the heirs of those who played it before remember their history. Nor will they allow us to forget it as we march into the future.

★   This is an updated and revised version of an earlier article 'India's Rising Profile in Central Asia' published in the journal *Comparative Strategy*. The views expressed here do not represent those of the US Army, Defense Department, or the US Government.

## Notes

1. New Delhi, *Hindustan Times* Internet Version, in English, 13 September 2000; Foreign Broadcast Information Service Central Eurasia, (Henceforth FBIS SOV), 13 September 2000.

2. Igor Khripunov and Anupam Srivastava, 'Contending with the "Bear-ish" Arms Market: US-Indian Strategic Cooperation and Russia', in Gary K Bertsch, Seema Gahlaut, and Anupam Srivastava (eds.), *Engaging India: US Strategic Relations with the World's Largest Democracy*, London and New York: Routledge, 1999, pp.245–46; Ross Munro, 'China, India, and Central Asia', Jed C Snyder, (ed.), *After Empire: The Emerging Geopolitics of Central Asia*, Fort Leslie McNair, Washington DC: National Defense University Press, 1995, pp.132–133.

3. Indian Foreign Policy, April 1999, News Reports, opinions, www.ipcs.org/archives/a-ifp-index/99-04-apr.htm; Julie A MacDonald, 'The Emergence of India as a Central Asian Player', *Central Asia-Caucasus Analyst*, 24 May 2000.

4. Meena Singh Roy, 'India's Interests in Central Asia', *Strategic Analysis*, March 2001, www.ciaonet.org/olj/sa/sa_mar01rom01.html.

5. Aabha Dixit, 'Conflict Resolution In Afghanistan: Does India Have a Role to Play?', Program in Arms Control, Disarmament, and International Security, University of Illinois at Urbana-Champaign, 1997; Poonam Mann, 'Fighting Terrorism: India and Central Asia', *Strategic Analysis*, February 2001, www.ciaonet.org/olj/sa/sa_feb01map01.html.

6. Julie MacDonald, 'India, Pakistan: Impact on Caspian Region's Stability', paper presented to the NBR Asia – SSI Conference on Caspian Sea Basin Security, Seattle, Washington, 29–30 April, 2003, pp.94–99.

7. Kishore C Dash, 'The Challenge of Regionalism in South Asia', *International Politics*, XXXVIII, No. 2, June 2001, pp.216–217.

8. Brigadier Vijai K Nair, VSM (Retd), PhD, 'Challenges for the Years Ahead: An Indian Perspective', paper presented to the Annual National Defense University Asian-Pacific Symposium, Honolulu, March 2001, www.ndu.edu/inss/symposia/pacific2001/nairpaper.htm.

9. Ibid., Jasjit Singh, 'An Indian Perspective', in Sandy Gordon and Stephen Henningham (eds.), *India Looks East: An Emerging Power and its Asia-Pacific Neighbours, Canberra Papers on Strategy and Defence*, No. 111, Canberra, Australia: Strategic and Defence Studies Centre, Research School of Pacific and Asian Studies, the Australian National University, 1995, p.57.

10. Kishore C Dash, op: cit., pp.216–217.

11. Ibid.

12. Richard Pomfret, *The Economies of Central Asia*, Princeton, N J: Princeton University Press, 1995, p.155; Munro, op, cit., pp.132–133.

13. Ross H Munro, 'China's Waxing Soheres of Influence', *Orbis*, XXXVIII, No. 4, Fall 1994, pp.585–606.

14. Jyotsna Bakshi, 'Russia's Post-Pokhran Dilemma', *Strategic Analysis*, XXII, No. 5, August 1998, p.721, quoted in Jerome M Conley, 'Indo-Russian Military and Nuclear Cooperation: Implications for the United States', INSS Occasional Paper No. 31, Proliferation Series, USAF Institute for National Security Studies, USAF Academy, Colorado Springs, Colorado, 2000, pp.24–25.

15. S Enders Wimbush, 'India's Perspective, Central Intelligence Agency, Russia in the International System: A Conference Report', 1 June 2001 www.cia.gov/nic/pubs/conference_reports/russia_conf.html, p.31. *See also* Sumit Ganguly, 'India's Alliances 2020', Michael R Chambers (ed.), *South Asia in 2020: Future Strategic Balances and Alliances*,

Carlisle Barracks, PA: Strategic Studies Institute, US Army War College, 2002, pp.370–76.

16. Jennifer Siegel, *Endgame: Britain, Russia and the Final Struggle for Central Asia*, Foreword by Paul Kennedy, London and New York: I B Tauris, 2002.

17. Frederic Grare, 'Pakistan and Central Asia: Strategic considerations Versus Economic Opportunities', *World Affairs*, II, No. 4, October–December 1998, pp.106–122.

18. Astri Suhrke, Kristian Beg Harpviken and Arne Strand, 'After Bonn: Conflictual Peace Building', *Third World Quarterly*, XXIII, No. 5, 2002, pp.878–884, J N Dixit, 'Central Asia is Central', *The Indian Express*, 29 August 2002, www.indian-express.com/archive_full_story.php.

19. Quoted in Walter K Andersen, 'India in Asia: Walking on a Tightrope', *Asian Survey*, December 1979 in S Nihal Singh, *The Yogi and the Bear: A Study of Indo-Soviet Relations*, Riverdale, MD: The Riverdale Company, Inc., 1986, p.147.

20. Agam Shjah, 'New Afghan Leadership Team Turns to India for Assistance', *Eurasia Insight*, 14 December 2001, www.eurasianet.org.

21. Quoted in Ji Guoxing, *Asian Pacific SLOC Security: The China Factor*, Canberra: Royal Australian Navy Sea Power Centre, Working Paper No. 10, April 2002, p.36.

22. Mushahid Hussain, 'Indian Power Projection in South Asia and the Regional States' Reaction', Hafeez Malik in (ed.), *Dilemmas of National Security and Cooperation in India and Pakistan*, New York: St Martin's Press, 1996, p.155.

23. Gordon and Henningham (eds.), Ji Guoxing, Ian Storey and Carlyle Thayer, 'Scramble for Cam Ranh Bay as Russia prepares to Withdraw', *Jane's intelligence Review*, December, 2001, pp.34–37. Indeed, Indian diplomats long ago observed that South-east Asia would become an area of contention with China.

24. K Alan Kronstadt, 'The Asian Way to Insecurity: India's Rise and the Meaning of Increased Power Projection

Capabilities in South Asia', paper presented at the 42nd Annual Convention of the International Studies Association, Chicago, Illinois, 21 February 2001.

25. John Garver, 'The Security Dilemma in Sino-Indian Relations', *India Review*, I, No. 4, October 2002, pp.17–21; Ahmad Faruqui, *Rethinking the National Security of Pakistan: The Price of Strategic Myopia*, Burlington, Vermont: Ashgate Publishing Company, 2003.

26. Garver, op. cit., pp.17–21.

27. Amin Saikal, 'The Future of India and South-west Asia', in Ross Babbage and Sandy Gordon (eds.), *India's Strategic Future: Regional State or Global Power*, Senator, the Honourable Robert Ray, Foreword, New York: St Martin's Press, 1992, pp.122–141; Kanti Bajpai, *India's Strategic Culture*, Chambers (ed.), p.263, Hasan-Askari Rizvi, 'Pakistan's Strategic Culture', Ibid., p.312.

28. Aabha Dixit.

29. J N Dixit and Agam Shah, 'Karzai Seeks Foreign Investment From Indian companies', www.eurasianet.org, 28 February 2002.

30. P Venkateshwar Rao, 'Ethnic conflict in Sri Lanka: India's Role and Perception', *Asian Survey*, April 1988, p.422.

31. Beth Duff Brown, 'India Fears Taliban Will Join Kashmir Conflict', *Washington Times*, 4 December 2001, p.9; T S Gopi Rethinaraj, 'South Asian Rivalries Obstruct Energy Cooperation', *Jane's Intelligence Review*, December 2001, pp.38–40, Raju G C Thomas, 'Indian Security Policy in the 1990s: New Risks and Opportunities', Hafeez Malik (ed.), *Dilemmas of National Security and Cooperation in India and Pakistan*, New York: St Martin's Press, 1996, p.125.

32. Thomas W Simons Jr., 'Thoughts on the Current Crisis', Michael R Chambers (ed.), pp.31–33, Associated Press, 'Pakistan Was Prepared to Use Nuclear Weapons', *New York Times*, 30 December 2002, Raju G C Thomas,

*India's Security Environment: Towards the Year 2000*, Carlisle Barracks, PA: Strategic Studies Institute, US Army War College, 1996, pp.3–5.

33. Ibid.

34. Sir John Thomson, 'Policy Paths in South Asia: Intersections Between Global and Local', Chambers (ed.), p.17; Jim Hoagland, 'Staying On in Central Asia', *Washington Post*, 20 January 2002, p.B7; Stephen Blank, 'A Sacred Place Is Never Empty: The External Geopolitics of the Trans-Caspian', Jim Colbert (ed.), *Natural Resources and National Security: Sources of Conflict & the US Interest*, Washington DC: Jewish Institute of National Security Affairs, 2001, pp.123–142.

35. Ibid.

36. Nadeem Iqbal, 'Pakistan's Arms Industry Aims High', *Asia Times Online*, 4 October 2002.

37. Mann, 'Fighting Terrorism', 'India Seeks Uzbek-made Aircraft to Enhance Capability Against China', www.UzReport.com, Tashkent, in English, 3 September 2002, Retrieved from Lexis-Nexis, 'India has Acknowledged Establishing an Air Base in Tajikistan', p.19.

38. Islamabad, *al-Akhbar*, in Urdu, 26 May 2001, *FBIS SOV*, 27 May 2001.

39. 'Rising India and US Policy Options in Asia', *South Asia Monitor*, Centre for Strategic and International Studies, No. 40, Washington DC, 1 December 2001, www.csis.org/saprog/sam40.htm.

40. Ibid., Rizvi, p.312, 'India: Prime Minister Interviewed by Arabic-Language London Paper', *Al-Sharq al Awsat*, in Arabic, 4 September 2002, Retrieved from Lexis-Nexis. To be fair, Amin Saikal in 1992 strongly disputed this point but today arguable things have changed, Saikal, p.141.

41. Thomas, pp.3–5.

42. 'Kazakhstan To Create Strong System of Defence From

Terror-President', *Khabar Television*, Almaty, 15 November 2002, Retrieved from Lexis-Nexis; Michael R Chambers, Compiler, 'US Military Perspectives on Regional Security in South Asia', Chambers (ed.), p.236.

43. Washington Post Foreign Service, 'Nuclear-Free Zone for Central Asia; 5 Ex-Soviet States Act to Distance Themselves From Russia', *Washington Post*, 5 October 2002, p.A14.

44. Singh, p.225.

45. Farhan Bokhari, 'Musharraf Vows to Back, "Kashmir Freedom Struggle"', *Financial Times*, 16 January 2002, p.4; Beth Duff-Brown, 'India Fears Taliban Will Join Kashmir Conflict', *Washington Times*, 4 December 2001, Thomas, *Indian Security Policy in the 1990s: New Risks and Opportunities*, p.125.

46. K Subrahmanyam, 'Covert Operations Pose New Challenges for Indian Security: In Search of Security After the Cold War', *World Affairs*, (New Delhi) I, No. 4, October–December 1997, pp.38–43; *also* B Raman, 'Covert Action and Counter Proxy War', *Bharat Rakshak Monitor*, IV (5), March–April 2002, www.bharat-rakshak.com/Monitor?Issue-5/raman.html.

47. Ibid.

48. Ibid., Tara Kartha, 'The Diffusion of Light Weapons in Pakistan', *Small Wars and Insurgencies*, VIII, No. 1, Spring, 1997, pp.71–87, Stephen Blank, 'Central Asia, South Asia and Asian Security', *Eurasian Studies*, II, No. 3, 1995, pp.2–22, Anatol Lieven, 'The Pressure on Pakistan', *Foreign Affairs*, LXXXI, No. 1, January–February 2002, pp.106–118.

49. For an overview of the broader processes of globalisation as they affect India's and other countries' defence industries see *Defense Industry Globalization*, A Compendium of Papers Presented at a Conference on: 'Defense Industry Globalization', Washington DC, on 16 November 2001,

Atlantic Council of the United States, 2002; Vivek Raghuvanshi, 'India Opens Arms Factories to Foreign Investors', *Defense News*, January 14–20, 2002, p.4; 'India Furthers Strategic Goals by Reaching out to Arms Markets', www.stratfor.com, 29 October 2002.

50. Owais Tohid, 'Taliban Fighters Infiltrating Back Into Afghanistan from Pakistan', *Eurasia Insight*, www.eurasianet.org, 5 May 2003, A Gizabi, 'Sinking Into the Afghan Swamp', *Jane's Terrorism and Security Monitor*, 14 February 2003, www4.janes.com/search97cgi/s97; Anthony Davis, 'Afghan Security Deteriorates as Taliban Regroup', *Jane's Intelligence Review*, 1 May 2003, www4.janes.com/search97/cgis97; Scott Baladuf and Owais Tohid, 'Taliban Appears to Be Regrouped and Well-Founded', *Christian Science Monitor*, 8 May 2003, www.csmonitor.com/2003/0508p01s02-wosc;

'Musharraf: Bin Laden May Be in Pakistan', 1 May 2001, Kathy Gannon, 'Al-Qaeda's No. 3 Says He Met Bin Laden, Who is Alive and in the Region', *Associated Press Worldstream*, 6 March 2003, Retrieved from Lexis-Nexis.

51. Frederic Grare, pp.106–122.

52. Ibid.

53. J N Dixit.

54. Poonam Mann, 'Fighting Terrorism'.

55. K Alan Kronstadt.

56. Jerome M Conley, Igor Khripunov and Srivastava, pp.238–261.

57. Anil Sharma, 'Indian Drive to Increase Arms Exports', *Asia Times Online*, 6 November 2002, 'India Furthers Strategic Goals by Reaching out to Arms Markets'.

58. Poonam Mann, 'Fighting Terrorism'.

59. *Defense Industry Globalization*.

60. Subhash Kapila, 'India-Israel Relations: The Imperatives for Enhanced Strategic Cooperation', *South Asia Analysis Group*, Papers No. 131, www.saag.org/papers2/papers131.html;

Caroline B Glick, 'Comrades in Arms; The Indian-Israel Connection', *Wall Street Journal Europe*, 23 January 2002; Vivek Raghuvanshi, 'Indians, French Poised To Sign Accord', *Defense News*, 25 June–1 July 2001, p.20; Brigadier Feroz Hassan Khan, 'Pakistan's Nuclear Future', Michael R Chambers (ed.), p.171.

61. Martin Walker, 'Attacks Ally, India, Turkey, Israel', *The Washington Times*, 19 January 2002, Glick.

62. Brahma Chellaney, 'China Seeks to Stem India's Building Military ties with the US', *International Herald Tribune*, 19–20 January 2002, www.iht.com; Andrew Scobell, '"Cult of Defense" and "Great Power Dreams": The Influence of Strategic Culture on China's Relationship With India', Michael R Chambers (ed.), pp.329–359, Ganguly, pp.370–376.

63. For example, John W Garver, 'The China-India-US Triangle: Strategic Relations in the Post-Cold War Era', *NBR Analysis*, XIII, No. 5, 2002; James Kynge and Edward Luce, 'Frosty Relations Between Asian Giants Begin To thaw', *Financial Times*, 14 January 2002, p.12; 'China No Threat to India, Says Zhu', *Hindustan Times*, 15 January 2002, www.hindustantimes.com/nonfram/ 150102/detfro03.asp.

64. This proposal dates back at least to 1994, Ramesh Thakur, 'Between East and West, from North to South', in Gordon and Henningham, (eds.), pp.20–21. For Putin's revival of it *see* 'Indian Daily Interviews Putin on Iraq, Pakistan, India', *The Hindu Web Site*, Madras, in English, 1 December 2002, Retrieved from Lexis-Nexis; Robert Marquand, 'Putin Pushes "Strategic Triangle" With China, India', *Christian Science Monitor*, 6 December 2002, p.7. For Chinese views, *see* Ganguly, pp.370–76, 381 and, New Delhi, *Dainik Jagran*, in Hindi, 7 August 2001, *Foreign Broadcast Information Service, Near East South Asia* (Henceforth *FBIS NES*), 9 August 2001, Sultan

Shahin, 'Delhi-Beijing-Moscow Axis: Old Romance Rekindled', *Asia Times Online*, 7 December 2002 and Garver, passim., Stanislav Menshikov, 'Geopolitical Geometry: The Eurasian Heavyweight', *Moscow Tribune*, 6 December 2002.

65. 'Rising India and US Policy Options in Asia'.
66. Mohan Malik, 'The Proliferation Axis: Beijing-Islamabad-Pyongyang', *Korean Journal of Defense Analysis*, XV, No. 1, Spring 2003, pp.57–100.
67. 'ONGC Arm Seeks Nod for Stake in Overseas Fields', *Financial Times Information*, 20 February 2002, Retrieved from Lexis-Nexis.
68. Meena Singh Roy, 'India's Interests in Central Asia', Shankkar and Shishir Gupta, 'Energy: Striking it Rich', *India Today*, 18 November 2002, Retrieved from Lexis-Nexis.
69. Mark Berniker, 'Trans-Afghan Pipeline Project Moving Forward, Faces Risks', www.eurasianet.org, 19 December 2002; Brigadier General (Retd) M Sakhawat Hussain, 'Behind the US Diplomatic initiative in South Asia', *The Independent*, 19 June 2002, Retrieved from Lexis-Nexis.
70. Ibid.
71. Again this is a very long-standing affair and perception going back to Nehru's time, Singh, passim.
72. Berniker, Sakhawat Hussain, Stephen Blank, 'Afghanistan's Newest Victimization', *Asia Times Online*, 13 May 2003, Stephen Blank, 'The Indian-Iranian Connection and its Importance for Central Asia', www.eurasianet.org, 12 March 2003.
73. '"Shanghai Five" Change Turns China in a New Strategic Direction', *Kyodo*, 18 June 2001, Retrieved from Lexis-Nexis Robert A Karniol, 'Shanghai Five in Major Revamp', *Jane's Defence Weekly*, 27 June 2001, p.5; Bates Gill, 'Shanghai Five: An Attempt to Counter US Influence in Asia?' *Newsweek Korea*, May 2001,

www.brookings.edu/views/op-ed/gill20010504.htm.

74. 'India Planning to Join Shanghai Cooperative Organization', ITAR-TASS, 29 October 2002, Retrieved from Lexis-Nexis.

75. 'The Indian-American Love-in', *Jane's Foreign Report*, 5 December 2002, www4.janes.com/search97/cgis97_cgi.

76. Julie A Macdonald, *Indo-US Military Relationship: Expectations and Perceptions*, Washington DC: Booz Allen, Hamilton with permission from the Office of the Secretary Of Defense/Net Assessment, 2002.

77. James Morrison, 'India Express', *Washington Times*, 11 December 2002, p.15; Rahul Bedi, 'US India Building Bridges', *Jane's Defence Weekly*, 28 November 2001, p.23.

78. Mutahir Ahmed, 'Afghanistan and Tajikistan: Destabilizing Factors for South and Central Asian Region', *Perceptions*, III, No. 1, March–May 1998, p.141.

79. Mann, 'Fighting Terrorism'.

80. John Hassell, 'An Update on the Great Game: Power Plays in the Graveyard of Empire', *San Diego Union-Tribune*, 1 September 2002, p.G-5, Retrieved from Lexis-Nexis.

81. Anupam Srivastava, 'Living With the Dragon: Re-Calibrating India's Relations With China', Amitabh Mattoo and Kanti Bajpai (eds.), *The Peacock and the Dragon: India-China Relations on the 21ˢᵗ Century*, New Delhi: Har Anand Publishers, 2000. This is taken from Dr Srivastava's manuscript which he generously gave to me.

82. I K Gujral, *A Foreign Policy for India*, New Delhi: External Publicity Division, Ministry of External Affairs, Government of India, 1998, p.135; Maya Chadda, 'Indo-Russian Relations in the Post-Cold War Era', in Hafeez Malik, (ed.), *The Roles of the United States, Russia, and China in the New World Order*, New York: St Martin's Press, 1998, p.119; S P Gupta, 'India's Increasing Eastern Orientation in Trade and Investment: Context and Challenges', in

Gordon and Henningham (eds.), pp.83–87; Teresita C Schaffer, 'A Changing India', Chambers (ed.), p.50. Vijay L Kelkar, 'South Asia in 2020: Economic Outlook', Chambers (ed.), p.87.

83. Gujral, op. cit., pp.181–191; Kelkar, op. cit., p.87.

84. Chadda, pp.106–107; Ganguly, pp.364–365.

85. S Frederick Starr is cited in National Intelligence Council, *Central Asia and the South Caucasus: Reorientations, Internal Transitions, Strategic Dynamics*, Washington DC, 2000, p.41.

86. 'Gazprom Capitalizes on Insecurity', *Indigo Publications Intelligence Online*, 5 December 2002, Retrieved from Lexis-Nexis; Vladimir Radyuhin, 'Russia Revives Gas Proposal', *The Hindu*, 7 August 2002, www.hnduonnet.com/stories/200280703531200.htm.

87. Igor S Ivanov, *The New Russian Diplomacy*, Foreword by Henry A Kissinger, Washington DC: Brookings Institution Press, 2002, p.123; Moscow, *Rossiyskaya Gazeta*, In Russian, 4 October 2000 *FBIS SOV*, 4 October 2000; Elizabeth Roche, 'Indo-Russian Trade Vital for Momentum in Relations: Analysis', *Agence France Presse*, 1 December 2002, Retrieved from Lexis-Nexis.

88. Poonam Mann, 'Fighting Terrorism'; Meena Singh Roy, 'India's Interests in Central Asia'.

89. This is based on conversations with S Frederick Starr, director of the Central Asia Caucasus Institute of Johns Hopkins University in Washington DC.

90. For example, *see* Chennai, *The Hindu* in English, 12 April 2001; *FBIS NES*, 12 April 2001; Tehran, *IRNA*, in English, 12 April 2001, *FBIS NES*, 12 April 2001, Robert M Cutler, 'The Indo-Iranian Rapprochement: Not Just Natural Gas Anymore', *Central Asia-Caucasus Analyst*, 9 May 2001; Regine A Spector, 'The North-South Transport Corridor', *Central Asia-Caucasus Analyst*, 3 July 2002.

91. Nodari A Simonia, 'TKR-TSR Linkage and Its Impact on ROK-DPRK-Russia Relationship', *The Journal of East Asian Affairs*, XV, No. 2, Fall–Winter 2001, pp.180–202.

92. John Calabrese, 'Indo-Iranian Relations in Transition', *Journal of South Asian and Middle Eastern Studies*, XXV, No. 5, Summer 2002, pp.60–82; T S Gopi Rethinaraj, pp.38–40; C Raja Mohan, 'Fostering Strategic Stability and Promoting Regional Collaboration', in Gary K Bertsch et al., (ed.), pp.38–39; 'Pakistan Ready to Give Any Guarantee for India-Iran Gas Pipeline', *Asia Pulse*, 10 December 2002, Retrieved from Lexis-Nexis.

93. Mohammed Ayoob, 'Southwest Asia After the Taliban', *Survival*, XLIV, No. 1, Spring 2002, pp.60–65.

94. Mike Hurle, 'India Responds to Trans-Afghan Pipeline Invitation', *World Markets Research Ltd*, World Markets Analysis, 16 May 2003, Retrieved from Lexis-Nexis.

95. Blank, 'Afghanistan's Newest Victimization'; Blank, 'The Indian-Iranian Connection'.

96. Calabrese, pp.60–82, Smita Gupta, 'Threats of Terrorism Bring India, Iran Closer', *The Times of India*, 15 April 2001.

97. Calabrese, pp.60–82, Satyanarayan Pattanayak, 'Oil as a Factor in Indo-Gulf Relations', *Strategic Analysis*, June 2001, www.ciaonet.org/olj/sa/sa_june01pas02.html.

98. 'Iran Tries to Become Centre of Distribution of Energy to International Market', www.TehranTimes.com, 9 June 2002, Retrieved from Lexis-Nexis.

99. T S Gopi Rethinaraj, pp.38–40, Calabrese, pp.60–82.

100. Farah Naaz, 'Indo-Iranian Relations 1947–2000', *Strategic Analysis*, www.ciaonet.org/olj/sa/sa_jan01naf01.html; Naseem Khan, 'Vajpayee's Visit to Iran: Indo-Iranian Relations and Prospects of Bilateral Cooperation', *Strategic Analysis*, September 2001, www.ciaonet.org/olj/sa/sa_sep01khm01.html.

101. Blank, 'The Indian-Iranian Connection'.

102. Naseem Khan, 'Vajpayee's Visit to Iran', T S Gopi Rethinaraj, pp.38–40, Calabrese, pp.60–82.

103. Ibid., Naseem Khan.

104. 'Russian Paper Says Minister Trubnikov's Talks Mark "New Shift" in Russia-US Ties', *Kommersant*, 29 July 2002, Retrieved from Lexis-Nexis.

105. Blank, 'Central Asia, South Asia, and Asian Security', pp.19–22; John W Garver, 'The Future of the Sino-Pakistani *Entente Cordiale*', Michael R Chambers, (ed.), pp.397–401, 429–436.

106. Conley and Seema Gahlaut, 'Nuclear Dangers in South Asia: Survey of Russian Perspectives', *The Monitor*, VII, No. 3, Fall, 2001, pp.18–23, 'Potential for Cooperation with India is Nearly Exhausted', *Current digest of the Post-Soviet Press*, (Henceforth CDPP), LIII, No. 35, 26 September 2001, p.17; Moscow, *Kommersant*, in Russian, 5 October 2000; *FBIS SOV*, 5 October 2000; Moscow, *Kommersant*, in Russian, 6 October 2000, *FBIS SOV*, 6 October 2000; Moscow, *Kommersant*, in Russian, 5 June 2001, *FBIS SOV*, 5 June 2001; Rahul Bedi, 'India Will Borrow Bombers in Latest Deal With Russia', *Jane's Defence Weekly*, 31 October 2001; Simon Saradzhyan, 'India Set to Buy $10 Billion in Arms', *The Moscow Times*, 5 June 2001, Retrieved from Lexis-Nexis' Rahul Bedi, 'India May Acquire Russian "Missile Shield"', *Jane's Defence Weekly*, 14 November 2001, p.5.

107. Ibid., K Alan Kronstadt.

108. Rahul Bedi, 'Indian Base in Tajikistan "Quietly Operational"', *Irish Times*, 22 August 2002, Retrieved from Lexis-Nexis; Shaikh Azizur Rahman, 'India Strikes for Oil and Gas With Military Base in Tajikistan', *Washington Times*, 2 September 2002, Retrieved from Lexis-Nexis, Hassell, 'India has Acknowledged Establishing an Air Base in Tajikistan', p.19, 'High-

Level Tajikistan Defence Delegation Meets Fernandes', The Press Trust of India, 2 December 2002, Retrieved from Lexis-Nexis.

109. *Jane's Intelligence Digest*, 13 December 2002, www.4.janes. com/search97cgi/s97_cgi; Douglas Frantz, 'Around the World, Hints of Afghanistan to Come', *New York Times*, 26 May 2002, Section 4, p.5.

110. Vivek Raghuvanshi, 'India Eyes Markets Abroad', *Defense News*, 20–26 May 2002, p.36; Vivek Raghuvanshi, 'Indian Munitions Plants Fear Sales Losses, Seek Exports', *Defense News*, 14–20 January 2002, p.10. Nadeem Iqbal and Anil Sharma.

111. Ibid., *Defense Industry Globalization*, 'India Furthers Strategic Goals'.

112. Ibid.

113. Ibid.

114. MacDonald, 'India, Pakistan: Impact on Caspian Region's Stability', pp.89–103.

115. Stephen Blank, 'The Arming of Central Asia', *Asia Times Online*, 24 August 2002.

116. Poonam Mann, 'Fighting Terrorism'.

117. Mohan, pp.38–39, Hoagland, p.B7; Lloyd Richardson, 'Now, Play the India Card', *Policy Review*, October 2002, Retrieved from Lexis-Nexis.

## Chapter XVI

# INDIAN ENERGY STRATEGIES AND CENTRAL ASIA

Maj. Gen. (Retd) S C N Jatar

## The Need for an Energy Policy

There is perhaps a misconception that security pertains only to safeguarding the country from internal and external aggression. In the total security and defence strategy of a nation, energy strategy plays a vital role. In fact, secure access to energy is a prerequisite to ensuring sound internal and external security. Amongst the energy sources, oil is the only one that is fluid, best stored for strategic purposes and easily transportable. During the past several decades, oil has been the world's dominant source of primary energy and it is expected to remain in that position with a 40 per cent share of total energy consumption in the 1999–2020[1] period and, most likely, beyond.

Gas hydrates are now considered an alternative energy resource for the entire globe and is categorised under the unconventional natural gas resources like shale gas, tight gas sands, coal-bed methane and underground coal gasification, all of which are either expensive to extract or require new technology. The discovery of large amount of gas hydrates in the permafrost region of the Arctic and beneath the sea along the outer continental margins of the world's ocean has heightened interest in gas hydrates as a possible energy resource. India has commenced research in identifying gas hydrates in Indian waters and has entered into collaboration with countries and institutions abroad. India has planned to put a figure on its gas hydrate reserves by the year 2008. For this, the government has chalked up an elaborate plan for the acquisition of data, its processing and interpretation, and drilling. The countries that have advanced knowledge in this regard are Japan, Canada and the US.

Although Duncan's Olduvai Theory[2] was enunciated before the formulation of the current US policy of the 'axis of evil', it has been rephrased in 2002 by *Newsweek*[3] as a backdrop to the US invasion of Iraq. The bottom line, as Duncan puts it, is that although world oil production from 1979 to 1999 increased at an average rate of 0.75 per cent per year, world population grew even faster. Thus, per capita world oil production declined at an average rate of 1.20 per cent per year between 1979 and 1999. Further, although world energy production increased at an average rate of 1.34 per cent per year from 1979 to 1999, world population grew even faster. Consequently, per capita world energy production declined at an average rate of 0.33 per cent per year during these same twenty years. The relevance of this theory to the energy strategies of nations lies in the fact that oil and, in turn, energy production per capita, will fall to critical values in the next twenty-five to thirty years. Petroleum, particularly crude oil, has thus become the most important energy resource. It plays a pivotal role in defining the energy strategy of a country and, in turn, the security of the nation.

Oil production in oil-producing countries will peak by the end of the decade except for OPEC countries whose decline in oil production will start sometime between 2025 and 2030. The world will, thus, get divided into two distinct camps: the oil-rich and the oil-poor during this decade itself. Gulf War II has churned up Arab and Muslim sentiments against the United States. With the resurgence of Al Qaeda and other radical Islamists, particularly in Arab countries, West Asia is likely to remain unstable for a long time. Both China and Japan are making massive investments in pipeline projects to access hydrocarbons from the Central Asian region and Russia respectively. China is also increasing its presence in Saudi Arabia substantially. China is thus ensuring both its mid-term and long-term security by endeavouring to replace the US as a security guarantor to Saudi Arabia and to act as a land bridge for the energy requirements of East Asia. Japan, on its part, is reducing dependence on West Asia by accessing natural gas from Russia, which has the highest repository of natural gas in the world.

The Central Asian region, with its modest reservoir of hydrocarbons, compared to West Asia, is important to India due to geo-strategic and geopolitical reasons. These considerations along with energy security considerations in the short term suggest that India would make a greater effort to access hydrocarbons from the Central Asian region and also develop its own natural gas resources in the north-east on a priority basis. The option of accessing oil from the Atlantic coast, in case of disruption in West Asian supplies, is not a practicable solution. If India's relations with Bangladesh improve, it would lead to twin objectives: access to natural gas and reducing Bangladesh's anti-India stance that encourages militancy against India. By taking up Iranian concessions to produce natural gas and swap it with Japan or any other country, India can go a long way in meeting its energy requirements. This is a better option than laying a pipeline across Pakistan. Access to West Asian oil remains India's long-term answer to energy security. Thus, India needs to chart out an energy strategy so as to fulfil its needs in the short term within this decade, in the medium term up to 2030 and in the long term beyond 2030.

The importance of an energy policy that is arrived at after a public consensus and is updated periodically with a clearly stated energy budget, cannot be overemphasised. Such a policy should focus on reducing dependence on foreign oil, strengthening strategic petroleum reserve (SPR), balancing import of crude oil vis-à-vis refined products, and privatising upstream companies versus privatising the oilfields. The energy policy document should also discuss the issues of building up a nuclear industry; funding new technologies, promoting environmental concerns, supporting conservation, R&D for renewable energy development, strengthening public transportation to reduce dependence on petroleum, determining the terms for private participation in exploration and production, and reforming the energy sector.

There is an urgent need to make a thorough assessment and arrive at a Strategic Petroleum Reserve (SPR) of adequate size and mix that is managed by authorised personnel and can be accessed from suitable locations. A judicious mix of product and crude imports to suit varied civil and military requirements is a necessity. Over dependence on either crude oil or product imports could be disastrous for the country in an emergency. The surplus refining capacity in the country is an ominous pointer in this regard. India should consider 'privatising' oilfields so as to attract foreign equity along with state-of-the-art petroleum know-how while retaining operational control over public sector upstream oil companies due to the strategic nature of crude oil exploration and production industry.

## Significance of the Central Asian region for India

The hydrocarbon reserves of Central Asian region, as assessed on 1 January 2002, are 6.552 billion barrels of crude oil and 232.6 trillion cubic feet of natural gas (see Table I).

## Table I: *Central Asian Region Oil and Gas Reserves*

| Region/country | Oil (billion barrels) | Gas (trillion cubic feet) |
|---|---|---|
| Kazakhstan (7–9 billion barrels of Kashagan field not included) | 5.4 | 65.0 |
| Turkmenistan | 0.5 | 101.0 |
| Uzbekistan | 0.6 | 66.2 |
| Kyrgyzstan | 0.04 | 0.2 |
| Tajikistan | 0.012 | 0.2 |
| Total (as of 1 January 2002) | 6.552 | 232.6 |

*Source*: Energy Information Administration/International Energy Annual 2001.

In addition to Kazakhstan's 'proven' reserves, its 'possible' hydrocarbon reserves, both onshore and offshore, are an estimated thirty to fifty billion barrels mostly in the Kazakh sector of the Caspian Sea. In petroleum industry, the term 'proven' reserves or P90 indicates 90 per cent confidence level, 'possible' or P50 indicates 50 per cent confidence level and 'probable' or P70 a 70 per cent confidence level in accessing the reserves. The corresponding figures for oil and gas reserves for the world and for West Asia are presented in Table II and III.

## Table II: *World Oil and Gas Reserves*

| Region/country | Oil (billion barrels) | Gas (trillion cubic feet) |
|---|---|---|
| North, Central and South America | 150 | 528 |
| Western Europe | 17 | 161 |
| Eastern Europe and former USSR (includes CAR) | 58 | 1968 |
| Africa | 77 | 394 |
| Middle East | 686 | 1975 |
| Asia and Oceania | 44 | 433 |
| Total World (as of 1 January 2002) | 1032 | 5459 |

*Source*: Energy Information Administration/International Energy Annual 2001.

Table III: *Oil and Gas Reserves of West Asia*

| Region/country | Oil (billion barrels) | Gas (trillion cubic feet) |
|---|---|---|
| Iran | 89.7 | 812.3 |
| Iraq | 112.5 | 109.8 |
| Kuwait | 96.5 | 52.7 |
| Saudi Arabia | 261.8 | 219.5 |
| United Arab Emirates (basically Abu Dhabi alone) | 97.8 | 212.1 |
| Rest of Middle East (508.5 trillion cubic feet gas is in Qatar) | 27.3 | 568.2 |
| Total Middle East or West Asia (as of January 01, 2002) | 685.6 | 1974.6 |

*Source*: Energy Information Administration/International Energy Annual 2001.

The figures of reserves to production (R:P) ratios – the number of years that reserves of oil will last at current production rates – are revealing.[4] The R:P ratio is about eight to ten years for the US, Norway and Canada and between fifteen and twenty years for India. For Iran, it is 53:1, Saudi Arabia 55:1, the UAE 75:1 and Kuwait 116:1. Iraq, because of its inability to produce at optimum rates due to the sanctions and denial of requisite technology, has an R:P ratio of 526:1. US production peaked in 1970; Russia in 1986, China is to in 2005–06, Mexico in 2007, and in the Canadian and Central Asian regions production could reach their peak towards the end of the first decade of the millennium. OPEC production is predicted to peak between the years 2025 and 2030.[5]

OPEC's share[6] of world reserves is 77 per cent. The OECD[7] area, which consumes a little over 70 per cent of the world's daily production, produces less than 10 per cent of daily global oil production and, what is perhaps more significant, has only around 5 per cent of the world's reserves. The US, with 5 per cent of world's population consuming 26 per cent of the world's petroleum, is concerned about its energy security, as seen from its success in changing the regime in Iraq to control a major portion of the world's oil reserves and production. Significantly, Iraq remains 90 per cent unexplored and could yield another 200 billion barrels reserves of oil with inputs of the latest technology from the United States. Oil reserves are declining globally although production may rise. The production of oil, without replacing that production with new reserves, is leading to a decline in reserves.

It is evident that West Asia has vast reserves of both oil and gas. Only Russia can somewhat challenge West Asia in natural gas. In fact, Central Asia has one of the lowest quantities of reserves, next only to western Europe. Why is it then that the Central Asian region figures prominently in energy strategies of nations? The Central Asian region consists of the republics of Kazakhstan, Turkmenistan, Uzbekistan, Kyrgyzstan, and Tajikistan. The region is located in the centre of the Eurasian landmass, extending from the Caspian Sea in the west to the border of western China in the east. To the north lies Russia, and to the south are Iran, Afghanistan and China. To the north and south are countries rich in hydrocarbons – Russia and Iran. To the east and south is China, which is a long-term rival to both America and Russia. The Central Asian region is thus strategically situated to influence major power relationships. Considering Central Asia's modest quantum of hydrocarbon reserves, the 'great game' obviously is to control and deny these to rivals rather than actually access it – more so, because the land route for piped gas to South Asia is shorter from the Central Asian region. This point is of significance to India in the event of disruption of supplies from West Asia with India being forced to look to the

Atlantic coasts for fuel supply.

Strategically, the US military presence in the Central Asian region, Iraq, Afghanistan and Pakistan effectively surrounds Iran and seals its getaway routes. Presence in the Central Asian region is important for geo-strategic reasons. After 9/11, a realisation has dawned that the greatest danger to the world today is from terrorism and not from territorial disputes. The stronghold of terrorism is Islamist radicalism. The US believes that Iran, Saudi Arabia and Syria are the fountainheads of terrorism. The Central Asian region can also be a fertile breeding ground for Islamist extremists. The civil war in Tajikistan, which was instigated by Islamist conservatives, is a case in point. One of the major aims of US military presence in the Central Asian region is to keep a finger on its pulse and thwart any emerging terrorist activity. Russia and China are also concerned about terrorism in Chechnya and Xinjiang respectively. Xinjiang bordered by Kazakhstan, Kyrgyzstan, and Tajikistan to the northwest is a target of Islamist insurgency. Since American military power cannot be challenged today, the only way to have a presence in the Central Asian region is by participating in the development of hydrocarbon reserves and the export pipelines mainly of gas, across the landmass outside the Central Asian region. Of course, the Central Asian region's gas reserves (mainly in Kazakhstan, Uzbekistan and Turkmenistan) also offer mid-term (up to 2025) energy security. The long-term (beyond 2030) importance of the Central Asian region is more in its strategic location than in its hydrocarbon potential, notwithstanding the assessment of 'possible' reserves of another about fifty million barrels of oil and oil equivalent of gas in Kazakhstan. The reservoirs of oil and gas and their transportation outside the Central Asian region, with the attendant need for pipeline security, are tools that could help achieve larger and more critical geostrategic and geopolitical ambitions.

Japan, with no petroleum resources of its own, is the world's second largest oil consumer, and is eagerly supporting the construction of a 2,500-mile, five-billion-dollar oil pipeline that would bypass China, bringing Siberian oil to the Sea of Japan.[8] China used to be self-sufficient in energy but is today a net importer of crude oil. That is why Beijing is moving to ensure its security by building pipelines into Russia, Kazakhstan and Turkmenistan. The Kazakh deals involve the construction of a massive pipeline to China from the Kazakh gas fields[9] which will further connect Tarim Basin of Xinjiang to Shanghai at a cost of $18 billion[10] a 4,200-km long gas pipeline. China hopes to become a land bridge for future oil deliveries to Japan and South Korea, giving it important leverage in its strategic goal to replace the United States as the major power in East Asia. Chinese relations with Saudi Arabia are largely linked to its growing appetite for imported energy resources and the long-term goal of replacing the United States as the Persian Gulf's security guarantor. China cannot afford to neglect the Central Asian region. Geostrategic considerations and energy security have taken precedence over economics in the moves being made by Japan and China.

## Growing Uncertainty and Instability in West Asia

As stated earlier, the non-OPEC oil producers are expected to reach their peak production levels by 2010. After this, OPEC will control 100 per cent of oil exports. The situation will get critical due to the turmoil in West Asia, where all the oil is. The conflict in Iraq has already divided the world as never before. The eclipse of a 'secular' Iraq would also create social, religious and political tensions in the Arab world, which is a repository of crude oil. Only Saudi Arabia could come to the aid of the US by agreeing to increase oil production by two million barrels per day to make up for the shortfalls during the Iraq war. As oil wells cannot be turned off or on at will, Saudi Arabia had to gradually increase its production from January 2003 to reach 9.5 million barrels per day progressively by March 2003, just in time for Gulf War II.

Instability looms large over West Asia. It is an uncertain region for several reasons. The Israel-Palestine imbroglio continues to defy a peaceful solution. Further, if Sunni terrorism – headed by the Al Qaeda and Hamas networks with sponsors in Saudi Arabia and Syria – and Shia terrorism – spurred by Iran-backed Hezbollah – merge, the region will become virtually unmanageable. Despite its firepower, the US military power can never hope to destroy such deadly stray groups completely by invading the country-sanctuaries that harbour these groups.[11]

Osama Bin Laden, in one of his videotapes, said that Jordan, Morocco, Nigeria, the country of the two shrines (Saudi Arabia), Yemen and Pakistan are 'ready for liberation'.[12] The US Embassy in Riyadh and two consulates in Saudi Arabia were closed on 21 May 2003 because of an 'imminent' threat of more terrorist attacks inside the kingdom. Officials in Britain and Germany also said they would close their embassies temporarily.[13] In another tape released on 21 May 2003, Al Qaeda's second-in-command urged Muslims to carry out more suicide attacks, called for the use of violence instead of peace talks and condemned Arab countries that helped the US-led campaign, naming Saudi Arabia, Kuwait, Qatar, Bahrain, Yemen and Jordan.[14]

## Criticality of Energy Security for India

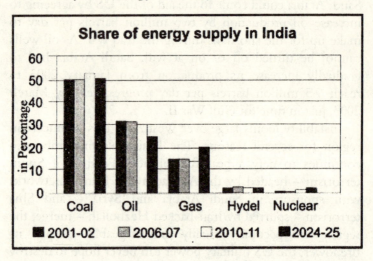

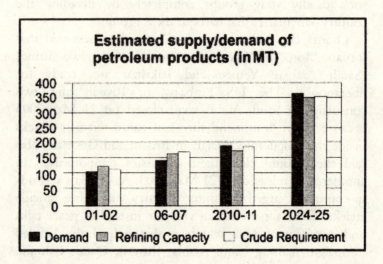

Oil and gas continue to play a vital role in meeting India's energy requirements. Forty-five per cent of the country's energy needs are met through oil and gas. India is endowed with twenty-six sedimentary basins covering an area of over three million square kilometre including deep waters. In these twenty-six basins (covering isobath up to 200 metres) with an area of about 1.784 million sq km the prognosticated reserves have been assessed at 18.51 billion tonnes[15] of Oil + Oil Equivalent of Gas (O+OEG) out of which ONGC has reserves of about 5.5 billion tonnes with the discovery of 270 prospects. The sedimentary basins of India have been classified into four categories as follows:

Category I: Basins with commercial production, e.g. Cambay, Upper Assam, Bombay Offshore, Krishna-Godavari, Cauvery and Assam-Arakan.

Category II: Basins with known occurrences of hydro–carbons, but from which no significant commercial production has yet been obtained, e.g. Kutch, Andaman and Rajasthan.

Category III: Basins in which significant quantities of hydrocarbons have not yet been found, but which on general geological considerations are assumed to be energy-rich, e.g., Mahanadi and Kerala-Konkan.

Category IV: Basins which on analogy with similar hydrocarbon-producing basins in the world, are deemed to be prospective, e.g. Pranhita-Godavari, Satpura-South Rewa, Damodar, Narmada, the Deccan Syneclise, Vindhyan, tectonised zone of the Himalayas, Karewa, Spiti-Zanskar, Cuddapah, Bhima-Kaladgi, Bastar and Chattisgarh.

As of now the main oil-producing areas in India are Upper Assam, Cambay basin in Gujarat and the Maharashtra-Gujarat offshore area, with the ONGC-discovered Ravva field the only sizeable one on the east coast. No significant oil discoveries have been made since 1987. Crude oil is being produced almost entirely from fields discovered before 1988. The private sector/joint venture companies in the country are producing from fields discovered by ONGC or Oil India Ltd. Oil or gas fields discovered entirely by the efforts of the private sector have yet to begin production. From 1950 onwards the demand for petroleum has been rising on an annual basis. In terms of crude oil self-sufficiency, the peak value of 67 per cent was reached in the late 1980s. Currently, the country is around 32.5 per cent self-reliant but this figure is expected to further decline to around 25 per cent by the end of the Tenth Plan period (2006–07) with demand reaching about 115 million tonnes per year by 2008. Self-reliance will reach a critical stage by the end of this decade as the economic growth of India picks up.

India imported oil worth US $12.7 billion (Rs 61,000 crores) in 2002–03. A one-dollar increase escalates the oil bill by $1.7 million or Rs 8.2 crores. India is still 63 per cent dependent on West Asian crude oil as opposed to over 83 per cent a decade earlier. Reducing dependence on West Asia is at best a mid-term measure because West Asian oil will outlast all other oil. India has to carve out a strategy to access West Asian oil for its long-term (beyond 2030) energy security.

In this scenario, India should chart out its energy strategy to cater to the short term (within this decade), medium term (up to 2030) and the long term (beyond 2030). The planning should consider factors such as the global geopolitical situation and geostrategic considerations, moves of the sole superpower towards consolidating its military presence in the Central Asian region and West Asia and the ominous Chinese moves to encircle India.[16] The location and extent of global hydrocarbon reserves are of importance. India's evolving relationship with the Central Asian states and the traditional bonds with hydrocarbon-rich Russia and Iran are also significant factors.

However, India does not have a stated energy policy. A plethora of ministries and departments of the government such as power, petroleum, coal, atomic energy, etc., deal with energy. The result is a splintered policy that appears directionless. Indian strategic plans for external and internal security do not lay sufficient emphasis on the need for secure access to energy resources. Advanced countries not only have an energy policy but also an annual energy budget. The focus of any energy policy is on reducing dependence on foreign oil, strengthening strategic petroleum reserve (SPR), balancing import of crude oil vis-à-vis refined products and privatising upstream companies versus the oilfields.

## Reduce Dependence on Oil Imports

India is engaged in exploration of oil and gas in nine countries. ONGC Videsh Ltd has signed contracts with Vietnam, Russia, Sudan, Iraq, Myanmar, the USA, Iran, Libya and Syria to access about 800 million tonnes of recoverable reserves of oil and thirty trillion cubic feet of gas. These are not large reserves considering our annual requirement of about 100 million tonnes of oil and three trillion cubic feet of gas, but it is a good beginning. Except for the one with Vietnam, all other contracts were initiated and signed during the last few years. India is also negotiating with Qatar, Sudan, Vietnam and Bangladesh to access acreage.

In March 2003, ONGC Videsh completed the acquisition of its first oil-producing property, investing Rs 3,500 crores (US $700 million approx.) for a 25 per cent equity in the Greater Nile Oil Project, Sudan. This investment entitles ONGC Videsh to three million tonnes of Nile blend crude per year valued at Rs 2,500 crores (US $500 million approx.) at current prices. The first cargo of 80,000 tonnes of Nile blend crude from ONGC's equity in the Greater Nile Oil Project, Sudan, was delivered to ONGC's refinery at Mangalore on 15 May 2003.[17]

ONGC Videsh has made an investment of $1.7 billion in acquiring 20 per cent interest in the Russian oilfield Sakhalin-I. This agreement would ensure equity oil of about two to four million tonnes besides five to eight million cubic metres of gas. India's share of oil and gas would be swapped with countries like Japan, China and Korea, which are closer to Sakhalin.[18]

The earliest production-sharing contract of ONGC Videsh from amongst the existing ones is with PetroVietnam dated 19 May 1988. ONGC Videsh has a 45 per cent stake in the production and so far 2.04 trillion cubic feet of gas has been discovered. India will get about 266 million cubic feet of gas from 2004 until 2019 from this contract.

ONGC Videsh is currently negotiating an exploration block in the Caspian Sea offshore, southwest of Kashagan field, and participating in two discovered fields in Kazakhstan in the Central Asian region.

While the thrust to acquire overseas oil and gas is indeed laudable, much more needs to be done, especially in acquiring foreign equity gas. Some energy 'experts' espouse import of natural gas from Bangladesh as a solution without assessing the real extent of reserves and attendant security threats emanating from such a situation. The gas reserves of Bangladesh are only 18.6 trillion cubic feet and of Myanmar ten trillion cubic feet as of 1 January 2002.[19] Bangladesh University of Engineering & Technology has assessed the reserves at twenty-four trillion cubic feet.[20] Further, the US Geological Survey has estimated that Bangladesh contains an additional 32.1 trillion cubic feet in additional 'undiscovered reserves', (US Department of Energy, Energy Information Administration, Country Analysis Brief – Bangladesh). Our own gas reserves are: Mumbai High, 10.6 trillion cubic feet; Bassein, 13.2 trillion cubic feet; Assam, 3.36 trillion cubic feet; Arunachal Pradesh, 1 trillion cubic feet; and, Tripura, 1 trillion cubic feet. The gas resources of Assam, Arunachal Pradesh and Tripura could not yet be fully exploited due to insurgency and lack of market. It is, thus, rather odd to go further east to access gas with attendant political and security problems. The pipeline from Myanmar would be longer and possibly more insecure. There are political issues which have not only affected Bangladeshi approval to such a venture but are likely to be a hindrance even if an approval is forthcoming. Some of these concerns are serious: persecution of Hindus, resurgence of fundamentalist Islam, state encouragement to anti-India militancy including setting up of Al Qaeda cells in the country, and illegal immigration of Bangladeshis into India. India has floated a public sector company called India International Gas Company with the Indian Oil Corporation, Gas Authority of India and Oil and Natural Gas Corporation as equity partners to access gas from Bangladesh and lay a pipeline.[21] If relationship with Bangladesh improves, its support to insurgents will go down. Thus, improving relationship with Bangladesh is an imperative for energy security. An interesting point to note is that Bangladesh exports lean gas from which liquefied petroleum gas cannot be extracted. Thus, import of gas from Bangladesh will not help in mitigating the projected deficit of LPG in the country estimated at between 3.38 and 5.88 million tonnes in 2006–07. LPG cannot be extracted from CNG either and hence import of LPG for all time has to be an important plank of our energy security.

Considering the extent of gas reserves and the political and security problems, it appears that Bangladesh could at best offer a mid term (up to 2030) solution to our energy needs. This too would depend on factors such as technical

317

and economic feasibility of the pipeline and the development of a viable market. Compare the 20 trillion cubic feet – or the higher estimation of 34 trillion cubic feet – gas reserves of Bangladesh and Myanmar with the massive 1,975 trillion cubic feet of West Asia (including 812 of Iran), 1,680 of Russia and 233 trillion cubic feet of the Central Asian region. Given these numbers, the answer to our mid (up to 2030) and long term (beyond 2030) energy security concerns becomes clearer.

The pipeline from the Central Asian region or Iran has to traverse through Afghanistan and Pakistan. Insurgents in Afghanistan and the government in Pakistan can easily block gas supply at crucial times on a land route and India would not even know who blocked it on the sea route. Insurance cover gives only notional security because monetary reimbursement (even if it is forthcoming) cannot compensate for the economic loss and the adverse social and political fallout due to the sudden stoppage of gas. The only alternative appears to be to swap natural gas in case Iran agrees to grant India concessions for exploration and production and if India strikes economically viable quantities of gas or oil in Iran. This is an involved affair because a market nevertheless has to be found for the gas so discovered.

An alternative could be to negotiate with Japan whose ever-increasing appetite for CNG can be satiated by Iranian gas. India should think of the same strategy to access Central Asian region and Russian gas, that is, of acquiring concessions and then trading equity gas either with oil or other commodities or making an outright sale of it at international prices for which a market has to be developed. The significance of such a swapping arrangement lies also in the fact that accessing petroleum from the Atlantic coasts is time-consuming and costly due to the distances involved.

## Strategic Petroleum Reserves (SPR)

SPR is required during times of war to deal with increase in consumption and to cope with any disruption of supplies. Disruption of supplies could occur due to an unstable West Asia or could even be due to a ban on supplies by the oil producers or due to UN sanctions during a war, especially with Pakistan. The US, due to its very large requirement of over twenty million barrels of oil per day, also uses its SPR of 600 million barrels to dampen oil prices by releasing petroleum from it. Our strategic petroleum reserves are only for twenty-six days and that too in the pipelines and thirty-five days of products at the refineries. Terming crude oil in pipelines as strategic reserves is unconventional. This is because crude oil in pipelines is not immediately available for treatment by the refineries due to the need to remove BS&W (bottom sediments and water) from it, which could take more than twenty-four hours. One can then even stretch the definition by including producible reserves of petroleum as strategic reserves. For a short war such long term 'reserves' are not useful. Security of supplies for gaseous fuels such as natural gas, CNG or LPG will always remain a problem.

By definition, SPR should be available immediately for deployment at pre-assessed locations and in a predetermined time frame. The authority to access the SPR is to be delegated appropriately. India must allocate different locations for the SPR after considering issues of defence and security. The SPR is normally located near the theatres of war, which in our case are far away from the ports. The quantity, locations and methods of storage (basically whether underground or over) can thus be firmed up. It is prudent to keep petroleum reserves away from urban centres and a large number of dummies should be created to ensure their protection. Our planners need to give adequate thought to these aspects of SPR planning. In the absence of such detailed planning, India's defence capabilities could be severely impacted. It could even force a ceasefire in future or potential hostilities, if not resolved in advance.

## Import of crude oil versus refined products

India does not have a long-term (beyond 2030) policy on import of crude oil vis-à-vis products, based on strategic considerations. The refining capacity planned at the end of the Eighth Plan (31 March 1997) was 61.55 million tonnes per annum (Mtp.a.), 114.67 Mtp.a. at the end of the Ninth Plan (31 March 2002) and 220.75 Mtp.a. at the end of the Tenth Plan (31 March 2007)[22]. Out of 220.75 Mtp.a., about 77 Mtp.a. is new capacity (25 – public sector units; 21 – joint ventures; and 31 – private sector units. Of the private sector units, 23 Mtp.a. is Reliance's contribution).

In either case, there is enormous overcapacity in refining. With a requirement of about 115 million tonnes by 2008, there is likely to be a surplus capacity in refining of between 23 and 106 Mtp.a. (provided all new refineries come up). This will result in over-dependence on crude oil for strategic storage. Consequently, there will be a loss of flexibility in planning and provisioning for SPR. The infrastructure for transportation and storage of petroleum products would also be neglected.

A subgroup of the 'R' Group set up by the Government of India for the Ninth Plan period in 1994 went into the question of 'whether it is necessary to set up new refining capacities or India can manage by importing the products directly'. It appears that the subgroup has only considered heavy dependence on one or the other and implied that importing crude oil for the entire requirement is tantamount to self-reliance. It has dismissed the higher volatility of crude oil prices. 'It is too simplistic to assume that any country can meet its deficits in a large scale by importing larger quantities of finished products,' the report comments. The subgroup has acknowledged:

> The associated economics of importing products versus setting up refining capacity cannot be taken as the only criteria for decision-making as there are large swings and unpredictable crude and petroleum product prices and even a temporary dislocation or product availability problems internationally can have significant debits to the national exchequer.

It has argued that there would be a tight product market in the years to come because global refining capacity utilisation has increased to 90 per cent. The subgroup has cited national security and self-reliance as the primary reasons for preferring an increase in the refining capacity and has contended that massive infrastructure is needed for import and transportation of products, ignoring the enormous capital and infrastructural requirements for refineries. The subgroup has not considered the fact that while product pipelines can be used for all products, crude pipelines cannot be used for products.

Table IV: *Refining Capacities in the Country*

| Year | Refining capacity in million tonnes per annum (Mtp.a.) |
|------|--------------------------------------------------------|
| 1.4.1997 | 62 |
| 1.4.2002 | 116 |
| 1.4.2005 | 132 |
| 1.4.2007 | 138 may go over to 150 Mtp.a. if the demand grows by over 5% p.a. |

*Source*: Petroleum Planning & Analysis Cell (PPAC), MoP&NG.

The committee set up by the Ministry of Petroleum & Natural Gas[23] for security of supply of auto-fuels has noted 'the government policy of attaining self-sufficiency in refining for meeting the domestic demand of petroleum products at minimal costs'. India Hydrocarbon Vision 2025 document states that 'maintaining around 90 per cent consumption of the middle distillates from domestic refining is one of the policy objectives'. It is thus apparent that the government first took the decision to depend heavily on the import of petroleum products and then 'situated the assessment' to support the decision. Costs, and not national security interests, appear to be the raison d'être of the policy. The committee further states:

> Meeting the country's demand by processing imported crude oil in the country as against product imports has the following apparent advantages:
>
> - Value addition in the country, apart from generating employment, results into savings in the country's import bill.
> - Low cost overseas transportation of crude oil makes its sourcing from distant sources possible which enables diversification of crude oil supply sources crucial for the oil supply security of the country.
> - International crude oil markets being deep and broad based in comparison to the product markets, price risks associated with oil market volatilities are minimised.
> - Requirement of port facilities and storage terminals for importing crude oil being lower than for products, port infrastructure costs are saved.

All the above cited reasons pertain to prices and costs. Considerations of security of the country, whether from the points of view of defence or energy, have been totally neglected. The government committee has drawn attention to another disadvantage of excess refining capacity. It points out that for its smooth functioning, an oil refinery needs to unload its production stocks continuously either in domestic markets or in foreign markets through exports. The inland refineries, numbering nine out of a total of sixteen, can dispose of their products in the domestic market only. Build-up of stocks further puts pressure on storage capacities and the refining process can come to a halt in case of uncleared inventory. 'Under such circumstances, the refinery has to close down on account of product containment,' says the report.

Clearly, the R Group and the government 'Committee' have not considered the security angle. The option considered was heavy dependence on import of either crude oil or refined products and not a judicious mix, which has not been assessed. Nor have they considered the option of importing products directly rather than importing crude and then refining it in case of an urgent requirement. Crude oil has no direct end-use application. It is often easier and more practical to purchase products in an emergency from a friendly country even if it is a net importer of petroleum. Thus, there is greater flexibility in importing products. Further, the SPR should have a component of products, which will be difficult to maintain in case of excess refining capacity. If the SPR is used up, it will have to be replenished with products, and not crude oil, during times of conflict or other emergencies when the country runs out of crude oil or the refineries are sabotaged. We, therefore, need to have a running contract for imports of products in peacetime. Pipelines are the quickest and safest means of transportation. There is an urgent need to assess whether product pipelines of adequate capacity are available from ports to the locations where SPR would be located.

Indian experts are beginning to reconsider the decision to develop new refineries. It is necessary to focus on finalising import of products, even if some products from Indian refineries have to be exported. A judicious mix of product and crude imports to suit varied civil and military requirements is an important part of energy security. It is surmised that the US keeps a mix of 50:50 between crude oil and petroleum products as its SPR. The United States had an inventory of a minimum of 300 million barrels of crude over a five-year period up to December 2002 and a maximum of 330 million barrels in May 2002.[24]

## Upstream Privatisation vis-à-vis Privatising the Oilfields

India needs foreign private capital for import of sophisticated equipment and access to latest technology. There is also a need to build confidence amongst international operators and strengthen ONGC to give a boost to exploration efforts in the country. ONGC should initially privatise oilfields totalling 50 per cent of its balance recoverable reserves. A collaborative joint venture with reputed international oil companies that have proven records in exploration and production activities could lead to the development of these oilfields. A competitive bidding process could help identify the right partners.

ONGC has about 1,100 million tonnes or about 8,000 million barrels of balance recoverable reserves of O+OEG. If half of these reserves were jointly developed, ONGC would generate for the country about US $24 billion at a very conservative net present value of oil reserves @ US $6 per barrel. And ONGC would still hold control over the fields with only 50 per cent reserves for joint development and access to state-of-the-art technology. Joint ventures do offer the opportunity to public sector companies to upgrade their know-how, imbibe a high-quality work culture and adopt cost-effective production processes from their international partners. However, there is also a risk that government may end up becoming an insignificant partner and may eventually lose control of the company and the oilfields. Already, the government has divested 35 per cent equity from its 84 per cent holding in ONGC. It now has just a 49 per cent stake in ONGC. This translates into roughly about US $20 billion for the government's share.[25]

## Conclusion

The emergence of Central Asia as a region with hydrocarbon potential offers India the opportunity to beef up its energy security in the short term up to 2025. A fact not normally appreciated is that OPEC oil – 659 billion barrels are contributed by its five West Asian members Iran, Iraq, Kuwait, UAE and Saudi Arabia – will outlast all other oil and its decline is likely to commence only after 2025. Considering the uncertain conditions in West Asia after Gulf War II, it would be prudent for India to access hydrocarbons from Bangladesh and the Central Asian region while speedily developing its own largely untapped hydrocarbon reserves.

## Notes

1. International Energy Outlook 2002, Highlights, Energy Information Administration.
2. 'The peak of world oil production and the road to the Olduvai Gorge', by Richard C Duncan, PhD, Pardee Keynote Symposia, Geological Society of America, Summit 2000, Reno, Nevada, 13 November 2000.
3. *Newsweek*, April 2002.
4. Rifkin, Jeremy, in *Hydrogen Economy*, quoted in 'This looming war is about oil', Fisk, Robert, 1 World Communication.
5. Puplava, Jim from website acknowledged through hyperlink to: www.financialsense.com
6. Of this, 659 billion barrels are in the five large member countries of OPEC: Iran. Iraq, Kuwait, UAE and Saudi Arabia, located in the West Asian region.
7. The Organisation for Economic Cooperation and Development. Current membership: Australia, New Zealand, Japan, the United States, Canada, the United Kingdom, France, Germany, Italy, Spain, Portugal, Belgium, Luxembourg, the Netherlands, Denmark, Norway, Sweden, Switzerland, Eire, Austria and Greece.
8. Brooke, James, 'Koizumi Visits Energy-Rich Russian Region', *Seeking Oil*, 12 January 2003.
9. Woodrow, Thomas, 'The Sino-Saudi Connection', *China Brief*, 24 October 2002, from: http://china.jamestown.org/pubs/view/cwe/002/021_003.htm, Thomas Woodrow was a senior China analyst at the Defense Intelligence Agency.
10. Goodman, Peter S, 'A Pipeline to the Future, Clogged by China's Past? Politics, Economics Complicate Natural Gas Push'. *Washington Post Foreign Service*, 20 August 2002; Page E01.

11. Narayanan, Dr Kottillil, former exploration adviser to the Government of Tanzania; chief technical adviser, UNIDO, UNDP Project URT 028/74; petroleum adviser, Norwegian Petroleum Directorate, Royal Norwegian Government; chairman, Advisory Council, Directorate General of Hydrocarbons, Govt. of India, in an informal paper, 22 May 2003.

12. 'Audiotape had hinted at Al Qaeda strikes on Morocco, Saudi', PTI report in *The Times of India*, Pune, 19 May 2003, quoting a report in the *Sunday Times*, London.

13. Natta, Don Van, Jr, 'US Diplomatic Outposts to Be Shut in Saudi Arabia', *The New York Times*, 21 May 2003 and Finn Peter, 'US, Britain, Germany Close Riyadh Embassies', *The Washington Post Foreign Service*, 21 May 2003.

14. 'Al-Qaeda' urges fresh attacks, BBC News, 22 May 2003.

15. Includes oil that is already produced, still to be produced and not yet discovered.

16. China is encircling India with a pro-Maoist monarch in Nepal, a January 2003 defence pact with Bangladesh, and with Pakistan as its proxy.

17. 'ONGC Group, Building India's Oil Security', *The Indian Express*, Pune, 15 May 2003.

18. 'OVL buys stake in Sakhalin for $1.7 billion', *The Times of India*, Pune, 3 November 2001.

19. The figure includes oil so far produced, oil so far found and proved for numbers but is yet to be produced and, lastly, oil that is yet to be found. Energy Information Administration/International Energy Annual 2001.

20. Jawahar, K R, 'Bangladesh Gas Economy', *SAPRA India Monthly Bulletin*, September 2002.

21. Ibid.

22. Website of the Ministry of Petroleum & Natural Gas accessed on 20 May 2003.

23. Chapter 7 entitled, 'Availability, demand and security of supply of auto fuels', Official website, Government of India, Ministry of Petroleum & Natural Gas, accessed 21 May 2003.

24. Simmons, Matthew R, 'Are Oil and Murphy's Law About to Meet?', *Outlook*, 2003; United States Crude Oil Prices, *World Oil*, February 2003, Vol. 224, No. 2.

25. Working Calculations for Divestment:

    ONGC Equity – Rs 1426 crore with government holding of 84 per cent.

    Dilution of equity by 35 per cent to 49 per cent.

    Average price Rs 425/- per share. A premium of another Rs 425/- per share is taken.

    35 per cent of Rs 1426 crore is Rs 500 crore for 50 crore shares of Rs 10/- each.

    50 crore multiplied by Rs 425/- is Rs 21250 crore, which comes to about US $10 billion @ Rs 47.50 for a dollar.

    If we take a premium on ONGC's share and value it at double the price @ Rs 850/- per share, the government take would come to US $20 billion.

# Chapter XVII

# CENTRAL ASIAN ECONOMIES: PROSPECTS FOR INDIA'S TRADE AND INVESTMENT

T K Bhaumik

## Introduction

The collapse of the Soviet Union in 1991 led to the creation of five nations under the banner of the Central Asian Republics (CARs). With independence, Kazakhstan, Kyrgyzstan, Tajikistan, Turkmenistan and Uzbekistan were faced with the challenge of creating new economies and establishing their identity in a fast changing global economic environment. After the initial years of instability and turmoil, these economies are slowly beginning to consolidate. The most significant challenge for these countries has been to put things in order, kick-start the economic sectors and put in place mechanisms that will lead to economic growth. Most of these countries are still grappling with this challenge.

The collapse of the USSR and its command and control economy was the first jolt for the Central Asian economies. This was accompanied by significant losses in economic output or 'net material production'. In the post-Soviet era, there has been a steady decline in the CARs' trade relations with Russia. Even so, a large chunk of Central Asian trade continues to be with Russia. Getting connected to the world economy and markets is the second challenge that these economies face. Rebuilding the economies is the most significant task at hand for the CARs. The priority areas are:

- To streamline the public sector units that the CARs have inherited from the Communist regime and bring them up to speed in terms of technology, productivity, capacities and capabilities.
- To embark on a rigorous economic reform process that can make the existing economic structure fully functional and capable of achieving major economic objectives.
- To work towards economic development by formulating strategies and policies. However, lack of access to official funding, particularly in terms of external assistance, and poor creditworthiness of these countries make this task even more difficult.

## Prospects for Economic Development

Given such a scenario, what are the prospects for the region's economic progress? Economic linkages with Russia are weakening, particularly since the Russian economy is struggling to transform into a market economy. The region does not hold much appeal except as a source of energy resources and supplier of a few minerals and agricultural produce. The low incomes of its collective population of about fifty-seven million do not make for an attractive domestic/regional market. The region has more geopolitical than geoeconomic significance.

Even so, the economies of the region have enough potential to attract the attention of global players. The region possesses rich mineral resources, including energy resources, and some agricultural raw material production capacities. The industrial economy may not be strong and competitive but the basic industrial infrastructure is already in place. Stronger commitment to economic reform can lead these countries towards the path of economic progress. A key factor that will determine the region's economic progress is the extent of economic integration among the countries of the region. Intra-regional cooperation can pave the way for integration with the global economy and faster growth. This is also considered essential for future growth of the region.

Fortunately, the leaders of the CARs are well aware of these issues. New policy initiatives undertaken by these governments are directed towards the goal of regional integration and integration with the global economy. The Economic Cooperation Organisation (ECO) is already in place and formal membership of international institutions such as the World Bank, IMF, ADB, European Bank for Reconstruction and Development (EBRD), etc., has been obtained by all the countries. All these are steps in the direction of future development. Most countries have embarked on an economic restructuring and adjustment programme, including initiatives such as land reform, privatisation, establishment of market-oriented institutions, financial restructuring, etc. However, the transition to a full-fledged modern market economy is not going to be easy.

## Economic Scenario

Post-independence, most countries of the region experienced significant loss of economic output. For instance, in Uzbekistan gross domestic product (GDP) decreased by 1.9 per cent per annum, in real terms, during 1990–98. In Turkmenistan, real per capita income declined by 14.6 per cent per annum during 1990–97. The other states fared no better. Stability and growth could be restored only in early 1998.

Table I: *Economic Structure of Central Asian Republics*

| Countries | Population (million) as in July '01 | GDP ($ billion) (2001) | Shares in GDP (%) | | |
|---|---|---|---|---|---|
| | | | Agriculture | Industry | Services |
| Kazakhstan | 14.83 | 22.3 ($1506) | 2.6 | 32.0 | 65.4 |
| Kyrgyz Rep. | 4.97 | 1.5 ($308) | 38.0 | 23.0 | 39.0 |
| Tazikistan | 6.38 | 1.03 ($161) | 24.0 | 21.0 | 55.0 |
| Turkmenistan | 5.44 | 6.0 ($1083) | 26.0 | 38.0 | 36.0 |
| Uzbekistan | 25.10 | 7.5 ($299) | 34.5 | 16.1 | 49.4 |
| Total | 56.72 | 38.33 ($3357) | – | – | – |

*Note*: Figures within brackets are per capita incomes.
*Source*: The Europa World Yearbook, 2001.

By and large, the region is a conglomeration of small and poor economies, with per capita income ranging from $161 to over $1,500. With the exception of Kazakhstan, the undeveloped agricultural sector is a primary source of livelihood for the bulk of the population. This is particularly true of Uzbekistan, which has nearly half of the total population of the region. There is a high incidence of poverty in the region, except in Turkmenistan where the percentage of people living below the national poverty line was only 7 per cent in 2001. It was nearly 32 per cent in Kazakhstan, 48 per cent in the Kyrgyz Republic, as high as 83 per cent in Tajikistan and 29 per cent in Uzbekistan. In recent times, the economies have begun to register growth as a result of better economic management.

According to the World Bank (2001), Kazakhstan has recorded high growth since 1999. Inflation is under control and debt-service ratio is on the decline. Better economic performance is largely on account of higher oil production and growing oil revenue. Oil revenues are accumulated in a National Fund established in 2001. The objective is to ensure better utilisation of the revenue stream. However, this also increases vulnerability of the economy to external shocks. Effective management of oil revenues, therefore, remains a major challenge.

In Kyrgyzstan, the smallest country of the region in terms of population, the collapse of the Soviet Union saw a drastic reduction in income levels (between 1991 and 1995 the GDP declined to 50 per cent of 1990 levels). However, between 1996 and 2001, real GDP registered an average annual growth of 5 per cent. Recovery in the agricultural sector largely accounted for this growth. Further growth was supported by macro-economic and exchange rate stability and low inflation.

As is indicated by its per capita income, Tajikistan is the poorest country of the region. Its topographical conditions are primarily responsible for the extreme poverty. Economic reform measures are being put in place with World Bank assistance and the economy is gradually turning around. Inflation has declined from 164 per cent in 1997 to 12.5 per cent in 2001. Infrastructure, damaged during the post-independence civil war, is also being restored.

The economy of Turkmenistan is relatively better on purely quantitative terms with very low levels of poverty. However, it is yet to take significant steps towards economic reform, and continues to be a highly subsidised economy. According to the World Bank, 'Share of the private sector is... just 25 per cent. Basic commodities (water, energy, bread) are free or heavily subsidised.' Further, there is ample evidence of poor economic management. From the World Bank's point of view the country is less inclined to take tough reform measures, and therefore, runs a greater risk of unsustainable development. Uzbekistan also has been slow to accept economic reforms. The economy remains highly distorted as a result. Private sector development has also been tardy.

Overall, the prospects for the regional economy are

mixed. It is a region with vast economic potential, but with high incidence of poverty and inadequate social and economic infrastructure. The process of economic reform is under way with the guidance of the World Bank but is far from complete and is expected to take a long time. Due to inadequate availability of domestic capital, technical competence and high-quality human capital, these countries are unable to get the maximum returns from their natural resources.

In reality, it is a case of rebuilding the economies and not merely a transition of economic regimes. If necessary institutions are put in place – for example, legal systems, public administration, financial infrastructure, etc. – the overall investment environment will improve. The World Bank has adopted a two-pronged approach of assisting economic reform as well as enabling development of social and economic infrastructure. This involves restoration of the water supply system, irrigation system, urban transportation, health care system, and the development of energy telecom and rural sectors. The education system, especially professional education, also needs to be overhauled to meet the needs of an efficient market economy.

## Trade Structure in the Central Asian Republics

For India, the collapse of the USSR has had an enormous impact on its trade. India's trade relations were with the Soviet Union and not its individual republics. There is no available data on how much of Indian exports, and in what proportion, went to the Central Asian states. Similarly, there is a lack of data on exports of individual states of the USSR to India. Gross trade turnover, however, was significant. In 1990, for instance, two-way trade between India and the USSR amounted to Rs 80,000 million, accounting for 16 per cent of India's total trade. It was largely 'arranged' trade, where competitive principles were not at work. With the collapse of the USSR, the onus was on India to reorganise its trade with the new regime and the newly independent CARs. Most of the trade relations were limited to India and the Russian Federation, which also faced the challenge of propping up its battered economy.

For the Russian Federation, this meant equipping itself for the transition to a market economy while for India it meant establishing a new trading relationship with a new partner. For the first time, there was a need for capturing market share in a competitive manner in a scenario that was marked by declining growth, exchange rate instability and economic uncertainties. For a while, both sides had few clues as to how to put the business relationship back on track. For Indian exporters, the Russian Federation was the obvious replacement for the USSR. As a result, few exporters trained their sights on the newly independent states. It is only recently that the Indian industry and trade have begun to acknowledge the potential of Central Asia as a major market. Even so, except for sporadic forays into these markets by a handful of companies, there is no concerted effort to increase trading relations with these countries.

On their part, the CARs have not been able to snap their economic ties with the Russian Federation and trade with Russia continues to be an important aspect of their external trade. Russia still is the main trading partner for some of these countries. However, the CARs have begun to develop trade linkages with other countries (see Table II).

Table II: *Major Trading Partners of Central Asian Republics (Percentage of Exports and Imports, 2001)*

| Exports of, and Imports from | Kazakhstan | Kyrgyz Rep. | Tajikistan | Turkmenistan | Uzbekistan |
|---|---|---|---|---|---|
| Russia | 14.0 (45.0) | 10.6 (16.5) | 20 (10.0) | 3.0 (8.0) | 23 (16) |
| Tajikistan | – | 1.0 (–) | – | 3.4 (–) | 7 (15) |
| Italy | 5.0 (4.3) | – | 4.0 (–) | – | 7 (8.5) |
| Ukraine | 3.5 (2.0) | – | – | 14.0 (13.0) | 10.5 (6.5) |
| S Korea | – (2.0) | – (3.0) | – | – | 5.0 (7.0) |
| Germany | 8.2 (8.1) | 37.0 (8.0) | – | 11.0 (6.3) | 3.0 (10.0) |
| Kyrgys Rep. | – | – | – | – | 4.0 (4.0) |
| Turkey | –(3.0) | 2.0 (5.0) | 19.5 (–) | 15.0 (14.0) | 5.0 (4.0) |
| Kazakhstan | – | 6.0 (12.0) | 1.3 (12.0) | – | 3.0 (5.0) |
| France | – | – | – | – (2.6) | 2.0 (4.0) |
| The USA | 2.6 (3.1) | 0.3 (5.6) | – (4.5) | – (14.0) | – |
| China | 7.6 (5.5) | 5.0 (8.5) | – | – | – |
| Switzerland | 6.0 (–) | 8.0 (–) | 12 (–) | 7.0 (–) | – |
| The UK | 1.0 (2.3) | 2.0 (–) | – | 0.9 (–) | – |
| Netherlands | 0.8 (2.0) | – | – | – | – |
| Uzbekistan | – | 15.3 (20.3) | 16 (26) | – (2.0) | – |
| Romania | – | – | – | – | – |
| Moldova | – | – | 5.0 (–) | – | – |
| Belgium | – | – | – | – | – |
| Azerbaijan | – | – | – (15.0) | 3.0 (–) | – |
| Japan | – | – | – | – (2.0) | – |
| Iran | – | – | 2.0 (–) | 18.0 (5.0) | – |
| Turkmenistan | – | – (4.0) | – (6.0) | – | – |

*Notes*: (1) Over 16 per cent of Kazakh's exports go to Bermuda (not mentioned in this table); (2) Figures in brackets are percentage of imports. *Source*: The Europa World Yearbook, 2001.

In 2001, total imports for the five Central Asian Republics stood at around $12 billion with Kazakhstan's share at $6363 million; Kyrgyz Republic's $467 million; Tajikistan's $766 million; Turkmenistan's $1785 million; and Uzbekistan's* $2440 million. Kazakhstan alone accounted for over 50 per cent of total imports, with Russia as the dominant supplier, accounting for 45 per cent of total imports, followed by Germany, China and Italy. In Uzbekistan, the second largest market, imports declined from $3237 million in 1995 to $2,440 million in 2000. Besides Russia, Tajikistan and Kazakhstan are also major suppliers to Uzbekistan. In Turkmenistan, the third largest market, the major suppliers are USA, Turkey, Ukraine and Russia (see Table III).

Overall, the value of imports is small. The lack of growth in value of imports in absolute terms is a matter of concern. Total value of imports declined from around $13 billion in 1995 to $12.3 billion in 2001. Aggregate exports increased from around $13 billion to over $17 billion in the same period. However, this growth was largely due to a substantial increase in exports from Kazakhstan and Turkmenistan. Other countries saw a significant decline in their export earnings.

Table III: *Exports and Imports of CAR Countries: 1995–2001 (US $ Million)*

| Countries | Exports | | Imports | | Trade Balance | | Per cent Average growth | |
|---|---|---|---|---|---|---|---|---|
| | 1995 | 2001 | 1995 | 2001 | 1995 | 2001 | Exports | Imports |
| Kazakhstan | 5913 | 8647 | 6891 | 6363 | – 978 | 2284 | 6.5 | – 1.4 |
| Kyrgys Rep. | 409 | 476 | 522 | 467 | – 113 | 9 | 2.5 | – 1.8 |
| Tajikistan | 779 | 652 | 838 | 766 | – 59 | –114 | – 2.9 | – 1.5 |
| Turkmenistan | 2147 | 4632 | 1113 | 2097 | 1094 | 535 | 3.5 | 11.1 |
| Uzbekistan | 3475 | 2816 | 3237 | 2440 | 238 | 376 | – 4.1 | – 5.5 |

Note: *2001 figures for Uzbekistan are for the year 2000.
Source: The Europa World Yearbook, 2001.

## Does India Have a Place?

How does India figure in the CARs' trade scenario? A few key facts first:

- The entire region is economically poor with limited purchasing power.
- The countries are in the process of re-constructing their economies but the resources are limited, which means the development process will take time to gather momentum.
- The market size is not attractive enough. In fact, import growth is shrinking, even as most economies of the region are exhibiting positive growth.
- For most of the countries, the ability to trade in hard currency is limited.
- There are already several major suppliers to the region, most of whom have historical and traditional links with the CARs. Besides, the geographical factor also plays a key role.

For India, a fresh start will have to be made and efforts initiated to re-establish trade and economic linkages. Fortunately, Indian industry considers Central Asia as an emerging economic region and is ready to explore opportunities by doing the necessary groundwork. Attempts are being made to familiarise the people of the region with Indian products, skills and services. There is a need for India to adopt a new approach and develop closer economic ties with the region. But first, let us consider the existing bilateral trade.

The size of the current bilateral trade is insignificant: two-way trade adds up to just $130 million. A major portion of this trade is confined to Kazakhstan and Uzbekistan. India has been concentrating on exports to the region and the CARs too are focusing primarily on promoting their exports. In 2000, India's imports from the entire region added up to only $41 million, while exports were worth $85 million. Clearly, there is a certain disharmony of interests in the present trade situation between India and the CARs.

There has been an effort to liberalise trade policies in the region with the export objective in mind. These initiatives include elimination of quota for export of goods, reduction in the list of products subject to licensing, elimination of export duties, establishment of free trade zones, etc., among others. As far as imports are concerned, these are constrained by low income, poor purchasing power, lack of adequate investments and inadequate hard currencies.

In the light of the enormous economic challenges that the region faces, it is only natural that the CARs should prioritise their aims and objectives. For instance, for Turkmenistan, a major challenge is to explore 'viable and acceptable modalities' for gas exports. Similarly, its priority also includes exporting aluminium and cotton. Kyrgyzstan wants to export a range of light industrial products, machinery and metallurgical products of non-ferrous types. However, for most of the CARs, the biggest priority is to enlarge their export capacities through free trade zones and regional integration. Import regimes are, by and large, restrictive with a number of restrictions and government controls.

Indian industry can develop a long-term partnership with the region and help the CARs achieve their goals of export growth. Indian companies can play a major role by investing in sectors that have potential for exports. Some of the prominent export sectors of the region are aluminium, textiles, general purpose machinery, chemicals, agricultural products, oil and gas, and other energy products. Incidentally, these are also the potential sectors for foreign investment in this region. Given the fact that selling Indian goods to these countries is fraught with several risks, a strategy to boost Indian investment in the region may go a long way in strengthening economic linkages with the region. While such a strategy would contribute significantly to the CARs' economic growth, it would also enable Indian companies to explore new global markets. The CARs are a gateway to China and East Asia on the one hand and Europe on the other. Strategic investment in this region may, thus, offer access to larger markets in the future.

This, however, is not to suggest that the export initiative should be abandoned. Rather, investment in the region should be given the priority it deserves as a sustainable strategy for future growth of Indian exports. As far as direct exports are concerned, measures should be taken to facilitate these countries to buy Indian products by offering options such as barter trade in the medium term. However, such strategies can work only if initiatives are taken at the government level. Long-term export credit arrangements is yet another measure that would help boost exports to the region.

## Conclusion

In conclusion, it is important for India to keep in view the ground realities of the economies of the region. These economies are, by and large, poor and fall in the category of low developing countries (LDCs) and face dual challenges of substantial adjustments and economic rebuilding. External assistance will help these economies to achieve their potential at a faster pace and it is here that India has the opportunity for making investments in certain sectors. It would go a long way in fostering a stronger relationship with the CARs and would also be beneficial for India in the long run.

# SECTION FIVE
## Appendix

# Indranil Banerjie

Indranil Banerjie is the founder and Executive Director of the SAPRA India Foundation, a New Delhi based independent think-tank. Mr Banerjie set up the foundation in 1995 to promote strategic thinking and the understanding of national security issues in India. The Foundation has focused on research on terrorism, weapons of mass destruction, military, international relations and internal security. Apart from editing a monthly bulletin on terrorism, national security and world affairs, Mr Banerjie also runs a website (www.subcontinent.com) and conducts workshops for government and private sector organisations. As head of the Foundation, he has led two Indian delegations to Washington DC to interact with US Congressmen. Also, he has travelled widely in the region and has visited Pakistan, Afghanistan, Turkey, Nepal, Bangladesh, Bhutan, Myanmar, Thailand and Malaysia.

Mr Banerjie has been a journalist for over twenty years and has worked with reputed media organisations, including the Living Media Group (India Today), Ananda Bazar Patrika Group (The Telegraph & Sunday Magazine) and NDTV (The World This Week). He has made several documentaries and current affairs programmes on Indian national security issues, which have been telecast on the national television network, Doordarshan.

★

# Venera Galyamova

Venera Galyamova graduated from the Almaty State University (1993–1998) and has been working as a senior research fellow from June 2002 at the Kazakhstan Institute for Strategic Studies. During January–June 2002, Ms Galyamova worked as an expert at the Centre for Foreign Policy and Analysis under the Kazakh ministry of foreign affairs. Her areas of interest include international relations, contemporary China and China's internal and foreign policy, and political life in contemporary Central Asia. Ms Galyamova can speak Chinese, English and French languages apart from being proficient in Kazakh and Russian languages. She has participated in various international conferences including two that were held in China. Her publications include a chapter in 'The Interests and Policies of World Powers in Kazakhstan', published in 2002. She was selected as one of the beneficiaries of the UNESCO/Keizo Obuchi research fellowship programme in 2002. She is currently working on her thesis titled 'Political Transformation in People's Republic of China'.

★

# Gulsara Osorova

Gulsara Osorova is currently a senior expert at the International Institute for Strategic Studies under the president of the Kyrgyz Republic. Her doctoral thesis was on 'Non-traditional security threats in Central Asia'. Her areas of interest include international relations, civic society development and security studies/non-traditional issues. She has participated in various international seminars in Kyrgyzstan and abroad. Dr Osorova graduated from the School of Political Science and International Relations, University of Birmingham, UK. She is fluent in Kyrgyz, Russian and English languages. She has published articles in the *Central Asia and Caucasus Analyst*, a journal published by John Hopkins University. She could be contacted at: gosorova@hotmail.com, gulsara@iiss.gov.kg.

*

# Dr Archana Srivastava

Dr Archana Srivastava is presently working as a research associate in the Centre for Russian, Central Asian and East European Studies in the School of International Studies, Jawaharlal Nehru University, New Delhi, India. Her doctoral thesis was on 'Impact of Economic Growth on Environment in Centrally Planned Economy: A Case Study of Soviet Russia'. She is fluent in Hindi, English and Russian languages. Her areas of interest include Russia, Central Asia, geopolitics and economic issues. Dr Srivastava is a life member of the Indian Society of Remote Sensing. She has written extensively on Central Asia and Russia and has presented several research papers in India and abroad. She could be contacted at: asrivastava@mail.jnu.ac.in.

★

# Suchandana Chatterjee

Suchandana Chatterjee works on contemporary Central Asia at Maulana Abul Kalam Azad Institute of Asian Studies (MAKAIAS), Kolkata, with emphasis on socio-political processes of 'transformation' in Tajikistan and Kyrgyzstan. Since 1994, she has represented MAKAIAS in various national and international conferences on themes related to Central Asia and its neighbourhood. In 2000 and 2002, on behalf of MAKAIAS she presented papers at VII ESCAS Conference (Vienna) and VIII ESCAS Conference (Bordeaux). Her articles have been published in *Contemporary Central Asia* and in various seminar proceedings. Among her recent publications are (1) *Politics and Society in Tajikistan in the aftermath of the Civil War*, Hope India Publications (India) on behalf of MAKAIAS, 2002; (2) 'Empires, kingdoms and mobile frontiers in Central Asia', in Ranabir Samaddar (ed.) *Space, Territory and the State: New Readings in International Politics*, Orient Longman (Hyderabad), 2002; and (3) 'The Shaping of Alliances in Bukharan People's Soviet Republic (1920–24)' in *The Turks*, Vol. 5, Part 68, Yeni Turkiye Publications, Ankara, 2002. Her book reviews have been published in *Abstracta Iranica* (Teheran), *Central Eurasian Studies Review* (Harvard Forum of Central Eurasian Studies) and *Journal of Central Asian Studies* (Oklahoma). Her field trip to Tashkent (February–March 1998) was conducted with ICSSR financial support. The title of her thesis is 'The Emirate of Bukhara, 1868–1924: Encounters with Transition'. She can be contacted at: suchandanachatterjee@hotmail.com sukalyan@ehp.saha.ernet.in.

★

# Lena Jonson

Lena Jonson is an associate professor and senior research fellow at the Swedish Institute of International Affairs in Stockholm 1991. She has had a long term interest in Russian foreign and security policy, especially Russian policy towards Central Asia. In 1997–98 she was a senior research fellow in the Russia-Eurasia Programme at the Royal Institute of International Affairs in London. During six months in 2002 she was political officer in Dushanbe at the OSCE Mission to Tajikistan. She has written extensively about Russian policy towards Central Asia and also Russian handling of armed conflicts on former Soviet territory. Her publications include: *Central Asian Security: The New International Context* (edited together with Roy Allison, Washington DC: Brookings Institution Press/The Royal Institute of International Affairs, 2001); *Russia and Central Asia in a New Web of Relations*, London: The Royal Institute of International Affairs, 1998; *The Tajik War: A Challenge to Russian Policy*, London, The Royal Institute of International Affairs, 1998; *Keeping Peace in the CIS: The Evolution of Russian Policy*, London, The Royal Institute of International Affairs, 1999; *Peacekeeping and the Role of Russia in Eurasia* (edited by Lena Jonson and Clive Archer, Boulder, Colorado: Westview Press, 1996). She has also contributed to several books such as 'The Caspian Region: the Geopolitical Situation', in *The Caspian region: Oil and Security*, edited by Gennady Chufrin, SIPRI: Oxford University Press, 2001 and 'The Security Dimension of Russia's South Central Asian Policy', in *Russia Between East and West*, edited by Gabriel Gorodetsky, London and New York: Frank Cass, 2003. She is a member of the editorial board of the journal *Central Asia and the Caucasus* (Umea).

★

# Svante E Cornell

Svante E Cornell is the deputy director of the Central Asia-Caucasus Institute of the Paul H Nitze School of Advanced International Studies, John Hopkins University. He is the editor of the institute's bi-weekly publication, the *Central Asia-Caucasus Analyst* (http://www.cacianalyst.org/). He is also the course chair of Caucasus area studies at the Foreign Service Institute, George P Schultz National Foreign Affairs Training Centre, US Department of State.

Cornell is the founder and executive director of Cornell Caspian Consulting, LLC, a strategy firm with offices or representatives in seven countries, which counsels governmental institutions and private companies on political and economic issues in the wider Caspian region (http://www.cornellcaspian.com/). In 2002, he co-founded the Silk Road Studies Programme of Uppsala University, Sweden, where he is research director and lectures on security studies in the former Soviet Union.

Previously, Mr Cornell lectured in international security at the Royal Swedish Military Academy and the department of Peace and Conflict Research of Uppsala University. He holds a PhD degree from the department of peace and conflict research of Uppsala University, an honorary doctorate from the Behmenyar Institute of Law and Philosophy of the Academy of Sciences of the Republic of Azerbaijan, and a degree in international relations from the Middle East Technical University, Ankara, Turkey.

His specialisation is on security issues, regional politics, conflict management, and state building in the Caucasus, Turkey, and South-west and Central Asia. He authored *Small Nations and Great Powers: A Study of Ethnopolitical Conflict in the Caucasus*, (2000), and *Autonomy and Conflict:*

*Ethnoterritoriality and Separatism in the South Caucasus* (2002). He is the author of numerous academic and policy articles that appeared in *World Politics*, *The Washington Quarterly*, *Current History*, *Journal of Democracy*, *Foreign Service Journal*, *Orbis*, and other journals. His commentaries occasionally appear in the American, Swedish, Turkish, and Pakistani daily press.

★

# Dr Anita Sengupta

Dr Anita Sengupta has been working in the areas of state formation, boundaries and identities, the question of minorities and gender, economy, culture, regional security and problems of transition in Central Asia, with Uzbekistan as the area of specific interest, for the past ten years. As a part of her doctoral and post-doctoral studies, she has worked in libraries and archives in Uzbekistan and Berlin.

She has been an invited speaker at various seminars and conferences organised by the European Society for Central Asian Studies; Zentralasien Seminar, Humboldt University, Berlin; Centre for Russian, Central Asian and East European Studies, Jawaharlal Nehru University, New Delhi; the Centre for Eurasian Studies, Mumbai University; the Department of International Relations and Strategic Studies, Jadavpur University; and the Department of South and South-east Asian Studies, Calcutta University. Her articles have been published in journals like *Central Asian Survey*, *Journal of Central Asian Studies*, *Economic and Political Weekly* and *International Studies* and in volumes on Central Asia. She is the author of *Frontiers into Borders: The Transformation of Identities in Central Asia* (2002).

A graduate in political science from Presidency College, Kolkata, Anita did her masters from Jawaharlal Nehru University, New Delhi. She was awarded her doctorate in January 2001 from the University of Calcutta in political science, on the theme, 'Language, Religion and State Formation in Central Asia – A Case Study of Uzbekistan'.

Anita is currently a fellow at the Maulana Abul Kalam Azad Institute of Asian Studies, Kolkata.

★

# Dr Sanjay Deshpande

Dr Sanjay Deshpande, who lost his left leg above knee in an accident in his childhood, pursued his higher studies at Moscow and returned to India with a PhD in Eurasian studies. During his stay in Russia, he taught Indian and South Asian history at the People's Friendship University, Moscow. Dr Deshpande has travelled extensively in the former Soviet Union and Europe. After returning from Russia, Dr Deshpande joined the Centre for Central Eurasian Studies, University of Mumbai. Dr Deshpande has written several research papers and articles on Russian and Central Asian problems. He has also participated in many national and international seminars. Dr Deshpande's area of specialisation includes pre-Soviet/Soviet/Russian/ Central Asian history, polity, socio-economic problems, foreign policy, and India's relationship with former Soviet republics. Dr Deshpande is a member of the Indian Association for American Studies. Dr Deshpande could be contacted at: desh_sanjay2001@yahoo.co.in.

★

# Prof. Nirmala Joshi

Prof. Nirmala Joshi of the Centre for Russian, Central Asian and East European Studies in the School of International Studies, Jawaharlal Nehru University, has been teaching and guiding research on Russia and Central Asia for several years. She was the chairperson of the Centre for two years (1997–99) and was later appointed director of the University Grants Commission's (UGC) programme on Russia and Central Asia in the Centre for three years. She has contributed several articles to books and scholarly journals covering a wide range of issues on the subject. Professor Joshi is the author of *Indo-Soviet Relations Unofficial Attitudes and Contacts: 1917–1947* and has edited *India and Hungary: Perspective on the Changing World Order* and *Central Asia: The Great Game Replayed: An Indian Perspective* (2003). Presently, she is working on *Central Asia's Security Concerns: Implications for India.*

Prof. Nirmala Joshi has been a member of the Indo-Russia Joint Commission for Cooperation in Social Sciences. She was nominated a member of the executive council of the Indian Council of World Affairs, New Delhi. She is a member of the standing committee of the UGC's Area Studies Programme. Professor Joshi has widely travelled to Russia, Europe and the United States of America. She could be contacted at: nirmalajoshi2002@hotmail.com.

★

# Prof. Stephen Blank

Stephen Blank is professor of Russian national security studies at the Strategic Studies Institute of the US Army War College. Dr Blank has been an associate professor of national security affairs at the Strategic Studies Institute since 1989. During 1998–2001 he was Douglas MacArthur professor of research at the War College. Prior to this appointment Dr Blank was associate professor for Soviet studies at the Centre for Aerospace Doctrine, Research, and Education of Air University at Maxwell AFB. Dr Blank's MA and PhD are in Russian history from the University of Chicago. He has published over 300 articles and monographs on Soviet/Russian military and foreign policies. His most recent book is *Imperial Decline: Russia's Changing Role in Asia*, Duke University Press, 1997, which he co-edited with Professor Alvin Rubinstein of the University of Pennsylvania. Dr Blank is also the author of a study of the Soviet commissariat of nationalities, *The Sorcerer as Apprentice: Stalin's Commissariat of Nationalities*, Greenwood Publishing Group, 1994, and the co-editor of The Soviet Military and the Future, Greenwood Publishing Group, 1992. Dr Blank has published over 290 articles, studies and books on foreign and military policy and international security in Europe, Asia, the Middle East and the CIS, US defence policy, and future war.

★

# Maj. Gen. (Retd) S C N Jatar

A civil engineering graduate from the College of Engineering, Pune, and a fellow of the Institution of Engineers, Maj. Gen. (Retd) S C N Jatar was commissioned in the Bombay Sappers, Corps of Engineers, Indian Army with seniority from 07 June 1954. He was instructor at the Infantry School, Mhow, (1965–66), head of the Indian military training team and chief instructor at the Nigerian Defence Academy, Kaduna, Nigeria, (1968–71), commanded an engineer regiment in the war in the Poonch Sector in 1971, was staff officer to the Expert Committee for reorganisation of the Indian army and to assess the threat to India in a twenty-five-year time-frame under the chairmanship of General K V Krishna Rao (1975–76), and commanded infantry brigades in the Kashmir Valley and Rajasthan desert (1977–1981).

Major General Jatar's association with the petroleum sector commenced in early 1981 when he was sent on deputation to Oil India Limited, then a 50:50 joint sector company of Burmah Oil and Government of India. This was in the wake of the oil blockade when all work in the oilfields had come to a halt. Jatar was successful in restarting the operations and in the very first year brought up the production from almost zero to over three million tonnes (60,000 barrels per day). Realising the strategic importance of oil and its close relationship with security and defence of the country, he made a deep study of the oil industry and learnt the intricacies of exploration and production operations. He opted for premature retirement from the army in 1983 and rose to become the chairman and managing director of Oil India Ltd. During his tenure he was successful in putting Arunachal Pradesh and Rajasthan on the oil map on India.

He was later chairman and managing director of ONGC Videsh Limited, the overseas arm of Oil & Natural Gas Corporation Limited. He was instrumental in negotiating the first ever production-sharing contract (with PetroVietnam) where an Indian company was the operator.

During his stint with the public sector he was elected as the chairman of the Standing Conference of Public Enterprises (SCOPE), the apex body of the central public sector. He was also president of the Petroleum Sports Control Board for five years.

After his superannuation from the public sector, General Jatar served as consultant to Hindustan Petroleum Corporation Ltd for the formation of their exploration and production company, Prize Petroleum. He was also project advisor, Standing Conference of Public Enterprises. He has served in the private sector as president of RPG Petrochem Limited and managing director of Garware Shipping Limited. He has been on the governing board of Pune Stock Exchange. He has specialised in security aspects in the oil and gas industry and chaired a government committee that went into these aspects for the entire upstream petroleum sector. He is currently a member of the steering committee of India's National Gas Hydrate Programme and technical consultant to ICICI Bank on oil and gas matters. He is a founder member of a non-governmental organisation called Initiative for Peace, Arms Control and Disarmament, and an associate of Security and Political Risk Analysis (SAPRA) India Foundation.

★

# T K Bhaumik

T K Bhaumik is senior adviser (policy) with the Confederation of Indian Industry since February 1993. He is also head of the WTO Research and Consulting Division of Confederation of Indian Industry.

Mr Bhaumik did his postgraduation in economics from Jadavpur University, Kolkata, in 1972. He holds a diploma in econometrics and planning from the Indian Statistical Institute, Kolkata. In addition, he has undertaken a certificate course in export promotion management from the Bremen Institute of Economic Research, Germany and also CBI Netherlands.

He headed the CII Team that worked with Prof. Michael A Porter on CII-Harvard Business School study of competitive advantage of Indian industry. Mr Bhaumik has also been a member of the Indian-ASEAN Expert Group on Cooperation in Trade and Investment, constituted by the ASEAN secretariat.

In addition, Mr Bhaumik has been a UNIDO consultant and undertaken UNDP projects. He has been active in the formation of Indian Ocean Rim Association for Regional Cooperation and Bangladesh-India-Myanmar-Sri Lanka-Thailand Economic Cooperation Group as industry representative.

He played a leading role in the CII delegation to the third and fourth WTO ministerial conferences in Seattle and Doha respectively. He has very close interaction with the WTO secretariat and the ministry of commerce, Government of India.

*